# *The* BEST *of*
# THE OLD FARMER'S ALMANAC

# *The* BEST *of*
# THE OLD FARMER'S ALMANAC

## *The First 200 Years*

### Judson Hale, Editor

RANDOM HOUSE   NEW YORK

Owing to limitations of space, all acknowledgments of permissions
to reprint previously published material and to use illustrations will
be found on pages 243-44.

Library of Congress Cataloging-in-Publication Data

The Best of The Old Farmer's Almanac: the first 200 years/
Judson Hale, editor.
        p. cm.
ISBN 0-679-74264-6
I. Hale, Judson D.
AC5.B228 1991
031–dc20 91-52660

Manufactured in the United States of America
98765432
First Paperback Edition

*To Lorna Sagendorph Trowbridge*

# Acknowledgments

I'M CONVINCED THIS BOOK would not be in your hands today were it not for the packaging and developmental editing skills of Sharon Smith. Her judgment, persistence, and dedication to the project made everything possible. Also, a very special thanks to my editor at Random House, David Rosenthal; to Jill Shaffer for all the design and art direction; to Jamie Kageleiry for the art research; to Linda Kaye, production manager at Random House; and to Almanac publisher John Pierce and Almanac managing editor Susan Peery for invaluable advice and consultations from the beginning discussions to the final deadline.

I also would like to thank the following: Barbara Jatkola for copyediting and proofreading; Mary DesRosiers for fact checking; Dougald MacDonald and Melanie Menagh for historical research; and Maureen DeGrenier, Lynn Lagasse, Linda Ottavi, Cindy Schlosser, and Carol Stowell for all manner of supportive and essential functions during the compilation and production process.

Finally, thanks to my wife, Sally, for invaluable practical advice, for giving up so much of what we'd planned to do during the weekends of the winter of 1991, and for all those bowls of soup.

# Contents

# Introduction

THE OLD FARMER'S ALMANAC has been a part of my life since 1939, the year my family purchased it from Little, Brown & Co. in Boston. From then on it was stuffed into my Christmas stocking every year, but, of course, I never read it. To me, it was virtually unreadable — just a confusing mass of small type intermixed with mysterious astronomical symbols signifying God knows what. Certainly nothing relevant to me or *my* life. It was apparent, however, that the adults in my house enjoyed it. "Going to be a tough winter," my father would invariably announce to anyone around as he leafed through it for the first time each year. (It was *never* going to be a *mild* winter.) Then everyone would laugh and banter about weather for a few minutes. So I associated the Almanac with weather forecasting and let it go at that.

Then, in 1958, fresh out of the U.S. Army, I began working for my uncle on *The Old Farmer's Almanac* (along with *Yankee* magazine, which he'd begun in 1935). My first Almanac task was to find and edit puzzles for the "Old-Fashioned Puzzles" page of the 1960 edition. It was also my job to unload several hundred cartons of the new edition from the back of the trailer truck that delivered them to our offices here in Dublin, New Hampshire. I was far more comfortable with the latter responsibility.

Over the next few years, I learned some editing skills and became better acquainted with the Almanac. In the process, I began to realize its primary function didn't have much of anything to do with weather forecasting. Rather, I came to understand, the Almanac's first and foremost annual responsibility was to present the astronomical structure of the forthcoming year as it relates to us here on earth. The Almanac lists the precise times of sunrise and sunset, moonrise and moonset, and high tide for every day of the year; it also gives the exact dates for eclipses, phases of the moon, changes of season, and so forth.

Related to that basic reason for existence has always been all the data (based on a variety of factors) useful in determining the most propitious *times* for most anything from planting peas, to castrating your bull, to taking a vacation (I always pick a week when the moon is becoming full), to photographing a sunrise over the ocean at high tide. In other words, while for two hundred years the Almanac has served as a weekly, monthly, and annual calendar, it has at the same time offered a sort of human agenda in harmony with the earth's place in the universe. Coming along for the ride were always a great variety of features — and, yes, the weather forecasts.

While I became aware of all this early on, it wasn't until the spring of 1990, as we were beginning to make plans for the 1992 edition, that I decided I wanted to read every page of all two hundred editions, going back to the fall of 1792. Not, initially, in preparation for doing this book, although that's what it turned out to be. More as an attempt to truly understand why and how this little yellow-covered annual has not only endured but downright prospered for longer than any other periodical in America. Why it has remained relevant not only to the rural eighteenth and nineteenth centuries but to the urban twentieth century as well.

When I unlocked the metal cabinets containing my uncle's collection of old almanacs one Saturday morning last May, I suddenly remembered we donated our best complete set to the Smithsonian several years ago and our best first edition to the White House during the Kennedy years. (The White House cornerstone was laid the same year and month the Almanac began — October 1792.) But I found two other somewhat battered sets, their early copies brown with age, their pages torn, flaky around the edges, and often with fading hand-scribbled weather or appointment notations along the margins. And so it was these I took to my office in boxes and carefully arranged on tables around my desk. Then, with trepidation at the extent of the task before me, with concern my eyes would be incapable of holding up through the mass of tiny, closely compacted type, and, at the same time, with eager anticipation of the surprises I'd discover over the ensuing months, I slowly picked up the original 1793 edition and began . . .

# PART I
## *The First 200 Years*

# CHAPTER ONE
## 1793 – 1846

# *Begun When* WASHINGTON *Was* President

*We look, as we pride ourselves in looking, a little old-fashioned, a little too independent to hang our dress for each "new-fangled notion" — a little t'other side of fifty.*
— Robert B. Thomas, 1842

UNDER THE GUIDING HAND OF ITS FIRST editor, Robert B. Thomas, the Almanac arrived on the scene in the fall of 1792, with its format and contents established and ready for the longest publishing tenure in American history. In the decades of its formative years, it would advise "blowing tobacco smoke into the fundament" of a drowning person, correctly predict snow for the summer of 1816, complain about the competition, and become older than all other American publications long before the Civil War. ✦

*George Washington was president at the time the first edition of* The Old Farmer's Almanac *was published.*

# SERIOUS WEATHER OBSERVING, INSTANT SUCCESS & A HINT OF SEXISM

"COLD AND FROSTY. . .LOOKS LIKE SNOW," says the first Almanac weather forecast, covering January 1–9, 1793. For the next day, "Blustering weather," a pretty safe forecast for most winter days in New England. I should be fair, however. The Almanac's founder and first editor, Robert B. Thomas, was serious about his weather forecasting.

How did he predict the weather? He devised what later became known as his "secret weather forecasting formula," which still exists and is kept safely tucked away in a black tin box at our Almanac offices in Dublin, New Hampshire. Basically, it's a rather complex series of weather cycles Thomas and others of his time observed.

Serious weather observing and predicting were common in the late eighteenth century. Everyone took into account nature's signs, carefully observing the thickness of the skin on onions and the width of the stripes on the woolly caterpillar. These things were all part of European folklore adapted to the somewhat different weather conditions of the colonies. Besides all that, many people believed that certain weather conditions following the change from one moon phase to the next depended on the precise time of that change (see the table on page 63). It follows that right from the start, the Almanac provided readers with those times — just in case they decided to ignore Thomas's predictions and make their own.

"As to my judgment of the weather," Thomas writes in his 1793 preface, "I need say but little; for you will, in one year's time, without any assistance of mine, very easily discover how near I have come to the truth." We hold to the same philosophy today. Weather forecasting in 1792 was what you might call an imperfect science. Today, two hundred years later, it still is.

In the same 1793 preface Thomas explains the title of his publication:

## WHY THE "FARMER'S ALMANAC"?

Having for several years past, paid some attention to that divine science, Astronomy, the study of which must afford infinite pleasure and satisfaction to every contemplative mind, it is this, with the repeated solicitations of my friends, that has induced me to present you with these Astronomical Calculations for the year 1793; which I have thought proper to entitle the Farmer's Almanac, as I have made it my principal aim to make it as useful as possible to that class of people. . . .The arrangement of this Almanac is

FACING PAGE: *This portrait of Robert B. Thomas hangs in the American Antiquarian Society in Worcester, Massachusetts. The Antiquarian Society also houses the largest collection of almanacs in the country.* BELOW: *The black tin box in the Dublin, New Hampshire, offices of Yankee Publishing Inc. — repository of R. B. Thomas's weather forecasting secrets.*

novel, though I have the vanity to believe it will be found as useful and convenient as any other almanac either of a double or single calendar. I have taken peculiar care to make the calculations accurate in every respect; and beside the more than usual astronomical calculations, I have added the rising, setting, or southing of the seven stars for every evening through the year.

I can't let Thomas's statements pass entirely without comment. First, "that class of people" — farmers — included almost everyone, even the president of the United States. Second, the arrangement of his Almanac was not "novel" — in fact, it was similar (I'll refrain from calling it a rip-off) to many of more than a hundred almanacs being published at that time. In those days — not so very unlike today — almanacs and the Bible were the nation's best-selling publications.

Even the concept of an almanac was not novel in Thomas's time. The first calendars appeared more than five thousand years ago, and the earliest almanacs, in the form of wooden blocks inscribed with the seasons and astronomical phenomena, followed soon after. The ancients sometimes referred to almanacs as "calendars of the heavens." The difference, then and now, is that while a calendar records time, an almanac records and predicts astronomical events, tides, weather, and other phenomena with respect to time. A calendar may exist without almanac information, but not the reverse. So today when you see a publication without astronomical or calendar information calling itself an almanac — it isn't.

[Nº. 1.]

THE

FARMER's ALMANAC,

CALCULATED ON A NEW AND IMPROVED PLAN,

FOR THE YEAR OF OUR LORD
1793:

Being the first after Leap Year, and seventeenth of the
Independence of America.

Fitted to the town of BOSTON, but will serve for any of
the adjoining States.

Containing, besides the large number of ASTRO-
NOMICAL CALCULATIONS and FARMER'S CA-
LENDAR for every month in the year, as great a vari-
ety as are to be found in any other Almanac,
OF NEW, USEFUL, and ENTERTAINING MATTER.

BY ROBERT B. THOMAS.

"While the bright radient sun in centre glows,
The earth, in annual motion round it goes;
At the same time on its own axis reels,
And gives us change of seasons as it wheels."

Published according to Act of Congress.

PRINTED AT THE Apollo Press, IN BOSTON,
BY BELKNAP AND HALL,
Sold at their Office, State Street; also, by the *Author*
and M. Smith, Sterling.
[Sixpence single, 4s. per dozen, 40s. per groce.]

## So Who in the World Was Robert B. Thomas?
### (1766–1846)

BORN IN GRAFTON, Massachusetts, nine years before the start of the American Revolution, Thomas was brought up on a farm in what was then Shrewsbury, Massachusetts. As a result of constantly changing town boundaries, he once noted, "It is rather paradoxical but no less a fact, that I have resided in four incorporated towns and two distinct parishes and one precinct, yet never moved from the same farm." The four towns were Shrewsbury, Lancaster, Sterling, and, finally, West Boylston. The foundations of the old Thomas homestead are now about thirty feet under the waters of the Wachusett Reservoir.

Thomas's grandfather was a graduate of Cambridge University in England, and his father had a passion for literature. Thomas, on the other hand, was fascinated by science. At age sixteen, he read Ferguson's *Astronomy*, which he came across in his father's library. He later wrote that "it was from the pleasing study of this work I first imbibed the idea of calculating an almanack."

With this dream in mind, he became a bookseller, taught school, built a store and bindery near the family farm, and studied astronomy in his spare time. In early 1792, he went to Boston to study mathematics under the tutelage of another almanac maker, Osgood Carlton, and that fall delivered the copy for the first edition of what he then called *The Farmer's Almanac* to printers Joseph Belknap and Thomas Hall. For a few years, the only payment he received was one-tenth of the copies printed, which he would then sell in his store. Only when the Almanac became very profitable did he receive a cash payment in addition to the extra copies.

Eventually, the Almanac made Robert B. Thomas a prosperous man. During his long life, he served as West Boylston's town clerk, chairman of the selectmen, a representative to the State Constitutional Convention in 1820, a justice of the peace, and founder of the local science club. But the Almanac remained his primary means of support for fifty-four years.

He died at age eighty, leaving his wife of forty-three years, Hannah, and two nephews. Today Robert B. and Hannah Thomas lie side by side in the cemetery in Sterling, Massachusetts. Although it's been almost 150 years since he died and eleven Almanac editors have followed him, no other name but his has ever appeared on the cover of *The Old Farmer's Almanac*.

**Keep your family from the abominable practise of backbiting.**

*1811*

*The old farmhouse in West Boylston, Massachusetts, where Thomas lived for most of his life. Its foundations now lie beneath the waters of the Wachusett Reservoir.*

ASTRONOMICAL CALCULATIONS.

| Days. | ☉ | Days. | ☉ | Days. | ☉ |
|---|---|---|---|---|---|
| 1 | ♊ 11 19 | 13 | ♊ 22 47 | 25 | ♋ 4 14 |
| 3 | 13 14 | 15 | 24 42 | 27 | 6 8 |
| 5 | 15 9 | 17 | 26 36 | 29 | 8 3 |
| 7 | 17 3 | 19 | 28 31 | | |
| 9 | 18 58 | 21 | ♋ 0 25 | | |
| 11 | 20 53 | 23 | 2 20 | | |

☉ place.

☽ Laſt quarter, 1 day, 4h. 49m. morning.
○ New moon, 8 day, 10h. 33m. morning.
☽ Firſt quarter, 16 day, 1h. 16m. evening.
● Full moon, 23 day, 7h. 24m. morning.
☽ Laſt quarter, 30 day, 10h. 30m. morning.

| M. D. | W. D. | ☉ riſes & ſets. | L. D. | ☉ F. A. | F. ſea. | ● place. | ● riſ. &ſets. H. M. | ● ſo. | 7's riſ. |
|---|---|---|---|---|---|---|---|---|---|
| 1 | Satur. | 4 33 | 8 14 54 | 2 23 | 5 31 | feet | 0 32 | 6 16 | 3 27 |
| 2 | SUN. | 4 32 | 8 14 56 | 2 24 | 6 21 | head | 1 7 | 7 6 | 3 23 |
| 3 | Mond. | 4 31 | 8 14 58 | 2 25 | 7 11 | head | 1 44 | 7 56 | 3 19 |
| 4 | Tueſd. | 4 31 | 8 14 58 | 2 26 | 8 1 | head | 2 10 | 8 46 | 3 15 |
| 5 | Wedn. | 4 31 | 8 14 58 | 2 27 | 8 50 | neck | 2 45 | 9 35 | 3 11 |
| 6 | Thurſ. | 4 30 | 8 15 0 | 2 28 | 9 40 | neck | 3 19 | 10 25 | 3 7 |
| 7 | Friday | 4 30 | 8 15 0 | 1 29 | 10 30 | arms | 3 55 | 11 15 | 3 3 |
| 8 | Satur. | 4 29 | 8 15 2 | 1 0 | 11 20 | arms | ☽ ſets. | even. | 2 58 |
| 9 | SUN. | 4 29 | 8 15 2 | 1 1 | even. | breaſt | 8 22 | 0 56 | 2 54 |
| 10 | Mond. | 4 29 | 8 15 2 | 1 2 | 0 | breaſt | 9 10 | 1 45 | 2 50 |
| 11 | Tueſd. | 4 28 | 8 15 4 | 1 3 | 1 48 | breaſt | 9 54 | 2 33 | 2 46 |
| 12 | Wedn. | 4 28 | 8 15 4 | 0 4 | 2 35 | heart | 10 33 | 3 20 | 2 42 |
| 13 | Thurſ. | 4 27 | 8 15 6 | 0 5 | 3 21 | heart | 11 7 | 4 6 | 2 38 |
| 14 | Friday | 4 27 | 8 15 6 | 0 6 | 4 5 | belly | 11 39 | 4 50 | 2 33 |
| 15 | Satur. | 4 27 | 8 15 6 | 0 7 | 4 48 | belly | morn. | 5 33 | 2 29 |
| 16 | SUN. | 4 27 | 8 15 6 | 0 8 | 5 30 | belly | 0 8 | 6 15 | 2 25 |
| 17 | Mond. | 4 27 | 8 15 6 | 1 9 | 6 13 | reins | 0 35 | 6 58 | 2 21 |
| 18 | Tueſd. | 4 27 | 8 15 6 | 1 10 | 6 58 | reins | 1 3 | 7 43 | 2 17 |
| 19 | Wedn. | 4 27 | 8 15 6 | 1 11 | 7 45 | ſecrets | 1 32 | 8 30 | 2 13 |
| 20 | Thurſ. | 4 27 | 8 15 6 | 1 12 | 8 35 | ſecrets | 2 5 | 9 20 | 2 9 |
| 21 | Friday | 4 27 | 8 15 6 | 1 13 | 9 28 | ſecrets | 2 40 | 10 13 | 2 5 |
| 22 | Satur. | 4 27 | 8 15 6 | 2 14 | 10 25 | thighs | 3 21 | 11 10 | 2 0 |
| 23 | SUN. | 4 27 | 8 15 6 | 2 16 | 11 24 | thighs | ● riſ. | morn. | 1 56 |
| 24 | Mond. | 4 27 | 8 15 6 | 2 16 | morn. | knees | 8 10 | 0 9 | 1 52 |
| 25 | Tueſd. | 4 27 | 8 15 6 | 2 17 | 0 25 | knees | 9 1 | 1 0 | 1 48 |
| 26 | Wedn. | 4 27 | 8 15 6 | 3 18 | 1 25 | legs | 9 46 | 2 10 | 1 44 |
| 27 | Thurſ. | 4 27 | 8 15 6 | 3 19 | 2 23 | legs | 10 26 | 3 8 | 1 39 |
| 28 | Friday | 4 28 | 8 15 4 | 3 20 | 3 19 | feet | 11 2 | 4 4 | 1 35 |
| 29 | Satur. | 4 28 | 8 15 4 | 3 21 | 4 12 | feet | 11 39 | 4 57 | 1 31 |
| 30 | SUN. | 4 28 | 8 15 4 | 3 22 | 5 4 | head | morn. | 5 49 | 1 27 |

In florid beauty all appears,
And nymphs, a crown of roſes wear,
See the pigmy corn in rows,
And farmers buſy with their hoes.

*Days of the Month.*

| Saturday | 1 | 8 | 15 | 22 | 29 |
|---|---|---|---|---|---|
| SUNDAY | 2 | 9 | 16 | 23 | 30 |
| Monday | 3 | 10 | 17 | 24 | |
| Tueſday | 4 | 11 | 18 | 25 | |
| Wedneſday | 5 | 12 | 19 | 26 | |
| Thurſday | 6 | 13 | 20 | 27 | |
| Friday | 7 | 14 | 21 | 28 | |

| | Calendar, Courts, Aſpects, Weather, &c. | FARMER's CALENDAR. |
|---|---|---|
| 1 | Middling tides. *Pretty* | I now ſuppoſe the buſy ſeed |
| 2 | 1ſt p. Trin. *hot weather.* | time nearly over, tho' it may do |
| 3 | Artil. Elect. Boſton. *Rain.* | to plant potatoes, peas, beans, &c. |
| 4 | DFC.Boſt.& Port. CP.Pow- | Weed Indian corn. |
| 5 | *Thunder* 8 ♈ ☿ [nal. | Bleed horned cattle of all kinds. |
| 6 | *and lightning.* | Weed carrots, parſnips, onions, |
| 7 | Scorp. H. ſou. 11, 12. | &c. before weeds overrun them. |
| 8 | Middling tides. | Sow buck wheat. Melons and |
| 9 | 2d p. Trin. *Pleaſant.* | cucumbers, attacked by bugs or |
| 10 | *Some* | flies, fumagate with brimſtone, |
| 11 | St. Barn. *flying clouds,* | or tobacco ſmoke. |
| 12 | *and ſhowers.* | Salt your cattle often. |
| 13 | ♃ ſou. 9, 57. ☽ Apogee. | Croſs harrow fallows. |
| 14 | *Clear, and very warm,* | Hoe cabbages often ; nothing |
| 15 | 3d p. Trin. *for ſome days.* | will make them flouriſh better. |
| 16 | Low tides. | Continue to ſow radiſhes, peas, |
| 17 | Bat.Bun.hill,1775. ♀ Stat. | &c. Water tender plants. |
| 18 | SJC. Ipſwich. | Look often to melons, cucum- |
| 19 | *Hot, dry weather.* | bers, &c. and ſee that bugs do |
| 20 | Longeſt day. | not deſtroy them. Weed flax. |
| 21 | *Signs of* | Plough fallows while the dew is |
| 22 | *rain.* | on in the morning. |
| 23 | 4th p. Trin. Mid. tides. | Water tender plants. |
| 24 | St. John Bap. | Begin to half hill Indian corn. |
| 25 | SJC.Yor. ♃ ſo.9.3. 6 ⊙ ☿ | Plant cucumbers for pickling. |
| 26 | ☽ Perigee. | Begin to cut your clover ; rake |
| 27 | *Great ſigns* | it when it is very early in flower. |
| 28 | *of rain.* | Let it have one day's ſun, then |
| 29 | St. Peter. | cart it, and when mowing, to ev- |
| 30 | 5th paſt Trinity. | ery ton put half a buſhel of ſalt. |

*The two 1793 calendar pages for the month of June — in the format that has remained virtually unchanged for the past two hundred years.*

Thomas's first edition — "Fitted to the town of Boston, but will serve for any of the adjoining States," as the title page proclaims — established the format and type of material that would continue in the publication to the present day. There was no editorial experimenting. Thomas knew what he wanted, and he went ahead and did it the same way every year until his death fifty-four years later. All eleven editors who came after him, including myself, simply followed suit.

People often ask me why I think the Almanac has been so successful and has endured for so long. Nothing readily apparent about that first edition explains why the circulation jumped from three thousand copies in 1793 to more than nine thousand in 1794. The price was about the same as that of the other almanacs — sixpence (about nine cents) a copy or forty shillings a gross. Printed at the Apollo Press in Boston, it was on sale in Boston stores along with no fewer than nineteen other roughly similar almanacs, and, with others, it was distributed throughout the New England countryside by peddlers. So why in the world is it the only one of the many eighteenth-century almanacs to survive?

I usually answer with vague references to the long tenure of most of the twelve Almanac editors; or to the fact that my family is only the fourth owner, possibly signifying a commitment the other almanacs lacked; or to the Almanac's good luck, such as the famous snow prediction for the summer of 1816, the 1858 Armstrong murder case in which Abraham Lincoln was involved, and the well-publicized German spy episode of World War II. But more on those later.

The point is, I don't really know. We can only surmise that possibly, as Thomas proclaimed in his early editions, the Thomas Almanac's astronomy *was* more accurate than that of the competition, the hints were more useful, and the features were just plain more entertaining.

My torn, yellowed, and somewhat falling-apart copy of the 1793 edition illustrates what our ancestors were reading by dim candlelight on cold winter evenings even as George Washington was finishing his first term in office. That 1793 Almanac has several pages devoted to federal and state courts, with their dates of sessions; the vacation schedules for Dartmouth and Harvard; four pages of distances between New England towns, along with the names of innkeepers; and the first Jewish history printed in this country, titled "A Brief Account of the Persecution of the Jews." There are also mathematical puzzles, the twenty-four calendar pages (two per month), and innumerable anecdotes and words of wisdom. For instance:

FOUR THINGS [THAT] SHOULD NEVER
FLATTER US
*(For These Things Are Not of Long Duration)*
1. Familiarity with the great
2. The caresses of women
3. The smiles of our enemies
4. A warm day in winter

If you've detected a hint of sexism in number 2, you're right. Thomas and the other almanac editors of his day designed their material for men. It was a male-dominated society, and although New Englanders were generally more literate than most Americans, American women everywhere lagged behind American men in literacy. Girls were often kept from school, while boys were generally

**THE UNITED STATES IN 1792**

- The Bill of Rights has just been ratified.
- The U.S. population, according to the 1790 census, is 3,929,672.
- Total U.S. land area is 891,364 square miles, including 26,618 square miles under water.
- Kentucky, formerly part of Virginia, becomes the 15th state.
- The invention of the cotton gin is 1 year away.
- Robert B. Thomas publishes the first edition of his *Farmer's Almanac.* With 48 pages and a total circulation of 3,000 copies, it sells for sixpence.

taught the rudiments of reading, writing, and "calculating." So early Almanac jokes are based on all the old stereotypes, especially that of the talkative woman. The theme is repeated again and again, starting with that very first edition:

> Question: Will you instruct your daughter in the different languages?
> Answer: No, sir. One tongue's enough for a woman.

## ATTACKING THE COMPETITION, DISGUSTING TALES & FIFTY-CENT SLAVES

AT THE TIME the Almanac began, there was another Thomas putting out another "farmer's almanac." In fact, if the truth be known, *that's* the one our own Robert B. Thomas sort of, well, copied. The competitor's name was Isaiah Thomas, but he was no relation. He lived in Worcester, Massachusetts, founded the American Antiquarian Society located there today, rode around like Paul Revere warning the countryside that the British were coming, fought as a minuteman at Lexington, and later published many almanacs and books, including *The History of Little Goody Two-Shoes.*

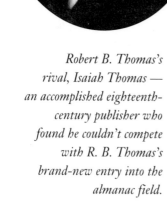

*Robert B. Thomas's rival, Isaiah Thomas — an accomplished eighteenth-century publisher who found he couldn't compete with R. B. Thomas's brand-new entry into the almanac field.*

I see, however, from *The Old Farmer's Almanac*'s 1794 preface that our Robert B. Thomas was not impressed. Or maybe he figured his best defense against the charge of, God forbid, *imitation*, was a good offense. "A selfish editor," he writes of his competitor Isaiah, "who appears to be much chagrined at our success has not only privately endeavoured to injure us, but publickly attacked our reputation by charging us with making copious extracts from his former almancks. . .[but] his almanack will be found to be fraught with error. In his astronomical calculations there were no less than fifty-six real errors."

Now, an almanac editor can quite comfortably abide incorrect weather predictions — I mean, after all! — but his "astronomical calculations," which are also predictions, *must* be 100 percent accurate. Fifty-six errors! Worse, Robert B. Thomas was correct. There really *were* that many errors. Well, Isaiah fought back in his subsequent editions, but he never fully recovered and was, within a few years, out of the farmer's almanac business. And by 1803, *our* Thomas could write that his sales were "unprecedented by any other Almanack published in the United States." But I'm jumping ahead of myself.

Besides the attack on poor Isaiah and the fare established the year before, the 1794 edition includes "A Cheap, Easy, and Clean Mixture for Effectively Destroying Bed Bugs" consisting of wine, turpentine, and a half ounce of camphor. And the next year there's a truly disgusting little tale emanating, supposedly, from the state of Delaware.

### A CURIOUS FACT

During several weeks of last summer, one of my milch-cows very frequently gave clotted blood from one of her tits, which, whenever this was the case, appeared scratched and inflamed. The milkmaid insisted she was sucked by a snake, but I paid little attention at first. Observing the animal so affected, I had her put into a separate pasture, and then nothing happened for several days. Thinking she might now be suffered to graze with the other cattle, she was put into her former pasture, and immediately her milk and tit were affected as above. She seemed very uneasy toward evening; always repaired to the same spot of the field at that time and lowed violently as if she had lost her calf. One evening as I was walking toward her, I saw a large black snake very near her, measuring nearly four feet. . . .I think we may reasonably suppose that the uncommon bloody appearance of her milk and tit must have arisen from being sucked by this huge reptile.

Are we to *believe* that? Equally appalling are the "directions for recovering persons apparently dead from drowning as recommended by the Humane Society." Specifically, one is to "blow tobacco smoke into the fundament with a fumigator." Difficult to imagine how blowing tobacco smoke up *there* would bring anyone around, but. . .

In each of the next four editions leading up to the turn of the century, there's an annual page titled "America's First Tax Bill on Houses, Lands, and Slaves." It stipulates that "a direct tax of two million dollars shall be hereby laid upon the United States" and apportioned to each of the sixteen existing states according to a table. For instance, Vermont was required to pay $46,864.19; South Carolina, $112,997.74; and so forth. There's an elaborate cal-

*The Almanac was an essential part of daily business for nineteenth-century readers, who often recorded important dates from farm and family life in the margins.*

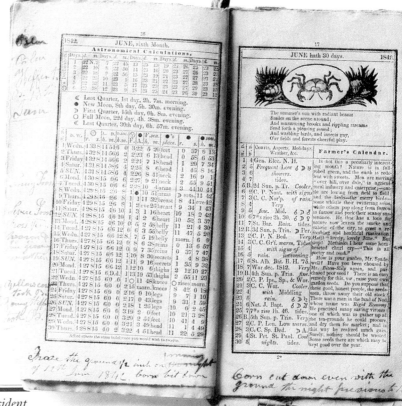

culation for land and "dwelling houses," but slaves were to be assessed at a simple fifty cents each.

## BEWARE INEXPERIENCED DRIVERS, BLEED YOUR CATTLE — AND IS THERE A WAR ON?

THE ARRIVAL OF a new century isn't mentioned in the 1800 edition, and the Almanac went to press prior to George Washington's death in December 1799, so there's no mention of that either. But one *can* learn that the Salem, Massachusetts, mail stage "starts from Major King's tavern every day in the week (Sundays excepted) at three o'clock in the afternoon and arrives in Boston every day at eleven o'clock in the morning." For those who prefer to travel on their own, there's a strong warning not to "suffer your horses to be frequently harnessed in a pleasure sleigh and be careful when they are, not to suffer them to be drove by young and inexperienced drivers."

The 1801 edition announces the "25th year of Independence of America," but Thomas doesn't make anything of it. It's obvious he's not one for frivolity and celebrating. "Cut your clover," he grumbles, "and mind your business."

In the 1803 edition, I found the first Almanac joke that made me smile. "When Pat shot at a hawk on the top limb of a tree and it fell to the ground with a thud, Mike said, 'Pat, you might have saved your powder and shot, for the fall would have killed it.'" (Well, I didn't say it was *hilarious*.)

Beginning in 1804, Thomas assigned Bartholomew Brown, a Boston lawyer, musical scholar, and storekeeper (how's that for a combination?) to write the twelve one-column "Farmer's Calendar" essays for each edition. As with all his contributors, Thomas acknowledges Brown by his

### FROM THE "FARMER'S CALENDAR" COLUMNS (1793)

- Feed your doves and spread ashes among their dung. (January)
- It will be a good plan now to sled out your winter dung . . .as you can carry much more on a sled than you can on a cart in April. (February)
- Set trees; be sure to set that side south that was south before. (April)
- Now all hands be haying; begin by mowing the ripest and thinnest first. (July)
- Turn your pigs into the woods to gather acorns. (September)
- Bleed your horses and fat cattle of all kinds. (November)
- Now come on the long and social winter evenings when the farmer may enjoy himself and instruct and entertain his family by reading some useful books. (December)

*The* BEST *of* THE OLD FARMER'S ALMANAC

initials only, a custom not to be duplicated until my uncle took over 140 years later.

Because Brown's well-read columns continued until three or four years after his death in 1854 (like Thomas, he prepared his copy well ahead of the deadlines), his "voice" in the Almanac — concentrating on rural life, nature, and plenty of advice — is an important element in these early editions. Here are a few samples from the "B.B." columns:

- Bleed working cattle to prevent their heating; give them potatoes and good hay. (1804)
- He that gets drunk is first a mad man, then an idiot. O, visit not the dram shop. (1806)
- It is every man's duty to make himself profitable to mankind; if he can, to many; if not, to fewer; if not so neither, to his neighbors; but always, however, to himself. (1807)

EPITAPH ON A VIOLENT SCOLD
(1801)

Beneath this stone, a lump of clay,
Lies ARABELLA YOUNG,
Who, on the twenty-fourth of May,
Began to hold her tongue.

With the 1810 edition, I'm relieved to find that the *s*'s are no longer indistinguishable from the *f*'s. That was most distracting — particularly, for instance, in the aforementioned snake/cow story of 1795, which, in my confusion, I thought at first was downright pornographic. The type in 1810, however, is now even smaller and more compact than in the first few editions — about the size of the print at the bottom of today's insurance policies. It's amazing to think that this was once pleasurable reading matter. I can only surmise that our ancestors enjoyed outstanding eyesight.

Moving right along, I find there's no hint of the War of 1812 in the 1812 edition. Timing wasn't right. The war began in June 1812, but the 1812 Almanac went to press in the late summer of 1811. The dissemination of news often required weeks in those days, but if you were to rely on the Almanac to know what was going on, the time delay could be as much as two years. It isn't until the 1814 edition, for instance, that you can find any indication that we were having some sort of trouble with Great Britain. It consists of a list of American ships, with those in italics being "vessels which have been captured from the British since the commencement of the present war."

Eli graduates might be interested to know that in 1815, Yale is finally included in the college vacation schedules. But it is plain in this edition — and others — that the Almanac did not recommend a college education. "What better estate can you give your offspring than a good education?" writes "B.B." in one of his columns that year. "However, I would not urge you to send them to college — or to an academy; but see that you have the best of teachers in your town schools."

**Think not that because it is winter, a farmer may lie idle. Busy, sir, busy! This is the word for all farmers at all times and seasons.**

*1819*

The dust from the 1815 eruption of Mount Tambora in the Dutch East Indies (now Indonesia) caused a worldwide lowering of temperatures during the summer of 1816, when the Almanac, legend has it, inadvertently but correctly predicted snow for July.

**Go not to your doctor for every ail, nor to your lawyer for every quarrel, nor to your pitcher for every thirst.**

*1802*

## PREDICTING SNOW FOR THE SUMMER OF 1816

OVER THE COURSE of the thirty-three years I've been with the Almanac, I've always kept my eye out for copies of the 1816 edition. When I occasionally find one, in some antiques shop or sent to me by a reader, I immediately turn to the July and August calendar pages to see whether they contain the famous snow forecasts Thomas supposedly made for both July and August. To date, all I've found is "Now expect good hay weather," "A storm is not far distant," or "Sultry with thundershowers." It's so disappointing.

However, I remain hopeful that a few copies still exist that do indeed predict "The Cold Summer of 1816," as that summer is known in history books. There's no question it *did* snow in New England and Canada during July and August of 1816. An 1815 eruption of Mount Tambora in the East Indies had left volcanic dust circling the globe, lowering temperatures as much as several degrees. But did the Almanac predict the snow that summer? Certainly the story that it did is an integral part of Almanac lore.

Some accounts say the printer inserted the snow prediction as a joke while Robert B. Thomas was sick in bed with the flu. The way I've always understood it, when Thomas discovered the "error," he destroyed all — or most of — the "snow" copies and reprinted the 1816 edition with the more conventional summer forecasts. It's said the word got out anyway, and during the winter and spring of that year, Thomas was repeatedly called upon to deny making such a ridiculous forecast for the following summer. Then, when it really *did* snow in July, he changed his tune and took full credit. "Told you so!" he allegedly said. If the story is true, it is one of the earliest and best examples of a subtle skill my uncle always referred to as "almanacsmanship."

## AN ODD TRADITION & WHY ALMANAC EDITORS ARE GRUMPY

THE 1819 EDITION marks the first time Thomas uses the famous words (well, famous to almanac buffs) that would become the traditional sign-off at the end of every year's preface or "To Patrons" page: "It is by our works and not our words that we would be judged. These, we hope, will maintain us [later changed to "sustain us"] in the humble though proud station we have so long held [in the name of your ob'd servant, Robert B. Thomas.]" The last part, in brackets, was added by Almanac editor John B. Tileston in 1870. Since that time, the entire statement has almost always been used by Almanac editors. And none of us has ever signed off with his own name.

**THE UNITED STATES IN 1816**

- James Monroe is elected president.
- Indiana becomes the 19th state.
- The U.S. population, according to the census of 1810, is 7,239,881.
- With the War of 1812 over for 2 years, the U.S. enjoys a period of peace.
- *The Old Farmer's Almanac*, according to legend, predicts snow in July.
- It snows in July.

Why are these words so important? Well, I suppose for most people, they're not. But you might be surprised at how strenuously a *few* readers complain to us if, as has inadvertently occurred a few times, a single word of that sign-off is changed or, worse, the sign-off is omitted altogether. When it comes to the Almanac, you just don't mess with tradition.

Almanac readers aren't the only ones who can be touchy. In the 1820 edition, Robert B. Thomas turns downright grumpy. But then there's nothing that irritates us Almanac editors more than seeing a bunch of cheap, fly-by-night imitators coming along attempting to fool the American public into believing their almanac is *the* Almanac. Like what's happening on newsstands today. Like, gulp, Thomas himself *sort of* did in 1792. And, judging from the following quote from his preface, like what was happening in 1820:

> GOOD ADVICE FOR 1820 — & FOR 1992
> To shew how well our little work has been appreciated by the public, we need no other evidence than to witness the many new publications of the kind annually springing up, whose Authors appear ambitious of a similarity to ours, by copying our plan and form, and some have even assumed our title, which will make it necessary for our friends and patrons to inquire for the "Farmer's Almanack by R. B. Thomas" to prevent any mistakes.

## WHEN'S THE BEST TIME TO CASTRATE YOUR BULL?

FROM THE BEGINNING, the Almanac has been calculated on astronomy, not astrology. But just as we include a few pages of astrology in each edition today, so too did Thomas include an annual table designating "The Names and Characters of the Signs of the Zodiac." After each sign is a body part — Virgo, belly; Sagittarius, thighs; Capricorn, knees; and so forth. These body parts appear in the left-hand calendar pages to indicate where in the heavens the moon will be located every day of the year.

Almanac readers were very familiar with "The Man of the Signs," sometimes called "The Moon's Man" or simply "The Anatomy." Before you had a diseased arm bled, for instance, you wanted to be very sure the moon was located in Gemini. (Gemini is in charge of your arms.) Along with the signs, or separate from them, the phases of the moon were used to determine the most propitious times for weaning a baby, planting certain vegetables, making butter — you

### THE UNITED STATES IN 1826

- John Quincy Adams is the nation's 6th president.
- The U.S. population, according to the 1820 census, stands at 9,638,359 persons — 93 percent of them living in rural areas.
- Total U.S. land area is 1,792,552 square miles, including 43,090 square miles under water.
- Thomas Jefferson and John Adams both die on the Fourth of July, the 50th anniversary of the Declaration of Independence.
- *The Old Farmer's Almanac* prints 96,000 copies.
- Since its first edition in 1792, the Almanac has printed a total of 1,800,000 copies.

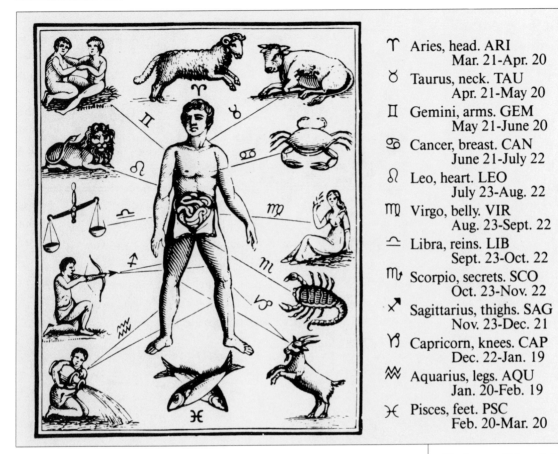

|  |  |
|---|---|
| ♈ | Aries, head. ARI Mar. 21-Apr. 20 |
| ♉ | Taurus, neck. TAU Apr. 21-May 20 |
| ♊ | Gemini, arms. GEM May 21-June 20 |
| ♋ | Cancer, breast. CAN June 21-July 22 |
| ♌ | Leo, heart. LEO July 23-Aug. 22 |
| ♍ | Virgo, belly. VIR Aug. 23-Sept. 22 |
| ♎ | Libra, reins. LIB Sept. 23-Oct. 22 |
| ♏ | Scorpio, secrets. SCO Oct. 23-Nov. 22 |
| ♐ | Sagittarius, thighs. SAG Nov. 23-Dec. 21 |
| ♑ | Capricorn, knees. CAP Dec. 22-Jan. 19 |
| ♒ | Aquarius, legs. AQU Jan. 20-Feb. 19 |
| ♓ | Pisces, feet. PSC Feb. 20-Mar. 20 |

name it. Providing an insight into the *timing* of day-to-day activities was a major function of the Almanac.

Just as in Thomas's time, our readers today use both our astronomical data and the astrological tables to determine timing. Common queries I receive, besides what the weather will be on a future date, have to do with when, according to the Almanac, it would be best to, say, have a tooth pulled or plant the peas. If the query is from Texas or Oklahoma, however, I know that more than likely it will be about castrating bulls.

"In the next ten days," a caller will ask, "when would the Almanac say would be the best time for me to castrate my bull?"

I always tell him to do it when the moon is waning (from the time it's full to the time it's new), as there should be less bleeding then. But sometimes the caller persists in having a more precise time, and that's when I recall the answer my uncle always gave in similar circumstances: "Why don't you try it," I'd hear him say into the telephone, "when he's asleep."

*The famous "Man of the Signs" or "Moon's Man" indicated what part of the human body was controlled by each sign of the zodiac.*

## Never, Never Drink Ardent Spirit

IN THE 1834 ALMANAC are ten illustrated pages designed to convince readers to stop drinking hard liquor, a dominant Almanac theme in the years to come. "Never drink ardent spirit," the article concludes, "even temporarily; for all drunkards were once temperate drinkers." Perhaps there's a smidgen of irony in the fact that not many pages removed from that advice is a chart indicating the distances "from one established tavern to another."

*A road map of New England, along with a list of distances between towns and taverns, was included in all nineteenth-century editions.*

I've found that when I give that answer, no matter how serious the caller may be about wanting the information, it invariably provides a few seconds of shared laughter.

## HUSKINGS ARE FRIVOLOUS — AND SO ARE BARN RAISINGS

IN THE 1832 EDITION, Thomas inserts the word *old* into his title. After all, the Almanac is almost forty, and back then, that was *old*. After the 1835 edition, he inexplicably drops it; the publication is simply *The Farmer's Almanac* again until 1848, two years after Thomas's death. Then, finally, *The OLD Farmer's Almanac* becomes the official and permanent title.

Two years after *old* first appears, Thomas reaffirms his no-nonsense, nose-to-the-grindstone approach to life. He actually comes out *against* good old-fashioned barn raisings and husking bees (social gatherings, common at that time, for the purpose of husking corn). "If you love fun and frolic and waste and slovenliness more than economy and profit," he notes, "then make a husking."

According to historian Jack Larkin (in his book, *The Reshaping of Everyday Life — 1790–1840*), New England farmers of this time took the Almanac's advice very seriously. The husking done at husking bees was not

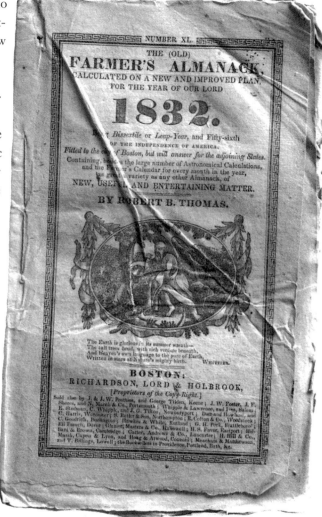

*In this edition, the word* Old *appears as part of the Almanac title for the first time.*

"clean," and much of it had to be redone after the party. Barn raisings involved lots of rum and hard cider. Bad. So, spurred on by the scoldings of the Almanac, gatherings combining socializing and work were on the decline.

## A FOND FAREWELL AFTER FIFTY-FOUR YEARS

FOUR YEARS PRIOR to his final (1846) edition, Thomas writes several compact pages about the previous fifty years of America and his Almanac, already the oldest continuously published periodical in the country. Seems as though he's even become a little sentimental in his old age. He titles the piece "Fifty Years Ago."

## Thomas Has a Close Call

In the course of the summer [of 1792], I made an excursion with a party to the fashionable resort *Fresh Pond*, Watertown, where we passed the day in different amusements and spent our money freely. I boarded in Milk Street, in the same house that Mr. D. Hill since owned and where he kept a grocery store adjoining. . . .In the latter part of August, the small-pox became very prevalent in Boston, which made me anxious to leave the town, not having had it myself. I left and came to L. Bemis, Esq.'s in Watertown, with whom I had an intimacy. Here I enjoyed myself some days. At length my father sent me a horse, and I returned home.

After tarrying a few weeks, and copying for press my first Almanack, I went to the hospital in Worcester, situated on the hill a mile north of the street, and was inoculated with the smallpox by Dr. J. Green, sen. When inoculated, I flattered myself and was flattered by the doctor, of being a good subject, and would have the disease light, having never exposed myself to heat and cold nor excessive labor, and had ever been temperate; but it turned out quite otherwise. I had the disease very severely. For many days my life was despaired of; and, in fact, it was, I afterward learned, currently reported in the neighboring towns that I was dead. I suffered much, but received every attention. . . .After spending five weeks here, the doctor gave me a clear discharge, though I made a most ghastly appearance and the people shunned me as I returned home, supposing me to be infectious. . . .

After I returned home I was weak and feeble for some months; after which I enjoyed good health, and, in general, have to this day, though advanced in life.

*From the last installment of Robert B. Thomas's autobiography, published in the 1839 edition of* The Old Farmer's Almanac.

### FIFTY YEARS AGO

Fifty years! It is life itself! In that time how many millions who were, half a century ago, living, breathing, and moving, full of hope, of young life, of energy and of vigor, have gone down to the silent grave! In that time what countless millions of the human race have been called "to sleep the sleep that knows no waking."

. . .Fifty years ago, the worthy fathers and mothers of the present generation were willing to dress in their own homespun. . . .[Now] the waterfall and steam engine, the improved spindles and other machines, manufacture millions of yards. . . .

. . .[T]hough we may not reach the 100th number of The Old Farmer's Almanac, yet we shall endeavor to improve as we progress. . .[and hope our Patrons] will not be disposed to cut our acquaintance, as a modern dandy would a rusty cousin from the backwoods. Because we look, as we pride ourselves in looking, a little old-fashioned, a little too independent to hang our dress for each "new-fangled notion" — a little t'other side of fifty.

In the Almanac for that year, I see the advertisements have been expanded to include more than just Bibles, psalm books, primers, schoolbooks, and stationery, all of which have been included — off and on — from the beginning. Now we also have steel pens and pen holders, slates, toothpowder, ink, and "camel's hair" pencils — as well as maps of all thirty states in the Union.

Thomas's last edition is not much different from his first. Both are forty-eight pages, although the 1846 edition includes four additional cover pages, and both include about the same type of "new, useful, and entertaining matter" as their title pages advertise.

His last weather forecast covers December 26–31, 1846. "Very fine for the season," it reads. To the end, he was not one to venture way out on a limb. Next to the final weather forecasts are these prophetic words: "So, then, my friends, with whom I have associated for many a year, I sincerely bid you a cheerful *good-bye*."

On May 19, 1846, he died in his home of typhus, nine years before his wife, Hannah. Much of his estate went to the sons of his then deceased brother, Aaron, whose house still stands in West Boylston, Massachusetts.

Now that I've reached this point in my reading of these old editions, I feel a little sad. There'll be no more Robert B. Thomas in the editions ahead. And I've become rather fond of this crusty, wise, blunt, sometimes witty, and, in his later years, sentimental New Englander who managed to maintain his enthusiasm in behalf of his readers for more than half a century. I'm going to miss him as I proceed along without him, my trusty magnifying glass close by, toward the far-off turn of the century and beyond . . . ✦

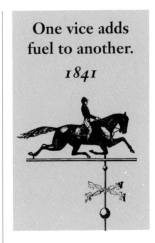

**One vice adds fuel to another.**

*1841*

## LEGAL KNOWLEDGE IN RELATION OF MAN & WIFE
### (1834)

- In law the husband and wife are considered as one person.
- The wife cannot sue in her own name.
- All contracts made between them before marriage are dissolved upon that event.
- Upon marriage, the husband becomes possessed of all right and title to her property.
- All debts due to the wife become, after marriage, the property of the husband.
- The husband is bound to provide his wife with all necessaries suitable to her condition in life and becomes liable for debts contracted by her for such necessaries, but not for superfluities or extravagances.

*During a 1966 restoration, this sour-faced portrait of Thomas's wife, Hannah, was found underneath a smiling version that was flaking with age.*

# Success & Prosperity *on the Road to* Disaster

*The Almanac is one of those old institutions which is perennially young in the appeal which it makes. From long custom we depend on it. It is an invaluable friend.*

— Franklin D. Roosevelt, 1938

A SERIES OF NEW EDITORS CARRY ON WITH VARYING SUCCESS, Abraham Lincoln uses the Almanac in a murder trial, the Civil War comes and goes, medicines are developed to cure *everything*, carriage fares are replaced by automobile laws, airplanes are charged with trespassing over private property, and the tenth editor commits the greatest Almanac blunder of all time. ✦

*The spring of 1928 in Vermont. The old ways of doing things still came in handy on occasion.*

## TEMPERANCE TAVERNS, JAPANESE ALMANACS & A THEORY ON LIGHTNING

WHEN ROBERT B. THOMAS DIED, the Almanac was being published by Jenks & Palmer, a successful Boston printing and publishing company, and it was John H. Jenks of that firm who became the second editor. In the 1847 edition, he pays Thomas a nice tribute, pledges to "continue the Almanac, the oldest in the country, through the present century at least," and says that Thomas's name "will always be connected with it in future as in past time." And so it has been.

A tide table is added "for all the New England coast" in the 1848 edition, and the "Mathematical Puzzles" section is expanded a bit, but little else changes. I see a reference to the existence of Temperance Taverns where no grog is served, but that information is tempered, so to speak, by the observation that follows: "O, how this world is given to lying."

There's also a lighter side to Jenks's material. "We have been favored with a sight of a Japanese Almanac," he notes in 1848. "It is printed on silk paper on both sides, is 10½ feet long and 6 inches wide, folding up in plaits. We found it easier to measure its length than to read its contents."

In spite of the holes and torn pages in my 1855 copy, I'm informed that "by calculations as to the mean strength of animals, it appears that a horse, drawing horizontally, and at the rate of two-and-a-half miles an hour, can work for eight hours in succession against a resistance of two hundred pounds." Not even a breather now and then?

**Fools will worship a mule that carries gold.**

*1849*

### WHAT TO DO WHEN A PERSON IS STRUCK BY LIGHTNING
#### (1855)

PERSONS STRUCK BY lightning should not be given up as dead for at least three hours. During the first two hours, they should be drenched freely with cold water and, if this fails to produce restoration, then add salt and continue the drenching for another hour.

### Why Is Benjamin Franklin on the Cover?

THE 1851 COVER WAS THE FIRST to feature the present-day "four seasons" drawing by Henry Nichols, a Cambridge, Massachusetts, engraver, although it was then dropped until 1855, when it finally became permanent. Thomas's face was included on the right-hand side as a tribute to him, but the reason for putting Benjamin Franklin on the left remains unclear. Franklin died in 1790, and his *Poor Richard's Almanac* had gone out of business long before that.

There's no evidence to indicate that Thomas and Franklin ever met. I can only surmise that Franklin, a popular historical figure with an almanac connection, was stuck on the cover simply to balance out the design.

## THE UNITED STATES IN 1863

- The U.S. population is 31,443,321, as of 1860.
- The Civil War drags on into its 3rd year, with a major Union victory at Gettysburg.
- President Lincoln issues the Emancipation Proclamation in January and delivers his Gettysburg Address in November.
- West Virginia becomes the 35th state.
- James L. Plimpton introduces roller-skating in the United States.
- *The Old Farmer's Almanac* distributes 225,000 copies.

The following year, editor Jenks espouses a theory about lightning. Apparently, there had been fewer thunderstorms than usual during the previous two summers, and Jenks attributes that to the proliferation of railroad tracks and telegraph wires. He writes that these expanding tracks and wires across the country tend to "draw off the electricity in the clouds. . .to make the storms of thunder and lightning less frequent than heretofore." Well, there *were* more railroad tracks in 1856 than before — judging from the fact that the annual (since 1841) "Railroads in New England" feature is now expanded from one page to two.

## ABRAHAM LINCOLN, THE ALMANAC & A MURDER TRIAL

IN OUR DUBLIN, NEW HAMPSHIRE, office hangs a reproduction of a painting by Norman Rockwell depicting Abraham Lincoln standing in front of a jury holding the 1857 edition of an almanac in his hand. Was it *The Old Farmer's Almanac?* It's difficult to prove conclusively, but everything I've read about the case — and certainly my examination of the 1857 edition — indicates that it was.

The occasion depicted in the Rockwell painting is the 1858 murder trial of an Illinois man named William "Duff" Armstrong. Armstrong was accused of murdering James Preston Metzker with a "slung-shot" — a weight tied to a leather thong, sort of an early blackjack — a few minutes before midnight on August 29, 1857. Lincoln was a friend of the accused man's father, Jack Armstrong, who'd just died, and so he offered to help defend young Duff Armstrong, without pay, as a favor to Jack Armstrong's widow.

The principal prosecution witness against Armstrong was a man named Charles Allen, who testified that he'd seen the murder from about 150 feet away. When Lincoln asked Allen how he could tell it was Armstrong given that it was the middle of the night and he was a considerable distance away from the murder scene, Allen replied, "By the light of the moon."

Enter the Almanac!

Upon hearing Allen's testimony, Lincoln produced a copy of the 1857 edition, turned to the two calendar pages for August, and showed the jury that not only was the moon in the first quarter but it was riding "low" on the horizon, about to set, at the precise time of the murder. There would not have been enough light for Allen to identify Armstrong or anyone else, said Lincoln. The jury agreed, and Duff Armstrong was acquitted.

| 21 | Fr. | { Earthquake in California, 1855. | *Coolish* |
| 22 | Sa. | ♅ □ ⊕ *Dull and change* | |
| 23 | D. | 11th Sun. af. Trin. | *able* |
| 24 | Mo. | St. Bartholomew. | *with* |
| 25 | Tu. | { C. C. Lawrence. | *rain* |
| 26 | W. | ☽ in apogee. *Fine again* | |
| 27 | Th. | { Battle of Long Island, 1776. *Low tides.* | |
| 28 | Fr. | *Some rain and wind.* | |
| 29 | Sa. | ☽ runs low. ♀ ☌ ♄ | |
| 30 | D. | 12th Sun. after Trinity. | |
| 31 | Mo. | { C. C. P. Worcester. | |

*Abraham Lincoln prepares to show an 1857 almanac to the jury during the famous Armstrong murder trial in the spring of 1858. The original of this Norman Rockwell painting hangs in the The Norman Rockwell Museum in Stockbridge, Massachusetts. The detail from the August 1857 calendar page contains the crucial information for Saturday, August 29.*

## COTTON BLOSSOMS & PATENT MEDICINES

JOHN JENKS SPENT the later years of his life as an invalid. That fact may account for his turning over the Almanac editorship — long before his death in 1869 — to one of his frequent contributors, Charles Louis Flint. Flint, the third Almanac editor, a graduate of Harvard University (1849) and Harvard Law School, Massachusetts's first secretary of agriculture, and one of the founders of the Massachusetts Institute of Technology (MIT), took over with the 1861 edition.

In the 1862 edition, he announces "a prominent feature of this number — the complete chronological record of events connected with the rise and progress of the rebellion against the national government." But it's not presented as a feature article. Instead, for the next six years, the chronological record of the war is jammed in among all the calendar and astronomical data on the calendar pages — and always in tiny four-point type.

An obvious trivia enthusiast, Flint includes on these same pages any number of off-the-wall tidbits of information such as "Cotton in blossom at this time in China" or "The Nile in Egypt is now at its height."

Patent-medicine advertisements increase during Flint's final two years. Readers can buy remedies for "Children Having Worms," as well as "Bronchial Troches" to relieve the throats of "Public Speakers, Singers, and those who over-tax the voice." A listing of testimonials for the latter includes one from Reverend Henry Ward Beecher, the most famous preacher in America during these years, in which he seems to become somewhat entangled in his prepositions: "I have never changed my mind respecting them from the first, excepting to think yet better of that which I began thinking well of." Pardon?

My research hasn't revealed why Flint gave up the helm of the Almanac with the 1869 edition (he would live for twenty more years), but give it up he did. The fourth editor, John B. Tileston, partner in the Dorchester, Massachusetts, firm of Brewer & Tileston, then the Almanac's publishers, took over temporarily while a search was undertaken for a permanent editor.

For his two years on the job — the shortest tenure of any Almanac editor before or since — Tileston was content mostly to repeat feature articles from past issues. The calendar pages in the 1870 and 1871 editions, so full of type during the 1860s, are now half empty, with the blandest, safest weather predictions of all time floating about in the spaces.

Loomis Joseph Campbell, a schoolteacher and textbook author, took over as editor beginning with the 1872 edition. Lasting only four years, he seems to have been equally uninspired. Like Tileston, he kept the Almanac going in the traditional format but added few of his own ideas. The title page poem in 1872 is, however, among my all-time favorite Almanac poems:

> Among the pitfalls in our way,
> The best of us walk blindly;
> So, man, be wary, watch and pray,
> And judge your brother kindly.

I expected that Campbell would make an effort to do some special things in the 1876 edition, but I find only one sentence regarding the nation's Centennial: "A hundred years this year since our fathers founded the Nation." That's *it*? Well, perhaps negotiations for selling the Almanac to the family-owned Boston publishing company William Ware & Co. were already under way by then and Campbell had lost whatever interest he'd had in the Almanac.

**THE UNITED STATES IN 1882**

- The population of Boston is 362,535; of Chicago, 500,000; of New York, a little more than 1 million.
- There are 10,357,981 horses in the U.S.
- Floods in Mississippi leave 85,000 homeless.
- The electric flatiron is patented by Henry W. Seeley.
- The nation's Indian wars are nearly over. It's been 6 years since Custer's Last Stand, but it will be only 6 more to the infamous Battle of Wounded Knee.
- William Horlick of Racine, Wisconsin, produces America's first malted milk.

# WHEN CLOCK TIME SLIPPED SIXTEEN MINUTES BEHIND BOSTON

*In 1878, editor Robert Ware was particularly concerned by the growing number of New Englanders heading west. He attributed the phenomenon to restlessness rather than the twin lures of California gold and easier farming. "Re-occupy the deserted farms," he pleaded, "and look more directly to mother earth for means of supporting a large and increasing population."*

ROBERT WARE, SON of the founder of William Ware & Co., took over as the sixth editor in 1877, but since his was a big company with many employees, he probably delegated many Almanac editorial tasks. Nonetheless, there seem to be fewer blank spaces on the calendar pages, and I no longer recognize many stories repeated from previous editions.

In the 1878 edition Ware shows considerable courage by specifically forecasting hail for Tuesday, July 23. Perhaps he was gambling on another miracle forecast like the one for the summer of 1816.

The 1885 edition is a milestone of sorts in that it's the first to be computed on standard time (adopted by the country in 1883), "sixteen minutes behind Boston local time." The Almanac seems suspicious of it, however. Until 1900 (I peeked ahead), it includes a table of New England cities followed by plus minutes or minus minutes in the event "greater accuracy is desired." For instance, for Keene, New Hampshire, add five minutes to standard time; for Portland, Maine, subtract three minutes. Can you imagine living your life like that?

## CURES FOR WHATEVER AILS YOU

MEDICINES ADVERtised in the 1889 edition included "cures" for ailments such as piles, scrofula, leprosy, eczema, "cancerous and ulcerated sores," and "all diseases of the skin and blood." There didn't seem to be a disease you couldn't cure with a medicine advertised in *The Old Farmer's Almanac*.

Considerably more upbeat (if less profound) was the first Coca-Cola advertisement in the 1898 edition. "A delightful summer and winter beverage," it said modestly, that cost "five cents a glass at soda fountains." Seven years earlier, the first Almanac ad for Arm & Hammer baking soda had appeared. Arm & Hammer continues to advertise in the Almanac today.

*Typical Almanac ads from the 1899 edition.*

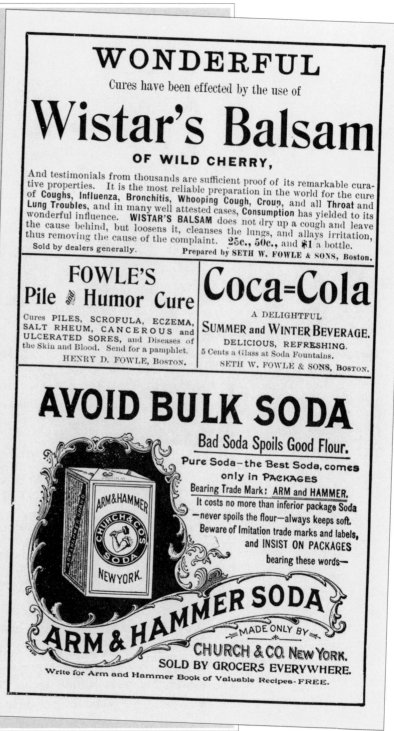

*Almanac reader Allyn Chase of Danvers, Massachusetts, recently found this photo of an early Almanac agent (salesperson) holding the 1893 edition.*

## A NEW WAY TO MILK TWO COWS SIMULTANEOUSLY

IN 1892, FORTY-SIX YEARS after Robert B. Thomas died, the "Centennial Number" remembers him well. In addition to a biographical feature about Thomas, editor Robert Ware and his publishers spring for an Almanac first — an insert of thick, glossy paper on which Thomas's portrait appears on one side and a photograph of the 1793 title page on the other.

Gentle scolding of readers for being idle, drunk, inconsiderate, and lazy continues each year as the nineteenth century draws to a close. But I notice there are more words of encouragement. "Be cheerful," the Almanac advises now from time to time. "If there is a virtue in the world at which we should always aim," says the 1893 edition, "it is cheerfulness." In the same edition, however, is a poem that's anything but cheerful:

## A HUNDRED YEARS FROM NOW

The surging sea of human life
Forever onward rolls,
And bears to the eternal shore
Its daily freight of souls.
Though bravely sails our bark today,
Pale Death sits at the prow,
And few shall know we ever lived,
A hundred years from now.

Why should we try so earnestly
In life's short, narrow span,
On golden stairs to climb so high
Above our brother man?
Why blindly at an earthly shrine
In slavish homage bow?
Our gold will rust, ourselves be dust,
A hundred years from now.

## THE UNITED STATES IN 1900

- William McKinley is re-elected president, with Theodore Roosevelt as his vice president.
- Carry Nation, leading the national temperance movement, begins raiding saloons with a hatchet.
- There are 45 states in the Union.
- More than 200 die when 3 steamships catch fire while docked at Hoboken, New Jersey.
- Wilbur and Orville Wright's historic flight near Kitty Hawk is just 3 years away.

With the 1900 edition, the Almanac editorship passed from Robert Ware to his brother Horace, a lawyer, banker, and member of the Massachusetts legislature. In the 1906 edition, Horace Ware introduces to the pages of the Almanac one of the major components of the twentieth century:

## AUTOMOBILES & MOTORCYCLES

- All states (in New England) except Connecticut require that a certificate of registration be issued for every vehicle in use.
- It is required in all states that registered numbers shall be displayed on the machines. . .and, except for Connecticut, carried in the machines.
- There are provisions to the rate of speed, to taking precautions against frightening horses. . .to carrying brakes, bells, horns, or other sound signals and lights.

A report on experimental milking machines, which could milk two cows simultaneously, appears in the 1908 edition, while the 1911 edition lists the dozens of docks in Boston from which transatlantic passenger ships left for destinations in Europe and North Africa. The jokes during these years remain hopelessly corny by today's standards, but here, from 1913, is one of the better ones (if you can believe it):

## A MUTUAL SERVICE

He — "I am very unfortunate; it seems I can please nobody."

She — "Come, cheer up; I have no one to admire me either."

He — "Tell you what. Let's found a society for mutual admiration. I, for instance, admire your beautiful eyes. And what do you admire in me?"

She — "Your good taste."

World War I ended in November 1918, a month or so after Horace Ware had gone to press with the 1919 edition. In it, he suggests that "during this period of bloodshed, of striving and sacrifice," Almanac readers would do well to "achieve that calmness of mind which is so often induced by a study of the Heavenly Bodies. . .or in the contemplation of the changing seasons with their perpetual renewing of life. . .and a better realization of the healing process which pervades all of Nature." Somewhere in that thought, as expressed by the Almanac's seventh editor, may well be a clue to this venerable publication's continuity, longevity, and success. It has always, as David Hartman once said to me on the "Good Morning America" television show, provided its readers with "a certain sense of perspective."

## A WARNING ABOUT TRESPASSING BY AIRPLANES & A MESSAGE FROM THE PRESIDENT

FOLLOWING WARE'S DEATH in 1919, the Almanac was acquired by Frank Buzzell Newton, another Boston lawyer, who expanded the advertising away from the patent medicines of earlier days and toward products such as Burpee seeds, King Arthur flour, and Arm & Hammer baking soda — which by now had become an old standby.

He also expanded the subject matter for the "Farmer's Calendar" columns. Instead of sticking to detailed hints and advice strictly for farmers, for instance, the July column of the 1926 edition advocates "the restorative powers of a bath"; September deals with signs of malnutrition in children; and October informs readers how to make concrete.

Carroll Swan, a Boston advertising man and author of *My Company*, a book detailing his combat experiences during World War I, was the next owner and editor of the Almanac. He called the 1933 edition (his first) "the largest Almanac ever published — 96 pages."

In past editions, I've noted the Almanac's worries about dangerous new phenomena such as electric wires, sleighs driven by teen-agers, telegraph wires, and husking bees. In 1933, it's airplanes:

### FARMER'S RIGHTS REGARDING AVIATION

Since the dawn of our common (English) law, the courts have jealously guarded the right of the landowner against trespassers. It has been held that a trespass may be committed by walking on the ground, by tunneling under the ground, or by invading the air space above the ground. This was on the principle that "he who owns the earth owns down to the center of the earth and up to the skies."

The development of the airplane. . .[makes] every inch of the plane's progress a trespass. . . .The ability of our law to retain the heart of the [trespassing] theory and still atone for the progress of civilization is shown by the uniform tendency of the courts to hold that flying at certain heights is not a trespass against the landowner.

The 1934 edition, published in the depths of the Great Depression, contains a special message from Franklin Roosevelt promoting planning, one of the Almanac's favorite themes down through the years:

*For some in the 1930s, flying airplanes was still a wild and crazy thing to do. This game of singles took place over Kansas.*

**Economy is a way of spending money without getting any fun out of it.**

*1927*

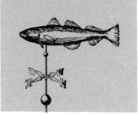

*Franklin Roosevelt used the Almanac several times in the 1930s to convey upbeat messages to the American public.*

## A MESSAGE FROM THE PRESIDENT

I am glad through the medium of *The Old Farmer's Almanac*, to extend my best wishes to the people of New England and to express my appreciation of the splendid cooperation you are giving.

Many hard lessons have taught us the human waste that results from lack of planning. Here and there a few wise cities and countries have looked ahead and planned, but our nation has "just grown." It is time to extend planning to a wider field. If we are successful we can march on, step by step, in a development of the great natural territorial units within our borders.

*Franklin D Roosevelt*

## THE GREATEST OF ALL ALMANAC BLUNDERS

AFTER CARROLL SWAN died in 1935, the Swan family licensed the Almanac copyright to Little, Brown & Co. of Boston, which appointed Roger Scaife, one of Boston's widely known literary figures, to be the tenth editor. "An almanac, perhaps more than any other type of publication, should recognize the March of Time and the changing conditions which govern everyday life," says the 1936 announcement of the change, thus ushering in the only period in the Almanac's long history in which it declined precipitously in circulation and financial stability. (The 1938 edition was down to 88,000 from probably twice that earlier in this century; circulation in 1863 is known to have been approximately 225,000.)

Maybe it wasn't all Scaife's fault. Perhaps the Almanac had come to represent a sort of nostalgia for the good old days that, after years of the Great Depression, the American public didn't feel was particularly relevant or entertaining. It's apparent that Scaife tried. His contributors include N. C. Wyeth, Robert Frost, and Joseph Lincoln, along with a host of widely known public officials such as Henry Wallace. Unfortunately, what these impressive-sounding officials write about might put anyone from any period in history to sleep. Among their articles are "The Value of the Study of Local History in the Public Schools," "Maine Agriculture," "The Supreme Court and the Constitution," and "Crime in America."

Scaife's one true blunder occurs in the 1938 edition. Although I knew about it long before my current reading, I'm still shocked: *there are no weather forecasts in that edition.* Instead, Scaife puts in temperature and precipitation averages along with statements like, for the end of March, "Nights are usually above freezing." Disaster.

My uncle told me that the public outcry was greater than when Teddy Roosevelt omitted "In God We Trust" from the nickel. (At least it showed that people still cared about the Almanac.)

Scaife reinstated the forecasts in the 1939 and 1940 editions, his last two, but it was too late to save his reputation in Almanac history. He'll always be remembered as the editor who left out the weather forecasts in *The Old Farmer's Almanac.* His considerable and impressive lifetime literary accomplishments? Long forgotten.

By 1939 the Almanac was losing money, and Little, Brown & Co. was looking for a way out. Along came my uncle, Robb Sagendorph, Harvard class of '22, who'd discovered the family steel business was not for him and had moved, with wife Beatrix and their two daughters, from Boston up to tiny Dublin, New Hampshire, to found *Yankee* magazine in 1935. "After more than one double martini," he later wrote of his meeting with the Little, Brown & Co. people, "I found myself the new owner and new editor of the Almanac."

The Almanac's future was about to be determined and nurtured by a man who was devoted to tradition and, at the same time, unpredictable by nature. An interesting and rather mind-boggling combination, as the next thirty years would prove. ✦

## THE UNITED STATES IN 1937

- Aviator Amelia Earhart disappears in the Pacific.
- The dirigible *Hindenburg* burns at Lakehurst, New Jersey.
- The Great Depression continues.
- War is approaching in Europe.
- There are 123,202,660 people in the U.S., according to the 1930 census, and 23,032,000 dairy cows.
- Rural electrification is bringing electricity to U.S. farms for the first time; 2 years ago, only 10 percent of American farms had electricity.
- The 1938 Almanac is the first — and last — edition with no weather forecasts.

# DISCOVERING *the Secrets of a* Healthy OLD AGE

*Tides, sunset and moonrise, holidays — as a maker of almanacs I find all these timetables useful in guiding us to what I like to call the edges of creation. In arriving there, we must have plans and calculations and all manner of manmade data. But once there, the open sky, sea, canyon, mountain peak, or stillness of a pond takes over and regulates our lives and thoughts. In Nature's own house we suddenly feel not careworn, but cared for.*

— Robb Sagendorph, 1957

DURING THE SECOND HALF OF THIS century, the Almanac, under the direction of one family, carries on its traditions, is almost banned by the U.S. government during World War II, becomes famous for a few outstanding weather forecasts and one inadvertent prediction that had nothing to do with the weather, defines *treason*, develops the fine art of "almanacsmanship," and tries to decide whether advertisements for miracle cures are, well, in questionable taste. ✦

*The Almanac's eleventh editor, Robb Sagendorph, in Dublin, New Hampshire, about 1965.*

## SUPPLYING INFORMATION TO THE ENEMY

ROBB SAGENDORPH, the eleventh editor, feeling that tradition was the Almanac's strongest suit, immediately reestablished its format and editorial style to be more like it had been under Robert B. Thomas. He even began using initials, as Thomas had, to credit contributors. "My respected friend J.C.D. is gratefully recognized for his acceptable annual contribution," he writes in the 1941 edition. "If he will be so kind as to call at the publisher's office, he will find remuneration for his labor." Must have misplaced J.C.D.'s address.

The upscale advertising — John Hancock Life Insurance, American Oil, and Underwood Deviled Ham — remains, but it's now mixed with old-style products. "Stop Your Rupture Worries" or "Piles So Bad I Couldn't Sit" are typical headlines. Readers can send away for glass eyes or order false teeth for $6.85 on a sixty-day trial basis. (Do you suppose those returned as somehow unsatisfactory were then shipped out to new customers?)

Because the 1942 edition went to press some five months before the attack on Pearl Harbor, the 1943 Almanac is the first in which one senses the country's embattled status. Roosevelt's picture joins that of Thomas and Franklin on the otherwise still traditional (since 1855) yellow cover, and the issue includes special wartime recipes (without meat) and pertinent observations by Sagendorph — who, by this time, was working for the U.S. Office of Censorship in Washington, D.C. In 1944 he notes, "The Almanac staff is at present in the armed forces or in war service. Thus is this edition born in the all-too-few hours of evenings and Sundays. . . in the candlelight of part-time labor."

The Old Farmer believes that our government will use every means to keep us out of war.

*1940*

Throughout the war, the following letter is included every year at the bottom of the "To Patrons" section. Apparently it is there as a result of one of the most famous episodes in Almanac history, ranking right up there with the summer snow forecast of 1816 and the Abraham Lincoln murder trial story of 1858.

The Office of Censorship
Washington, D.C.

August 30, 1943

YANKEE INC.
Dublin, N.H.

Gentlemen:

Thank you for submitting in proof form the weather indications for *The Old Farmer's Almanac* for the coming year. Due to your published statement that these are "weather indications," there is no application to them of the request in the "Weather" clause of the Code of Wartime Practices for the American Press that no weather *forecasts* be published except those issued by the U.S. Weather Bureau.

Your cooperation under the Voluntary Code is appreciated.

Very truly yours,
Jack Lockhart
Assistant Director (Press)

The story behind this letter, as told to me by Sagendorph many times, concerns a German spy who was apprehended by the FBI on a train going into New York City's Penn Station sometime during 1942. He'd landed on Long Island from a U-boat the night before. In the German's coat pocket was the 1942 edition of *The Old Farmer's Almanac*.

*When a German spy put ashore on Long Island by a U-boat was apprehended by the FBI, a copy of the Almanac was found in his pocket. Our government then decided that either the Almanac should be banned or the word "forecasts" should be eliminated. My uncle was always of the opinion that it was the tide tables the Germans had used. "Then again," he'd usually add, "maybe it was the forecasts. After all, the Germans went on to lose the war."*

Why were the Germans interested in the Almanac? Who knows? (Maybe they liked the jokes.) But the U.S. government speculated that the Germans might be using it for the weather forecasts. In other words, the Almanac was supplying valuable information to the enemy!

So to the "Code of Wartime Practices for the American Press" was added the stipulation that no weather forecasts were to be published in the United States except by the government itself. This put future wartime editions of the Almanac in jeopardy. According to Sagendorph, there was a real possibility that it would be banned "for the duration."

Somehow Sagendorph managed to get the government to agree that there would be no violation if the Almanac featured weather *indications* rather than *forecasts*. (It probably helped that Sagendorph worked for the Office of Censorship.) And so, until the 1946 edition, the usual "Weather Forecasts" cover line reads instead, "Weather Indications."

The Almanac remained on the newsstands — and even began claiming a slightly better accuracy rate for its "indications." By this time, one Abe Weatherwise was credited with all Almanac forecasts. "Old Mr. Weatherwise writes from his government job," Sagendorph notes in the 1944 edition, "that his Weather Indications of the past year, for the eight months he has been able to verify them, ran about 83 percent right." That's three points higher than the traditional 80 percent most Almanac editors claimed for their forecasts.

## WINTERS WILL BE "MILD," "TURBULENT," "WET," "WHITE" & THEN "ICY"

UNDER SAGENDORPH, the weather forecasts become a more important part of the Almanac. Over the years, he expands Thomas's "secret formula" of weather cycles to include the entire country (as he does with the editorial coverage in general), and he devotes far more space to weather matters, while continuing the usual two- or three-word forecasts that have been running down the right-hand calendar pages since 1793.

When reading the Almanac of those years, however, it's difficult to determine how seriously Sagendorph took his weather forecasting. In the 1945 edition, for instance, he positively gloats about the accuracy of his "mild winter" forecast for 1944, saying that "our forecast will remain a counterpart in years to come for the famous cold summer forecast of 1816." But then, two years later, he cautions

### THE UNITED STATES IN 1942

- As the U.S. enters World War II, sugar, gas, and coffee are rationed.
- Boston's Cocoanut Grove nightclub burns; 487 die.
- There are 132,165,129 people in the U.S., according to the 1940 census, and 24,940,000 dairy cows.
- U.S. Marines land on Guadalcanal.
- Zoot suits are in style.
- More than 200,000 copies of *The Old Farmer's Almanac*'s 150th edition are printed — and one of them turns up in the hands of a Nazi spy.

A TYPICAL SAGENDORPH REPLY TO A READER QUERY (1949)

LULU B., NEW Britain, Connecticut: You request the actual number of snowflakes that fell in New England during the month of December 1947. Our staff reports that the actual count they made, which came to quite a figure, remains inaccurate inasmuch as several of the flakes that fell on the eastern side of Mount Mansfield, near Stowe, Vermont, became mixed up with some that had blown up from the ground (already counted). Sorry.

readers against considering "the forecasts herein as anything more than guides or reminders as to what *may* happen."

He loved to summarize all his forecasts in one word. One word for the entire United States, for the entire winter. Then, in the following edition, he'd assess its accuracy — which, if one is to take *his* word, couldn't have been much better. In the 1949 edition, for example, he writes that "the past five winters — first 'mild,' then 'turbulent,' then 'wet,' then 'old-fashioned,' and, finally, last year's 'white, long, and cold' — followed exactly the predictions of Mr. Weatherwise."

Seemingly beginning to run out of good one-word forecasts, he predicts the 1950 winter will be "icy." And I guess it was, at one time or other. Briefly carried away by his success, he breaks with the traditional Almanac claim of 80 percent accuracy the next year by saying all the forecasts for the previous year — day by day as well as summaries — were "almost 100 percent accurate." (Well, at least he said "almost.")

These were heady times for the Almanac. Circulation was healthy again, profits were good, and every year seemed to generate more publicity nationwide. Over the next decade, Sagendorph was interviewed by *Colliers*, *Life*, and *The Saturday Evening Post*; appeared on television shows such as "What's My Line?" and "I've Got a Secret"; and generally became a familiar media character — all of which, as he writes in his "To Patrons" pages, "kept the Almanac a good distance this side of oblivion."

## BETTER A DOUBLE BED THAN A STONE JUG FOOT WARMER

IT'S CLEAR TO SEE that by this time Sagendorph has positioned his editorial matter in a finely tuned balance between humble and proud, whimsical and serious, useful and, at times, downright wacky. Each edition includes something thoughtful, too — usually provided by the contributions of a Peterborough, New Hampshire, apple farmer named Benjamin Rice, who, by the late 1940s, was responsible for the "Farmer's Calendar" essays. For example . . .

### DECEMBER 1949

In December, poised on the very rim of the icy cup of winter, it is as if we were given a clairvoyance with which better to see and understand the troubles and longings and beauty of this world — and men's hearts. Of the good green summer over, of the long gray winter ahead, our minds are sharp with contrasts. In the bite of twilight our thoughts, too, are keen and quickened. In looking to our own comfort and security — the filled woodshed, the well-banked house, the armory of food in the cellar — in looking to these, there comes a truer sense of the other fellow's lacks and hungers. Clear as Monadnock against the December sky we have the meaning of our own lives in this strange and lovely world — a world of want and plenty, peace and war — all that is worst in mankind and all that is best. No life has

*Along with the Declaration of Independence, the Almanac was included in the Grolier Club's 1946 list of "one hundred books, printed before 1900, remarkable for their influence upon American life and culture." Also on the list were Montgomery Ward's mail-order catalog, Webster's dictionary, and the Monroe Doctrine.*

## SAGENDORPH GOES BANANAS

BY THE END OF the 1940s, perhaps emboldened by the Almanac's success, Sagendorph began to innovate. Starting with the 1949 edition and continuing for the next ten years, he published multipage color inserts advertising the United Fruit Company's Chiquita bananas, of all things. To say they seemed out of place in the Almanac is an understatement, but the recipes for banana fritters, banana pancakes, banana doughnuts, and so on, all were scrumptious.

*A page from one of the sixteen-page, full-color banana inserts bound into every Almanac in the 1950s.*

So ...   Buyabanana
Tryabanana
Fryabanana
Diceabanana
Spliceabanana
Grababanana
Nababanana
Beatabanana
Eatabanana

HAVABANANA TODAY!

FREE! For free reprints of this booklet, send your name and address to United Fruit Company, Dept. OFA, Pier 3, North River, New York 6, N. Y.

UNITED FRUIT COMPANY

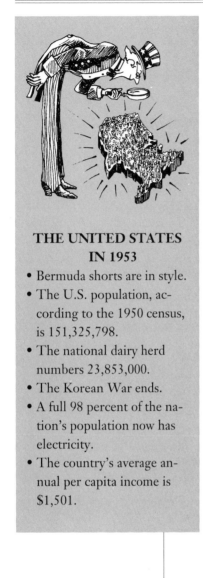

## THE UNITED STATES IN 1953

- Bermuda shorts are in style.
- The U.S. population, according to the 1950 census, is 151,325,798.
- The national dairy herd numbers 23,853,000.
- The Korean War ends.
- A full 98 percent of the nation's population now has electricity.
- The country's average annual per capita income is $1,501.

meaning save as it touches others and reaches out to as much of humanity as it may cheer and help.

In the country here we like to think that this "December" wisdom springs partly from the fact that we can look, when we will, over the long valley to the whitening shoulder of the mountain. But in truth we know that as much wisdom as we or any man may find can be sought and found in the windows or on doorsteps, at street corners or altars — or from mountains everywhere. It is a wisdom that springs from the heart alone. It is the heart that must see.

That's the more contemplative side of the Almanac, but there's another side, too. As always, year after year, Sagendorph maintains his friendly, informal, teasing relationship with his readers:

Mrs. B.D.R., Spokane, Washington: Your request as to where you may purchase a stone jug foot warmer as a substitute for your electric heating pad has been referred to the Society for the Return of the Double Bed. (1952)

The jokes and anecdotes also continue, but as you can see from the following, not only is Almanac humor beginning to more closely resemble what we consider amusing today, but the "talkative woman" stereotype of past editions has obviously given way to reality:

AS USUAL
"How did you get along with your wife in that last argument?"
"Oh, she came crawling to me on her knees."
"Yeah? What did she say?"
"She called me a coward and dared me to come out from under the bed."

## A HEAVY SQUALL & THAT'S NOT ALL

SAGENDORPH BEGINS rhyming some of his weather forecasts in the 1950 edition — "A few hours' thaw, then cold and raw" or "Gone are the leaves, all except Eve's." His most famous rhyming forecast appears in the 1953 edition. For the first six days of June, the prediction reads, "A heavy squall and that's not all." The next day's forecast, on the seventh, is just one word: "Nasty." Two days later, on June 9, 1953, New England's most disastrous tornado roared into Worcester County, Massachusetts, killing eighty-nine people. The rhymed Almanac forecast provided a light side to an otherwise grim story, and it was quoted extensively in newspapers throughout the country. From then on, Sagendorph made sure all his calendar page weather forecasts were in equally quotable rhyme. "No lounge lizard will enjoy this blizzard," was the prediction for early February 1955, and again it was right on target.

By 1956 Sagendorph's outstanding forecasting success had surely gone to his head. That's the only way I can explain his making such an outlandishly brazen forecast for the winter of 1956. "It will be," he flat out says in bold type, "as severe as any of the 20th century."

*An unidentified woman contemplates the destruction of her home by the Worcester County, Massachusetts, tornado of June 1953. The Almanac's forecast: "A heavy squall and that's not all."*

Well, it wasn't. So in the following edition, he demonstrates the backpedaling skills so essential to the success of a long-range weather forecaster — skills he was to refine even more in his later years.

## CONCERNING A
## QUESTIONABLE WEATHER FORECAST

The overall prediction made by staffer Abe Weatherwise for last winter read: "As severe as any of the 20th century." If immodesty on our part in pointing with pride to the success of this prediction will be forgiven, which we doubt, we would like to point out that with the exception of February, during which Europe took unto itself the bad weather Abe had expected here, the past winter will stand in the records of the 20th century as "severe.". . . As nearly as our limited means of observation can determine, and taking into account that even a Boston prediction for "rain" can be successful on the Common and on the same day wrong two blocks away . . . [etc., etc.]

From 1957 on, the predictions don't go as far out on a limb. Also, Sagendorph returns to quoting the traditional 80 percent accuracy rate of all previous Almanac forecasters. No more of the "almost 100 percent accurate" sort of claims. "If Abe is given zero for one error last winter," he writes in the 1961 edition, "his score is an even 80 percent."

Ironically, the Almanac "forecast" (if one can refer to it as such) that received the most reader reaction — letters from around the world, in fact — had nothing to do with the weather. Nor was it deliberate. Studying that November 1963 calendar page in front of me now brings back all the horror and disbelief of that incredible Friday, November 22, in Dallas, Texas.

"Two full moons this month — guard against crime" appears at the bottom of the page. Ben Rice's "Farmer's Calendar" essay is uncharacteristically gloomy, referring to a blue jay crying "havoc, havoc" and to guns and "human misery."

I recall Ben Rice telling me he meant nothing by these words, except that he'd always felt a sense of foreboding when there were two full moons in the month of November. Ben Rice was as sensitive a person as anyone I've known.

Two years later, the horror of that awful day is remembered. "Dear God," says the November 1965 calendar page, "please take care of your servant, John Fitzgerald Kennedy."

But life — and the Almanac — continued, and neither one was entirely somber and sad. The 1966 Almanac contains a feature describing in graphic detail "The Mating Habits of the Eastern Skunk," and I recall Sagendorph

The earth is building a pollution area between herself and the sun — the United States contributes half of it.

*1970*

hesitating to publish a wacky 1966 feature about body moles for fear some readers would take it seriously . . .

### THERE'S A FORTUNE IN YOUR MOLES

• A mole on the outside corner of either eye denotes the person to be of steady, sober, and sedate disposition, but will be liable to a violent death.

• A mole on the lip, either upper or lower, proves the person to be fond of delicate things and very much given to the pleasures of love, in which he or she will commonly be successful.

• A mole on the belly denotes the person to be addicted to sloth and gluttony, selfish in almost all articles, and seldom inclined to be nice or careful in point of dress.

As a 175th anniversary gift to Almanac readers, Sagendorph inserts into the 1967 edition two beautiful color reproductions from a fifteenth-century hand-inscribed *Book of Hours* he'd purchased on a trip to Europe. Well, it's

*November 22, 1963, the day the Kennedys landed in Dallas, was inadvertently noted by the Almanac as one marked for "human misery" as well as "murder, perhaps."*

*As a 175th anniversary "gift" to its readers, the Almanac presented this reproduction from a fifteenth-century Book of Hours. Well, not exactly a gift. Readers were encouraged to send in a dollar for three more.*

*sort* of an anniversary gift. Readers are invited to send to the Almanac for three of them "on postcard stock" for one dollar.

In the 1968 edition, Sagendorph explains why he has continued to use the all-but-illegible small type in the Almanac. "The continuity of this Almanac as an American and family tradition," he writes in his "To Patrons" section, "is desired by its readers . . . and although a larger format, bigger type, etc. might [sic] make it easier to read, the maintaining of the original 1793 format is now a *must*, and any major change in this format, more readable or not, would seem to us (and most of our readers) as almost treason." *Treason?*

I recall arguing with him on this point. "Uncle Robb," I'd say, "the Almanac may be America's best-loved publication, but with type as small as we're using, it's America's least-read publication." He wouldn't budge. Scenic photographs of Spain, religious paintings from Europe, Chiquita bananas — sure. But leave the tiny type alone. Well, he *was* stubborn about small matters (like type!), but he also was an innovator, a visionary, and, particularly in his relationship with his readers, an editorial genius. I surely loved the man.

## NEVER OUTGROW YOUR OWN PLUMBING CAPABILITIES

SAGENDORPH prepared his final Almanac, the 1970 edition, during 1969 while he was dying of cancer. There's an account of the 1969 moon landing by Armstrong and Aldrich, something readers were already knowledgeable about from the saturation of media coverage during the more than

"So that readers of this Almanac in future generations will have a record of exactly how it was," Sagendorph explained, the 1970 edition (his last) included an account of the Armstrong-Aldrich moon landing.

## THE UNITED STATES IN 1970

- Richard M. Nixon is president.
- Deep in the Vietnam War, the nation is rocked by student unrest.
- There are 2,949,000 farms in the U.S.
- The U.S. population is 203,211,926.
- It costs 6¢ to mail a letter.
- There are approximately 4 million tractors in the U.S.
- The country's average annual per capita income is $3,893.
- Robb Sagendorph, 11th editor and 20th publisher of *The Old Farmer's Almanac*, dies at age 69.

two months prior to this edition's publication date. So why include it? Because, like most of the previous Almanac editors, Sagendorph believed (as I do) that one of the Almanac's responsibilities is to in some way reflect each year of publication. The moon voyage, he writes, is included "so that readers of this Almanac in future generations will have a record of exactly how it was." (Yes, there'll be jillions of other records, but perhaps none in any publication that has heretofore demonstrated more continuity, stability, or promise of its future existence.)

The data on which the Almanac's weather forecasts were based were now being prepared by Dr. Richard Head, a distinguished solar scientist and formerly a chief scientist for NASA during the highly successful Mercury program. Dr. Head had recently resigned from NASA to join the Almanac staff on a full-time basis so he could continue his solar research and, as a by-product, prepare the annual Almanac forecasts. The secret formula had taken a back seat. But Sagendorph reserved the right to summarize Dr. Head's data, and his wording in doing so for the forthcoming winter of 1970 is a far cry from the "worst winter of the 20th century" prediction he boldly (and unwisely) proclaimed for 1956. I guess he'd mellowed.

### SAGENDORPH'S LAST WEATHER FORECAST
*or Almanacsmanship at Its Best*

This coming winter will be its atrocious, fickle, unpredictable self. The ingredients — make no mistake — for heavy snows, blizzards, frozen pipes, and toes are all here. BUT the averages say warmer than normal coast to coast.

WHILE LYING very ill at the hospital in Peterborough, New Hampshire, several weeks before his death on July 4, 1970, Sagendorph asked Rob Trowbridge, his son-in-law, and myself, his nephew, to approach his bedside together. He told us it was his wish that Rob succeed him as the Almanac and *Yankee* magazine publisher and that I succeed him as editor of both. Then, in almost a whisper, he said, "But don't grow any more, boys."

"Why not?" we asked, expecting great words of wisdom. Both *Yankee* and the Almanac had been expanding rapidly for ten years, and certainly we'd all discussed plans to continue that trend. "Because," he said, "the plumbing won't take it."

## What They Say About
### *The Old Farmer's Almanac*

AND THE 190TH ANNUAL EDITION of *The Old Farmer's Almanac* is out this morning. Some people read it for its weather forecasts, planting tables, recipes, secrets of the zodiac, phases of the moon. I like the ads, myself. The ads in *The Old Farmer's Almanac* are like no others. They're for windmills, denture cushions, buried treasure wands, abdominal appliances, choir robes, red suspenders. There's an ad in here for rooster pills, for men who feel run down, worn out, and lacking pep and spark. Those whom nature has dealt a losing hand. There's not a brittle, sophisticated ad in this whole edition. *The Old Farmer's Almanac* is willing to leave that market to *Playboy* and the *New Yorker*. These ads speak to the real America. The one that is worried about its false teeth falling out or its pants falling down; devout, a little superstitious, and suffering a decided lack of pep and spark. Publications come and go with their ads for designer gowns. *The Old Farmer's Almanac* offers remedies for aching feet. That's why it's lasted for 190 years.

*Charles Kuralt, 1981.*

---

*The late Walt Kelly sent the original of this cartoon to the Almanac offices, signing it, "From a fan."*

## THE UNITED STATES IN 1991

- There are 50 states in the Union.
- The U.S. population is 245.8 million, of which 80 percent live in or near a large city.
- The national dairy herd numbers 10,149,000.
- There are 2,143,000 farms in the nation, cultivating 988 million acres.
- It costs 29¢ to mail a letter.
- The country's average annual per capita income, as of 1990, is $18,480.
- The 200th edition of *The Old Farmer's Almanac*, with 6.4 million copies in print, sells for $2.95.

I felt let down. How could he be joking at a time like this? But as the years have passed, I've come to regard his last advice to us as not only prophetic (the plumbing situation in our buildings later became a continual nightmare) but, in a much larger sense, downright profound.

## ARE MIRACLE-CURE ADS IN GOOD TASTE?

SOMEHOW IT DOESN'T seem appropriate for me, now the twelfth Almanac editor, to comment on the twenty-two editions I've edited to date. Let me just say that the best of what we've published during those years, at least in my opinion, is represented in Part II.

The changes we've instituted have not been radical. Not even particularly noticeable at first glance. Well, yes, call it treason if you wish, but we did enlarge the type in the 1972 edition. (Sorry, Uncle Robb, but we just couldn't help ourselves.)

With Dr. Head in full scientific and solar stride, we've expanded the weather forecast coverage to the present sixteen regions across the United States, plus, eventually, the five regions we now have in our special Canadian edition. In other words, long-range weather forecasting, for all its pitfalls and uncertainties, has become a more substantial effort than at any other time in the Almanac's history, costing us well over $100,000 annually. Our accuracy? Still 80 percent. Of course.

We've added to the annual number of pages, slightly increased the overall dimensions, begun testing all recipes, attempted to clarify the all-important astronomical data on the calendar pages, enlarged the staff, and solicited good writers and illustrators from around the United States and Canada. Also, with the 1988 edition, we initiated an annual "Consumer's Guide" section designed not only to predict consumer trends but, more important, to reflect the current year of publication for, as Sagendorph put it, "readers of this Almanac in future generations." But we continue to punch the traditional hole in the upper left-hand corner, so the reader can hang it up, even though the cost of doing so has risen to more than $50,000 each year.

We still refuse all liquor and cigarette advertising, as well as any other advertising we determine is harmful. However, we also continue to debate the merits of certain products and generally divide all advertising into three basic categories: (1) advertisements in good taste (the vast majority); (2) advertisements in questionable taste (like maybe miracle cures or anti-aging

NEW ENGLAND SNOWFALL
(IN INCHES)

products); and (3) advertisements in bad taste (voodoo dolls, for instance, as well as many ads that could easily be labeled pornography). Each year, following heated debates, we happily accept ads in categories 1 and 2.

With all the subtle changes implemented over the years, I believe that were Robert B. Thomas to return to this world and pick up the two hundredth edition of his creation at a newsstand or bookstore, he'd recognize it. I'd also like to think he'd be pleased — and proud.

However, it is by our works and not our words that we would be judged. These, we hope, will sustain us in the humble though proud station we have so long held in the name of

Your ob'd servant,

*Rob. B. Thomas.*

September 1991

*The year is 1971, shortly after the death of Robb Sagendorph. Rob Trowbridge (left), Sagendorph's son-in-law, and yours truly, Sagendorph's nephew, had just taken over as publisher and editor, respectively. The chart behind us reflects actual snowfall from 1960 to 1971 — with the dotted line indicating our 1972 forecast. As I recall, it turned out to be about 80 percent accurate.*

# EDITORS OF *The Old Farmer's Almanac*

Robert Bailey Thomas (1793–1846)

John Henry Jenks (1847–1860)

Charles Louis Flint (1861–1869)

John Boies Tileston (1870–1871)

Loomis Joseph Campbell (1872–1876)

Robert Ware (1877–1899)

Horace Everett Ware (1900–1918)

Frank B. Newton (1919–1932)

Carroll Swan (1933–1935)

Roger Scaife (1936–1940)

Robb Sagendorph (1941–1970)

Judson Hale (1971–present)

---

# PUBLISHERS OF *The Old Farmer's Almanac*

Belknap & Hall (1793–1795)

Belknap (1796)

John West (1797–1812)

West & Richardson (1813–1819)

West, Richardson & Lord (1819–1820)

Richardson & Lord (1821–1829)

Richardson, Lord & Holbrook (1830–1832)

Carter, Hendee & Co. (1833–1836)

Charles J. Hendee (1837–1838)

G. W. Palmer & Co. (1839)

Jenks & Palmer (1840–1851)

Jenks, Hickling & Swan (1852–1854)

Hickling, Swan & Brown (1855–1857)

Hickling, Swan & Brewer (1858–1860)

Swan, Brewer & Tileston (1861–1862)

Brewer & Tileston (1863–1876)

William Ware & Co. (1877–1918)

The Old Farmer's Almanac, Inc. (1919–1935)

Little, Brown & Co. (1936–1940)

Robb Sagendorph, Yankee, Inc. (1941–1970)

C. Robertson Trowbridge, Yankee Publishing Inc. (1971–1989)

John Pierce, Yankee Publishing Inc. (1990–present)

# PART II
## *The Greatest Moments*

The following chapters, beginning with the weather,
feature the twelve editorial subject categories almost always
included in every edition of the Almanac. Representing
each category are the most interesting, the most unusual,
the most useful (and, in some cases, the most useless)
stories, quotes, charts, and tidbits I discovered in my
careful reading of every edition. In other words, they're the
*best*, the crème de la crème, of everything published in
*The Old Farmer's Almanac* over the past two hundred years.
But, of course, that's just *my* opinion . . .

# CHAPTER FOUR

# WEATHERWISE
# *& Otherwise*

*WHAT* THE OLD FARMER'S
ALMANAC *TOLD*

*It told when the tin peddler Swift was due;*
*It told when we paid the milk bill, too.*
*It told when we bought a barrel o' flour;*
*It told when Pa'd get his herrin' "dower."*
*Our ma, on weather, would have her say;*
*Our pa jes' thought "Old Farmer's" way.*

MAINTAINING WEATHER RECORDS WAS A
popular pastime when the Almanac began.
Three of the first four U.S. presidents, for
instance, including Washington, owned their
own weather instruments, from which they
recorded daily observations. In the margins
of some eighteenth- and nineteenth-century
copies of the Almanac are hand-written notations such as "rainy and cold" or "light
snow last night" — along with bits of personal history like those noted in the above
rhyme. Few Almanac readers today maintain
weather diaries, but their interest in weather
matters remains high. ✦

---

*A priest hears confession at a church in*
*Long Beach, Mississippi, wrecked by Hurricane*
*Camille on August 17, 1969. The Almanac's*
*prediction: "This storm is cold and to*
*the devil sold."*

# The Greatest Single Prediction of All Time

*Or was it a stroke of luck?*   By T. R. LeMaire

I N November 1868, Lieutenant S. M. Saxby of the British navy notified the London press that our world would be visited by a gale of frightful violence and unprecedented tides during the following year. Saxby named the day, October 5, and the hour, 7 A.M.

Saxby based his long-range prediction not on the simple instruments of the day but on astronomy. He observed that a lunar coincidence would place the moon directly over the earth's equator on that date. With moon and sun exerting their maximum pull at the same time, he reasoned, unusually high tides would result "— and nothing more threatening, I say, can occur without a miracle."

Saxby's calculations were refined by Frederick Allison of Halifax, who pinpointed the storm's landfall. Allison hardly endeared himself to the neighbors by announcing Halifax harbor as the target.

**When it rains pottage, hold out your dish.**

*1809*

As the fateful date of October 5, 1869, neared, Halifax citizens acted in very human ways. Many laughed at Saxby and Allison's "luny" notion of forecasting a hurricane eleven months in advance. Some saw doomsday a-coming and prayed for deliverance. Others began boarding up windows.

Unknown to all, a tropical storm was prowling up the Atlantic toward Nova Scotia — right on schedule. A beast of the sea, it swished its tail at Nantucket Sound, and the island's newspaper reported for October 4, 1869, "No material damage." Boston had a "short squall" about three thirty that afternoon, but at sea ships were being shattered.

The Saxby-Allison forecast had named Halifax as the target, with 7 A.M. as zero hour. The prediction was amazingly close — within about one hundred dred miles and twelve hours. The gale struck during the preceding night. Instead of plunging along the easterly shore of Nova Scotia, it attacked the west. Up the Bay of Fundy it roared, blasting the shores of Maine and New Brunswick. The Saxby Gale was a full-blown hurricane.

On the day following the Saxby Gale, a traveler covering the thirty rural miles between Eastport and Calais, Maine, counted ninety houses either blown apart or severely damaged. A crewless vessel was blown across Passamaquoddy Bay and up the St. Croix River, a distance of thirty miles.

The Saxby Gale was unique, however, not for wind but for water. The rain, the tides, and the floods in most areas were without equal. Although the eye of the hurricane had remained at sea, the Middle Atlantic and New England states drowned.

Rain gauges overflowed. At Goffstown, New Hampshire, nearly four and a half inches cascaded down

---

## SURE-FIRE(?) *Methods for Predicting the* WEATHER 1

### Yes, the Animals & Birds Know

- Sheep run to and fro, jump from the ground, and fight in their gambols before a change of weather.
- When cattle lie out, or pigs lie down for the night without covering themselves with litter, fine weather will continue.
- Asses hanging their ears forward or rubbing themselves against walls or trees prognosticate rain.
- Cats remaining indoors, devoid of vivacity, forecast wet or windy weather.

- Frogs croaking more than usual, moles throwing up more soil than usual, toads in great numbers, and oxen licking their forefeet all mean rain.
- Owls hooting and screeching during bad weather foretell fine weather near at hand.
- Swallows flying near the ground, robins coming near the house, and sparrows chirping a great deal all mean rain or wind.
- If the kingfisher disappears, expect fine weather.

on the town in only two hours. At Canton, Connecticut, an observer would not submit his rain report because he "measured 12.35 inches but do not think it could possibly have been so much." It was!

An enormous wall of water surged along the Fundy coast. Fundy tides, of course, are famous, reaching heights of forty-five and even fifty feet. But during the Saxby Gale, the tide literally left its mark on Parrsboro buildings near the head of the bay — and that mark was at fifty-seven and a half feet!

This amazingly accurate forecast has been called many things: a miracle of meteorology; one of the best near misses in the entire history of prediction; a stroke of luck. Guesswork, however, appears to be ruled out by the laws of probability. How high are the odds against anyone blindly picking a spot between Mexico and Newfoundland where a hurricane will strike next year — and being accurate within one hundred miles? It's possible. But also naming a time between June 1 and November 30, and being correct within twelve hours, seems to ask too much of rabbits' feet and horseshoes.

Despite the record rains, the floods, and the forecast fantastic, the Saxby Gale was forgotten by New Englanders. For decades, New England regarded itself as immune to tropical storms, well clear of the frequent devastation associated with the Gulf states' "hurricane alley." Then came September 1938, when the horrendous '38 hurricane ignored the Gulf of Mexico and stalked up the Atlantic seaboard instead. Tragically few people were aware that a tropical storm could strike so far north. They had forgotten the Saxby Gale. ✦

## SURE-FIRE(?) *Methods for Predicting the* WEATHER 2

### USING FLOWERS & VEGETABLES

- The common chickweed (*Stellaria media*) has a small white flower that, if closed, means rain is close at hand. In dry weather, it is regularly open from nine in the morning until noon.
- When the African marigold remains closed after 8 A.M. or before 5 P.M., rain may be expected.
- Many other flower varieties close their petals as rain or night approaches, opening them again after the rain or when morning comes. Examples include germander, speedwell, red campion, wood sorrel, Hieraciums, succory, common daisies, wintergreen, and white water lily.
- Watch for rain if any of the following open later or close earlier than usual: day lily (opens at 7 A.M., closes at 7 P.M.); dandelion (opens at 7 A.M., closes at 8 P.M.); lettuce (opens at 8 A.M., closes at 9 P.M.).
- Plenty of berries or acorns indicates a severe winter ahead. Thin and delicate onion skins mean a mild winter.

## SURE-FIRE(?) *Methods for Predicting the* WEATHER **3**

### A Table Foretelling the Weather Through All the Lunations of Each Year — Forever

THIS TABLE IS the result of many years' actual observation and shows what sort of weather will probably follow the moon's entrance into any of its quarters. For example, the weather for the week following November 10, 1992, would be rainy because the moon becomes full that day at 4:21 A.M. EST.

*Editor's note:* While the data in this table are taken into consideration in the yearlong process of compiling the annual long-range weather forecasts for *The Old Farmer's Almanac,* we rely far more on our projections of solar activity.

| TIME OF CHANGE | SUMMER | WINTER |
|---|---|---|
| Midnight to 2 A.M. | Fair | Hard frost, unless wind is south or west |
| 2 A.M. to 4 A.M. | Cold, with frequent showers | Snow and stormy |
| 4 A.M. to 6 A.M. | Rain | Rain |
| 6 A.M. to 8 A.M. | Wind and rain | Stormy |
| 8 A.M. to 10 A.M. | Changeable | Cold rain if wind is west; snow if east |
| 10 A.M. to noon | Frequent showers | Cold with high winds |
| Noon to 2 P.M. | Very rainy | Snow or rain |
| 2 P.M. to 4 P.M. | Changeable | Fair and mild |
| 4 P.M. to 6 P.M. | Fair | Fair |
| 6 P.M. to 10 P.M. | Fair if wind is northwest; rain if south or southwest | Fair and frosty if wind is north or northeast; rain or snow if wind is south or southwest |
| 10 P.M. to midnight | Fair | Fair and frosty |

This table was created more than 150 years ago by Dr. Herschell for the Boston *Courier;* it first appeared in *The Old Farmer's Almanac* in 1834.

**Cut your grass while the dew is on if you would have your scythe move smoothly.**

*1835*

# America's Most Destructive Storms

BECAUSE POPULATION and valuation differences make it impossible to assess earlier storms, for the most part this list is restricted to those occurring after 1890.

• **Most destructive tropical hurricane (measured in lives lost):** The Galveston, Texas, hurricane of September 8, 1900. The storm is estimated to have killed between 6,000 and 7,200 people, mainly in a 20-foot-high tidal surge that swept over the unprepared city. The highest exact-count hurricane death toll in the United States is 1,836 — from the San Felipe hurricane of September 17, 1928, which blew Lake Okeechobee, Florida, out of its bed and into the adjacent towns and farms.

• **Most destructive tropical hurricane (measured in over-all devastation):** The Great New England Hurricane of

*New Haven, Connecticut, was buried by the blizzard of March 11–14, 1888. "Raw, easterly winds," predicted the Almanac.*

September 21, 1938. All or parts of six states were devastated by high winds, tidal surges, and floods, the combination of which killed an estimated 600 people. From a strictly meteorological standpoint, Hurricane Camille, which hit the Mississippi coast on August 17, 1969, is believed

to be the most intense ever to hit the United States; warnings of Camille's approach held the death toll to 144.

• **Most destructive floods induced by hurricanes:** August 18 and 19, 1955, Pennsylvania to Massachusetts, brought on by Hurricane Diane, with 172 dead and $700 million in property damage. June 22, 1972, floods from Hurricane Agnes left Pennsylvania and New York with 122 dead and $2.1 billion in property damage.

• **Most destructive small-area flood:** Johnstown, Pennsylvania, flood of May 31, 1889. Cloudbursts broke the dam on the Conemaugh River; the city was wiped out, and 2,100 people were killed.

• **Most destructive single tornado:** March 18, 1925, with a track of 219 miles (the longest on record) from Redford, Missouri, to Princeton, Indiana; 695 people were killed, 2,027 were injured, and property damage totaled $17 million.

• **Most destructive single-location tornado:** Natchez, Mississippi, May 7, 1840. Most of the city was leveled, three steamboats were sunk, and 317 people were killed. Property damage was reported as at least $5 million in the currency of the period.

• **Most destructive snow-storm:** Probably the Great East Coast Blizzard of March 11–14, 1888. Snowstorms as a rule cause little direct destruction or loss of life, so comparisons are difficult. The 1888 blizzard, however, appears unrivaled for the magnitude of its disruption of commerce and transportation and for the number of people — estimated at 100 or more — who died of exposure in its drifts.

• **Most destructive ice storm:** January 28–February 1, 1951, in Tennessee and northern Mississippi, Alabama, and Georgia. Damage from downed trees, broken power lines, and collapsed roofs was estimated at $100 million; 25 people died, and more than 500 were seriously injured. ✦

*Compiled by Andrew E. Rothovius.*

*The Almanac has generally avoided predicting tornadoes like this one in Kansas — except for the famous Worcester tornado forecast in 1953.*

# How Come No Two Snowflakes Are Alike?

*In the 4 billion years of the earth's history, nobody's ever found twins.* By Chet Raymo

*Wilson A. Bentley dedicated almost his entire life to photographing and observing snowflakes.*

Is THERE ANY TRUTH to the old saw, "No two snowflakes are alike"? Of course, the question could be laid to rest if someone succeeded in observing two identical flakes. The person who had the best opportunity to do so was Wilson A. Bentley of Jericho, Vermont. Bentley was a farmer and amateur meteorologist. For fifty years, he dedicated himself to observing flakes of snow.

On his fifteenth birthday, Bentley's mother gave him the use of an old microscope. It was snowing that day, and the boy succeeded in getting a glimpse of a six-sided snowflake with the instrument; that was the beginning of a fascination that lasted the rest of his life. By age twenty, the unschooled farm boy had perfected a technique for photographing snowflakes. When death ended the adventure half a century later, Wilson Bentley had accumulated nearly five thousand microphotographs of snow crystals. He also had won worldwide fame as an expert on the meteorology of snow. In his own neighborhood, he was known simply as the "Snowflake Man." After his death, an editorial in the *Burlington Free Press* said, "He saw something in the snowflakes which other men failed to see, not because they could not see, but because they had not the patience and the understanding to look."

We have Bentley's word for it that no two snowflakes in his collection were alike. That fact was a source of satisfaction for him. In the simple snowflake, he stood face to face with one of nature's deepest mysteries, what the Greeks called "the problem of the One and the Many": how does any form endure in the face of almost limitless possibility? The snowflake exemplified for Bentley the kaleidoscopic balance of order and disorder that is the basis of beauty in nature and in art.

But five thousand snowflakes is a relatively small number. If we had the patience and understanding to inspect five million snowflakes, or five billion, might we find at least one pair of twins? The answer is almost certainly no.

A single crystal of snow weighs about a millionth of a gram. In a cup of snow, there are more than 10 million flakes.

I estimate that something like $10^{22}$ snowflakes fall on New England in a typical snowstorm. (That's 1 followed by 22 zeros.) During the 4-billion-year history of the earth, perhaps as many as $10^{34}$ snowflakes have fallen on it. (Add 12 more zeros.) Could it really be possible that among that unimaginably large number of flakes, no two have been alike?

Twentieth-century physics has made substantial progress toward understanding the genesis of the snowflake's form. The hexagonal symmetry of snowflakes has its origin in the shape of the water molecule. A water molecule consists of an atom of oxygen and two atoms of hydrogen. The hydrogen atoms are connected to the oxygen in such a way that the two hydrogen "arms" make an angle about like the arms on the side of this $x$. The angle of the arms ensures that when water molecules link together to form a crystal, the resultant symmetry will be hexagonal, just as the placement of the holes in the knobs of a Tinker Toy set determines the symmetry of the structures that can be built with the set.

Now we turn to the probabilities of combination. A deck of fifty-two cards can be shuffled into $10^{68}$ different combinations. A small Tinker Toy set may have something like a hundred pieces; consider, if you will, the huge number of different structures that could be built with such a set. A single snow crystal consists of something like $10^{18}$ (1 quintillion) molecules of water. The number of ways that many molecules can be arranged into six-sided crystals is astronomical — vastly larger than the number of snowflakes that has ever fallen on the face of the earth. The odds are very great indeed that no two flakes have ever been exactly alike.

Wilson Bentley once wrote, "The farm folks up in this north country dread the winter, but I was always supremely happy, from the day of the first snowfall — which usually came in November — until the last one, which sometimes came as late as May." For the Snowflake Man, snow was a continuing lesson in the way nature's beauty arises from a delicate balance of law and chaos, stability and change. ✦

*For Bentley, the snowflake exemplified the balance of order and disorder that is the basis of beauty in both nature and art. These images are made from his original glass plates.*

# Exactly What, Why & When Is Indian Summer?

*The answers are not as simple as you may think.*

AFTER LABOR DAY HAS passed, it seems that almost any warm day in the northern part of the United States is referred to by most people as "Indian summer." And while their mistake is certainly not of the earthshaking variety, these casual observers are, for the most part, in error.

Besides falling within specific dates, true Indian summer must meet certain other criteria. It must be warm, of course. In addition, however, the atmosphere must be hazy or smoky, there must be no wind, the barometer must be standing high, and the nights must be clear and chilly.

The more controversial aspect of Indian summer is the time of its occurrence — or whether there *is* a certain time. Most would agree that warm days in the fall do not of themselves constitute Indian summer unless they follow a spell of cold weather or a hard frost. Beyond that, many references to Indian summer in American literature indicate that it occurs in late fall.

For the past two hundred years, this publication, as well as many other nineteenth-century almanacs, has adhered to the saying, "If All Saints' brings out winter, St. Martin's brings out Indian summer." Accordingly, Indian summer can occur between St. Martin's Day (November 11) and November 20. If the conditions that constitute Indian summer do not occur between those dates, then there is *no* Indian summer that year. If a period of warm fall weather occurs at a different time, such a period could be correctly described as being *like* Indian summer.

Finally, why is Indian summer called Indian summer? Some say the name comes from the Indians, who believed that the condition was caused by a certain wind emanating from the court of their god Cautantowwit, or the southwestern god. Others say that the term evolved from the fact that around the time of Indian summer, or shortly before it, the deciduous trees are "dressed" as colorfully as Indians.

The most probable origin of the name, in our view, goes back to the very early settlers in New England. Each year they would welcome the arrival of cold wintry weather in late October, knowing that they could leave their stockades without worrying about Indian attacks and could begin preparing their fields for spring planting. The Indians didn't like attacking in cold weather. But then came a time, almost every year around St. Martin's Day, when it would suddenly turn warm again, and the Indians would decide to have one more go at the settlers. The settlers called this Indian summer. ✦

## THE OL' GOOSE BONE METHOD
### *By Warren Evans*

BACK AROUND the turn of the last century, in the days before the National Weather Service, the so-called goose bone method was a famous weather-forecasting technique. Here's how it worked:

Around Thanksgiving, Grandma would cook a freshly killed goose. She would roast it, carve it, and serve it, always being careful not to cut the breastbone from the carcass.

After the goose had been eaten, she would carefully remove the breastbone and cut away all the meat and fat left clinging to it. Grandpa would take the bone and put it on a shelf to dry, keeping an eye out for the coloration that would follow.

If the bone turned blue, black, or purple, a cold winter lay ahead.

White indicated a mild winter.

Purple tips were a sure sign of a cold spring.

A blue color, branching out toward the edge of the bone, meant open weather until New Year's Day.

If the bone was a dark color, or blue all over, the prediction was for a real bad winter.

That's it. And there was even an explanation. An overall dark color meant that the bird had absorbed a lot of oil, which acted as a natural protection against the cold. The darker the blue coloring, the tougher the winter ahead would probably be.

# Is Another Ice Age on the Way?

*Glaciers could scrape Chicago, New York, and Boston from the face of the earth — but it would take a little time . . . .* By CHET RAYMO

O NCE I STOOD WITH a friend on a high bluff in New Hampshire's White Mountains. "Do you realize," I said, "that fifteen thousand years ago, all of these valleys about us were filled with ice? Only the peaks of the highest mountains stood above the glacier, like islands in a frozen sea. If we had stood here then, the ice would have reached in every direction as far as the eye can see."

"I don't believe it," said my friend.

"But it's true," I insisted.

"Oh, I know it's true," he replied. "But I don't believe it."

*Nineteenth-century geologist Louis Agassiz (seated) was the first to suggest that large parts of the North American continent were once covered by glaciers.*

I can easily forgive my friend his incredulity. When the Swiss American geologist Louis Agassiz suggested early in the nineteenth century that large parts of the northern continents were once covered by glaciers, the idea met with general skepticism. But once people knew what to look for, the evidence for an ice age became persuasive. Today no geologist doubts that those continent-spanning glaciers once existed.

Ten times during the past million years ice has advanced from polar regions to cover one-third of the land area of the earth. When the glaciers achieved their maximum coverage, North America was mantled by ice as far south as Cape Cod, Massachusetts; Long Island, New York; and the valleys of the Ohio and Missouri rivers.

If the cycle of glaciation continues, then sometime within the next few thousand years, the planet will begin to slip into another era of ice. How would we recognize the initiation of an ice age? We wouldn't, at least not within a lifetime or even many lifetimes. There are too many short-term climate controls that would likely mask the initiation of a true ice age.

Major volcanic eruptions, for instance, can significantly affect the climate. The eruption of the volcano Tambora in the East Indies in 1815 caused the famous "Year Without a Summer," when snow and freezes ruined crops in New England in July and August. The explosion of Krakatoa in 1883 spread dust into the stratosphere that cooled the earth for several years.

Our own interventions in climate also might mask the return of the ice. By burning fossil fuels, we are dumping vast quantities of carbon dioxide into the atmosphere. By cutting down the tropical rain forests we are diminishing the earth's capacity to remove carbon dioxide from the atmosphere. Carbon dioxide in the atmosphere serves the same function as glass in a greenhouse: it traps the sun's heat. The trapped heat may tend to keep the earth warm. But carbon dioxide also can stimulate plant growth, and plants in turn give off oxygen. Oxygen has a *cooling* effect, so perhaps the whole thing will become a stand-off.

But sooner or later, most climatologists agree, the glacial cycle will prevail and an ice age will return. What then? Over a period of many millenniums, temperatures will tend to decrease. The average drop in global temperatures during the most recent ice age was about 10°F. In contrast, the temperature drop during both the Little Ice Age and the Year Without a Summer was less than two degrees. If the pattern of the last ice age is repeated, it will take eighty thousand years to reach the full ten-degree drop.

Meanwhile, glaciers will begin an inexorable glide down mountain valleys. Ice sheets will begin to grow on the tundra of central Canada, moving radially outward under the influence of their own weight. They will push down across the continent like mile-thick bulldozers, scooping, grinding, and breaking everything in their path. They will plane off the tops of hills and excavate valleys. They will scrape Seattle, Chicago, New York, and Boston from the face of the earth.

It was June when I challenged my friend to imagine New Hampshire buried by ice. We were standing at the rim of Tuckerman Ravine on the shoulder of Mount Washington. In the bowl-shaped valley below us, a few dedicated skiers took advantage of the last remaining fields of winter snow in all of New England.

Skiing in Tuckerman sometimes lasts into July. Then, a few weeks later, the first of the next winter's snow arrives. A modest drop of average temperature would allow snow to go unmelted from one winter to the next. Year by year, the snow cover would thicken and turn to ice.

"Keep your eye on this place," I said to my friend. "When the next ice age comes, one of the signs will be a new alpine glacier in Tuckerman Ravine." ✦

# CHAPTER FIVE

# MEN &
# WOMEN & LOVE &
# BABIES

*MAN*
*At 10 a child, at 20 wild,*
*At 30 tame, if ever;*
*At 40 wise, at 50 rich,*
*At 60 good, or never.*
— Written by a wise woman in 1856

BEFORE NEWSPAPER ADVICE COLUMNS and television talk shows, Americans looked to sources such as *The Old Farmer's Almanac* for information, advice, and ideas to do with courtship, marriage, love, beauty, and, yes, even raising children. ✦

*Clowning for the photographer (unusual in nineteenth-century photographs) are these happy couples on an outing in Connecticut.*

# What Men Find Beautiful in Women

*On the burning question of the ideal woman's face, the Almanac reported in 1989, it all comes down to tiny fractions of an inch.* BY GEOFFREY ELAN

> *'Tis not a lip, or eye, we beauty call,*
> *But the joint force and full result of all.*
> — Alexander Pope

SORRY, MR. POPE. The latest research on attractiveness shows it *is* a lip, eye, or some other feature of a woman's face that we call beauty. We even know how wide those lips and how high those eyes ought to be.

Dr. Michael Cunningham, a psychologist at the University of Louisville, showed 150 male college students pictures of 50 women's faces and asked his subjects to rate the attractiveness of those faces on a six-point scale. The students didn't know that 27 of the women rated were Miss Universe contestants. The others were randomly selected college seniors.

To no one's surprise, the beauty contestants scored much higher than the college seniors. The women rated most attractive had certain features in common: large, widely spaced eyes, small noses and chins, prominent cheekbones, narrow cheeks, arched eyebrows, wide smiles, and dilated pupils.

That happened to be just what Cunningham had expected. He had a theory that what men would find beautiful in a woman's face would be a combination of two things. One would be what he called "neonate features" — large, widely spaced eyes and small noses and chins — which we associate with children, thus triggering subconscious feelings of warmth and protectiveness. The other would be features that suggest sexual maturity and responsiveness: prominent cheekbones, narrow cheeks, arched eyebrows, wide smiles, and dilated pupils.

"The sum total of the features signifies someone who is slightly young and helpless, though sexually mature and friendly," Cunningham concluded in the *Journal of Personality and Social Psychology*. "And men find that combination compelling."

Cunningham and his assistants got out their micrometers and measured the faces of the highest-rated women to come up with an idealized model

*Nefertiti, immortalized by this bust of her discovered in 1933, has come to represent the timeless beauty of a woman's face. While most early Egyptian busts were stylized, this one is, according to scholars, close to an exact likeness.*

of a beautiful woman's face. The ideal mouth, they found, should be exactly half the width of the face at mouth level. The eyes should be one-fourteenth the height of the face and three-tenths the width of the face at eye level. The pupils should be one-fourteenth the distance between the cheekbones. The distance from the center of the eye to the bottom of the eyebrow should be one-tenth the height of the face. The chin should be one-fifth the length of the face, and the total area of the nose (length from bridge to tip times the distance between the outer edges of the nostrils) should be no more than 5 percent of the total area of the face.

Cunningham admits that this is not an absolute standard of female beauty but one that college men of this time and place agree upon. Every culture has its own image of the beautiful woman. Ill health was fashionable in the United States in the years before the Civil War. Many a woman starved herself — or suffered severe internal injuries inflicted by corsets — to achieve an eighteen-inch waist. Harriet Beecher Stowe wrote in outrage, "We in America have got so far out of the way of a womanhood that has any vigor of outline or opulence of physical proportions that, when we see a woman made as a woman ought to be, she strikes us as a monster."

By the 1880s, though, plumpness was in. The Statue of Liberty, dedicated in 1886, portrays a large-waisted, broad-shouldered woman. It is interesting that the richly endowed women of Dutch painter Peter Paul Rubens were popular when Holland was becoming a world power. When the United States started throwing its weight around on the world stage, actress

*Marilyn Monroe's beauty was, in part, associated with the color of her hair. But the twentieth-century fixation on blondes is nothing new. "The reign of the blonde in modern literature is but a continuation of her reign in Greece and Rome," wrote classical scholar M. B. Ogle. (Yes, that really was his name.)*

*Rubenesque proportions like those of Lillian Russell have almost always been considered ideal — that is, until relatively recently. Some have suggested that a nation's drive for expansion can be measured in the bustlines of its most popular women.*

Lillian Russell's Rubenesque proportions were considered ideal. Some scholars have wondered whether a nation's drive for expansion can be measured in the bustlines of its most popular women.

Whatever the reason, the pendulum swung back toward thinness and didn't stop until it reached the rail-like flappers of the Roaring Twenties. Then came the backswing to voluptuousness that peaked with Marilyn Monroe in the 1950s. And so it continues, even to this day.

But no matter how fashion may change, research by Cunningham and many others shows that women perceived to be beautiful benefit from those perceptions in a host of ways. Not only are they sought after for dating and marriage, but they also tend to get better grades in school, do better in job interviews, and get higher pay. They also are more likely to be acquitted by juries. The studies are virtually unanimous: it's better to be beautiful.

It's safer, too. In another experiment, Dr. Cunningham showed pictures of sixteen women's faces to eighty-two male college students and asked them for which of the women they would be most likely to do certain things. The men studied, Cunningham reports, would be most willing to lend money to a woman with a small nose. They'd be more inclined to donate a kidney to a woman with a small nose and greater-than-average eye height. And for women with small noses, greater eye height, and greater eye width, the men would leap on a terrorist hand grenade. "Such results," Cunningham concluded, "suggest that the possession of attractive facial features may be of survival value for adults."

So get out those rulers and calculators. If your total nose area is, say, 6 percent of the area of your face, plastic surgery may be worth the price. You can always get a loan from a college man — *afterward.* ✦

## CONCERNING KISSES (1858)

"THE KISS," SAYS AN ANCIENT woman-hater, "is the aurora of love but the sunset of chastity."

After the first kiss there follows a second, then a third, and so upward on the many-runged ladder of love to the ultima Thule. One kiss is very little and yet very much. It is the wordless interpreter of two hearts, which by this one breath tell each other more than by myriad words. The kiss is the high priest who initiates the heart into the Elysian mysteries of love.

The monks of the Middle Ages — great theorists — divided the kiss into fifteen distinct and separate orders:

1. The decorous or modest kiss
2. The diplomatic kiss, or kiss of policy
3. The spying kiss, to ascertain if a woman had drunk wine
4. The slave kiss
5. The kiss infamous (a church penance)
6. The slipper kiss (practiced toward tyrants)
7. The judicial kiss
8. The feudal kiss
9. The religious kiss (kissing the cross)
10. The academic kiss (on joining a solemn brotherhood)
11. The hand kiss
12. The Judas kiss
13. The medical kiss (for the purpose of healing some sickness)
14. The kiss of etiquette
15. The kiss of love — the only real kiss

*Long red hair like Lady Godiva's indicates, according to the Almanac, a fiery and impatient disposition.*

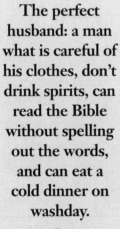

**The perfect husband: a man what is careful of his clothes, don't drink spirits, can read the Bible without spelling out the words, and can eat a cold dinner on washday.**

*1853*

# Falling in Love with His (or Her) Hair

*A treatise on this delicate subject as it was regarded in the year 1816.*

• If the hair is very black, short, and curly, the man will be given to liquor, somewhat quarrelsome, of an unsettled temper, amorous, and unsteady in his undertakings, though ardent at the beginning of an enterprise. He will be very desirous of riches but in general miss his aim, and he will be subject to much discontent. The same may be said of a woman.

• A man with dark brown, long, smooth hair generally will be of a robust constitution, obstinate in temper, eager in his pursuits, a lover of the other sex, fond of variety in his ordinary pursuits, exceedingly curious, and of a flexible disposition. In his amusements he will be very fickle, and he will not continue long attached to the same woman unless she takes extraordinary pains to please him.

• A woman of the same kind of hair will be nearly the same as the man but more steady in her conduct and attachments, especially in love. She will be of a good constitution, have many children, be much respected, and enjoy good health and a reasonable share of happiness.

• A man with light brown, long, smooth hair will be of a peaceable, even, and rather generous temper. He will prevent mischief if it is in his power, but when provoked he will strike furiously. He will be sorry for his passion, however, and soon appeased. He will be strongly attached to women and will protect them from any insult. He will be desirous of having money, more to do good than for the sake of hoarding. If he is guilty of infidelity to his wife, it will be very discreetly. Upon the whole, he will be an amiable character, affable and kind.

• A woman of the same kind of hair will be tenderhearted, but hasty in her temper. She will be neither obstinate nor haughty, and her inclinations to love will never be unreasonable. Her constitution will be good, but she will seldom be very fortunate.

• If the hair is short, bushy, and apt to curl by nature, the man will be more industrious and the woman more sedentary.

• A man with fair hair will be of a weak constitution, his mind much given to reflection, especially on religious matters. He will be assiduous in his occupation but not given to rambling. He will be very moderate in his amorous wishes and must take great pains to live to a middling age.

• A woman of this colored hair will, on the contrary, be of a good constitution, never to be diverted from her purposes, very passionate in love affairs, and never easy unless in company. She will delight in hearing herself praised, especially for beauty. She will take great pleasure in dancing, romping, and violent exercise and commonly will live to a great age.

• A man with long red hair will be cunning, artful, and deceitful. He will be very much addicted to traffic of some kind, restless in his disposition, and constantly roving.

• A woman of the same kind of hair will be glib of tongue, have words at will, and be talkative and vain. Her temper will be impatient and fiery and will not easily bear contradiction.✦

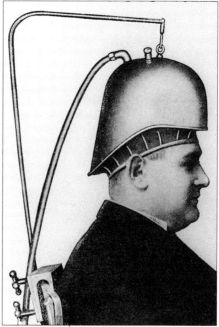

*It's hard to fall in love with his hair if he doesn't have any. The Evan Vacuum Cap was a nineteenth-century contraption designed to remedy that problem. It was made in St. Louis.*

# How to Find Your Perfect Mate

*Herewith, from science and folklore, 26 sure-fire techniques.*

### By Tim Clark

*Short-armed women married to long-armed men are, according to some experts, unlikely to be happy.*

• Roast hummingbird hearts, grind them into a powder, and sprinkle the powder on your beloved.

• Kiss as many people as possible. Dr. Bubba Nicholson of Tampa, Florida, says that kissing is a way for us to taste semiochemicals on another's skin. Semiochemicals transmit biological signals of compatibility and attraction, according to Dr. Nicholson, whose finding appeared in the *British Journal of Dermatology.*

• Practice the technique of Australian aborigines: prepare a love potion from the testicles of kangaroos.

• Follow the procedure described in Sir Thomas More's *Utopia* (1517), in which "the woman, whether maiden or widow, is shown naked to the suitor by a worthy and respected matron, and similarly, the suitor is presented naked before the maiden by a discreet man."

• Think of the one you love while you swallow a four-leaf clover, and your love will be returned.

• Sleep with a mirror under your pillow for three nights, the third a Friday, and you will dream of your true love on the third night.

• Swallow the heart of a wild duck.

• Hide the dried tongue of a turtledove in a girl's room; she will love you forever.

• Stand on your head and chew a piece of beef gristle, then swallow it.

• Follow the protocol of eighteenth-century France, in which a man would tell a woman three times that she was beautiful. The first time she was required to thank him, the second time to believe him, and the third time to reward him.

• Offer your lover a double-fudge sundae. Chocolate is rich in phenylethylamine, a substance related to amphetamines, which may be responsible for the erratic behavior of people in love.

• Swallow a white dove's heart, point downward, while resting your hand on the shoulder of the one you love.

• Hard-boil an egg, cut it in half, discard the yolk, and fill the egg halves with salt. Sit on something you have never sat on before, eat the egg, and walk to bed backward. You will dream of your future mate.

• On the last night in April, wash a handkerchief and hang it over a rosebush. When it dries in the morning, the initials of your true love will appear in the wrinkles.

• Walk around the block with your mouth full of water. If you don't swallow it, you will marry within the year.

• Pick an apple, prick it full of holes, carry it for a while under your left arm, and give it to your lover.

• Kill an eleven-month-old rooster and swallow his heart, blood and all, before it cools. If you don't choke on it, you will be married in eleven months.

• Peel an apple without breaking the peel, swing the peel around your head three times, and throw it over your shoulder. When it lands, it will form your lover's initial.

• Make a silent supper in the dark, late at night. Everything must be done backward — the place settings, the chairs, the walking to and fro — and in perfect silence. Then take your seat (backward) and wait for the stroke of midnight. You will see your true love's face before you.

• Hang your shoes out the window, and you'll dream of your love.

• Watch the way a person who interests you stands. If he or she tilts the head to one side, elevates the shoulders, and rotates the feet to a pigeon-toed position ("the meekness cue"), anthropologists say it means he or she is giving you permission to come closer.

*Watch the way a person who interests you stands. Is he giving you permission to come closer?*

• Count fifty white horses and a white mule, and the first unmarried man you shake hands with afterward will be the one you marry.

• Offer your prospective mate beer, lemonade, or cider containing a teaspoon of your own powdered fingernails.

• Always carry a tape measure. Genetic researchers Maria Pennock Watkins and Arlen Price studied 170 couples married for at least seven years and found a strong correlation between the relative length of people's forearms and the success of their marriages. Couples whose forearms (measured from elbow to tip of middle finger) were similar were more likely to have stable marriages. Short-armed women married to long-armed men were least likely to be happy.

• Cut your nails on nine Sundays in a row.

• Stop looking. Many experts agree that the search for a perfect mate is doomed to disappointment and marital discord. As one psychologist put it, "Be flexible. You have to give up the notion of finding and molding the perfect mate. It's a kind of strange commitment to the unknown." But if you must look, carry the heart of an owl with you at all times. ✦

## A Sad and Moving Scene of Long Ago

MINERS WORKING FAR underground came upon the body of a poor fellow who had perished in the suffocating pit forty years earlier. Some chemical agent to which the body had been subjected — an agent prepared in the laboratory of nature — had effectively arrested the process of decay. The miners brought the body up to the surface, and for a while, until it crumbled away through exposure to the atmosphere, it lay there, the image of a fine, sturdy young man. No convulsion had passed over the face in death; the features were tranquil, the hair as black as jet.

No one recognized the face — a generation had grown up since the day the miner had gone down his shaft for the last time. But a tottering old woman, who had hurried from her cottage at hearing the news, came up, and she knew again the fact that through all these years she had never quite forgotten: the poor miner was to have been her husband on the day after that on which he died.

They were rough people, of course, they who were looking on; a liberal education and refined manners were not deemed essential for the man whose work was to get up coal. But there were no dry eyes when the gray-haired woman cast herself upon the youthful corpse and poured into its deaf ear many words of endearment unused for forty years. It was a touching contrast: the one so old, the other so young. They had both been young those long years ago, but time had gone on with the living and stood still with the dead.

*Reprinted in the Almanac from the March 10, 1869, issue of* The Weekly New Era *of Fort Smith, Arkansas. Submitted by Robert L. Farmer.*

## How to Make Your Husband Happy
### (1877)

- Try to do not only *what* your husband wishes in household matters but also *when* and *how* he wishes.
- Do not neglect neatness of person and surroundings.
- Never speak slightingly or bitterly of or to your husband, especially in the presence of other people.
- Speak gently always, and do not allow your voice to become sharp and loud. Control of the voice helps to control the temper.

## How to Make Your Wife Happy
### (1877)

- Treat your wife as politely and kindly as when you were wooing her.
- If your dinner does not suit you, do not spoil her appetite by scolding her about it at the time, but give whatever suggestions are needed after dinner.
- Share your pleasures and your cares with her, and show that you value her society and her advice.
- Do not speak lightly of her cares and fatigues, but sympathize with her troubles, whether small or great.
- Try to gratify her fancies, such as a flower garden or conveniences about her work. She will be reminded of your consideration or neglect many times every day by these little things.

# The First Case of Artificial Insemination by a Bullet

*The young couple were definitely ahead of their time . . .*

### By Bernard Lamere

*Captain L. G. Capers (this may or may not be the captain) was an eyewitness to the incredible conception described herewith.*

URING THE CIVIL WAR, Union doctor Captain L. G. Capers was acting as a field surgeon at a skirmish in a small Virginia village on May 12, 1863. Some distance to the rear of the captain's regiment, a mother and her two daughters stood on the steps of their large country home watching the engagement, prepared to act as nurses if necessary.

Just as Captain Capers saw a young soldier fall to the ground nearby, he heard a sharp cry of pain from the steps of the house. When the surgeon examined the infantryman, he found that a bullet had broken the fellow's leg and then ricocheted up, passing through his scrotum. As he was administering first aid to the soldier, Captain Capers was approached by the mother from the house to the rear. Apparently one of her daughters also had been wounded.

Upon examining the young woman, Capers found a jagged wound in her abdomen, but he was unable to tell where the object had lodged. He administered what aid he could for such a serious wound, and he was quite pleased to see that she did recover from the injury.

Thereafter it was a full eight months before the captain and his regiment passed through the same area, at which time he was quite surprised to find the young woman very pregnant. Within a month, she delivered a healthy baby boy whose features were quite similar to those of the young soldier who had been wounded at nearly the same instant the girl had been struck nine months earlier. The surgeon hypothesized that the bullet that struck the soldier had carried sperm into the young woman's uterus and that she had conceived.

The theory has never been tested again, either involuntarily or by design, so the surgeon's hypothesis remains to be debated. For the wounded soldier and young woman, however, the end result of the incredible circumstances must have been appealing. They courted, fell in love, and married, later producing two more children using a more common technique. ✦

## Do You Obey These Laws?

ACROSS THE United States there are thousands of out-of-date, no-longer-enforced local and state laws concerning dating, marriage, and divorce that no one has ever bothered to remove from the books. Here are some we would not consider to be totally without merit.

- An old Riverside, California, health ordinance prohibits two people from kissing each other on the lips until they first clean their lips with carbolated rose water.
- An Indiana law does not allow a man to wear a mustache if he "habitually kisses human beings."
- An all-but-forgotten law in Owensboro, Kentucky, states that if a woman wants to buy a new hat, her husband must try it on first.
- A section of the municipal code in Ottumwa, Iowa, states, "It is unlawful for any male person, within the corporate limits of the city, to wink at any female with whom he is unacquainted."
- Orange County, New York, has a law that forbids a man to look at a girl "that way."
- It's against the law to whistle at a girl in Abilene, Texas, and tickling a girl with a feather duster is illegal in Portland, Maine.
- No liquor may be sold to a married man in Cold Springs, Pennsylvania, unless he first obtains the written consent of his wife.
- Macon, Georgia, doesn't allow a man to put his arms around a woman without a legal reason to do so.
- In Lebanon, Tennessee, a husband may not shove his wife out of bed, even if her feet are cold. The same law allows a wife to shove her husband out of bed at any time without a reason.
- In Minnesota it is considered a legal proposal of marriage to do any of the following in the presence of a girl's mother and father: hug the girl, kiss the girl, or present her with a box of candy.

*Courtesy of Vince O'Connor.*

*A Kentucky law requires that a man try on his wife's new hat before she buys it.*

A sour-faced wife is the liquor dealer's friend.

*1872*

> You are a bachelor — oh, haste then and be married, for he who hath no children or wife doth not know what love means.
>
> *1805*

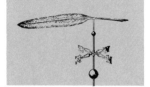

## WHEN TO WEAN YOUR BABY (1881)

WHEN A CHILD has shown any tendency to diarrhea, or is delicate and puny, he should not be weaned until after his second summer.

However, sometimes the mother furnishes an insufficient supply of milk for the child, which may be known by his constant hunger. In such case, if all his teeth are through — eight in each jaw — he may be either entirely or partly weaned, though summer is approaching.

## WHAT EVERY FARMER'S BOY SHOULD KNOW (1867)

- To dress himself, black his own shoes, cut his brother's hair, wind a watch, sew on a button, make a bed, and keep all his clothes in perfect order and neatly in place
- To harness a horse, grease a wagon, and drive a team
- To milk cows, shear sheep, and dress veal or mutton
- To reckon money and keep accounts accurately and according to good bookkeeping rules
- To write a neat, appropriate, briefly expressed business letter, in a good hand, and fold and superscribe it properly, and to write contracts
- To plow, sow grain and grass seed, drive a mowing machine, swing a scythe, build a neat stack, and pitch hay
- To put up a package, build a fire, whitewash a wall, mend broken tools, and regulate a clock

## What Every Farmer's Girl Should Know (1867)

- To sew and knit
- To mend clothes neatly
- To dress her own hair
- To wash dishes and sweep carpets
- To trim lamps
- To make good bread and perform all plain cooking
- To keep her room, closets, and drawers neatly in order
- To make good butter and cheese
- To keep accounts and calculate interest
- To write, fold, and superscribe letters properly
- To nurse the sick efficiently and not faint at the sight of a drop of blood
- To be ready to render efficient aid and comfort to those in trouble, in an unostentatious way
- To receive and entertain visitors when her mother is sick or absent

## Epitaph on a Gravestone in Penobscot, Maine

Here lies a poor woman
Who always was tired;
She lived in a house
Where help was not hired.
Her last words on earth were,
"Dear friends, I am going
Where washing ain't done,
Nor sweeping or sewing.
But everything there is exact to
   my wishes,
For where they don't eat,
There's no washing dishes.
I'll be where loud anthems will
   always be ringing,
But having no voice, I'll be clear
   of the singing;
Don't mourn for me now, don't
   mourn for me never,
I'm going to do nothing forever
   and ever."

# CHAPTER SIX

# When the Moon Comes Over the Mountain

## THE GHOSTS' HIGH NOON

*When the footpads quail at the night
   bird's wail,
and black dogs bay at the moon,
Then is the specters' holiday
   — then is the ghosts' high noon!*

THE MOON'S RISINGS, SETTINGS, PLACE IN the sky, and phases have been basic elements of all two hundred editions of *The Old Farmer's Almanac.* But through the years, the Almanac also has reflected the fascination and mysticism with which we regard that great, shining ball slowly rising over the eastern horizon — precisely on schedule. ✦

*Man's endless fascination with the moon was captured by Steven Spielberg in the movie* E.T.

# How Big the Moon?

*Before you start arguing with this theory, try a simple experiment.*

## By Lewis J. Boss

THE FACT THAT the moon looks remarkably larger when it is near the horizon than when it is high in the sky has been noted by almost everyone, philosophers and astronomers alike.

Karl Friedrich Gauss, an early nineteenth-century philosopher, astronomer, and eminent mathematician, suggested that the reason lay in the difference between the image perceived when the rising moon was viewed over a horizon, which provided a scale for the eye, and the image perceived when the eyes were raised to view the same object high overhead. In developing this theory, he came surprisingly close to the truth.

Actually, the phenomenon is probably a combination of physiological and optical effects, as can be demonstrated by the following experiment. Roll an eleven- or twelve-inch sheet of paper into a tube about one-half inch in diameter. With one eye, look through this tube at the seemingly enlarged full moon near the horizon. At once the moon's disk will contract to its normal proportions. Now close this eye and open the other one. Immediately the moon will resume its enlarged appearance. Repeat this action as often as desired, and you will find that the eye looking through the tube is never deceived. The reason is that there is a very thin ring of sky around the moon when it is viewed through the tube and none of the neighboring trees or buildings on the landscape at the horizon are visible.

As a matter of fact, the moon should appear very slightly larger to our eyes when it is at its zenith because it is then closer to us. This is shown in the accompanying diagram. Let the small circle M represent the moon and the large circle the earth. When the moon is on the horizon at a place A on the earth's surface and later on is observed from this place after it has moved into position B, the earth having turned on its axis by about ninety degrees, it is obvious that the moon is nearer to B than it is to A by almost the length of the earth's radius, C–B. The average distance of the moon from the earth, C–M, is about 240,000 miles. The earth's radius, C–B, is around 4,000 miles. Consequently, the zenith moon should appear to be slightly larger than the horizon moon by about one-sixtieth. Our instinctive opposite reaction is one giant optical illusion. ✦

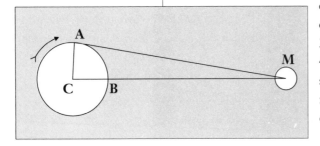

# When Does One-Quarter Equal One-Half?

*And other lunar riddles . . .*     BY ROBERT X. PERRY

I N CASE YOU DIDN'T KNOW IT, that half-moon you saw in the sky last night was the first quarter. How can a quarter actually be a half? In this case, the word *quarter* refers to time — one-fourth of a lunar month; it does not indicate the shape of the visible moon. But though this apparent contradiction is easily explained, over the years many calendars, newspapers, authors, and artists have offered incorrect sketches of these phases.

A great many sophisticated people devoted to the U.S. space program live on the east coast of Florida. Yet both of the local newspapers delivered to my doorstep in Cocoa Beach after the liftoff of *Apollo 17* — the last of the Apollo moon missions — committed common lunar errors. One showed each quarter incorrectly as one-fourth of a full moon. The other correctly showed them as half-moons but reversed the direction of the sketches. In correct moon diagrams, the first quarter is arched to the right; the moon is waxing. Figure 1 shows the four principal phases in their proper form, reading chronologically from left to right.

FIGURE 1

New    First Quarter    Full    Last Quarter

## WHEN WILL THE MOON RISE TODAY?

Another common lunar puzzle involves the timing of moonrise. Folks who enjoy the out-of-doors and the wonders of nature may wish to commit to memory the following gem:

> The new moon always rises at sunrise
> And the first quarter at noon.
> The full moon always rises at sunset
> And the last quarter at midnight.

Moonrise (and, incidentally, the time of high tide) occurs about fifty minutes later each day than the day before. To determine the time of moonrise for each day of the month, just add fifty minutes for each day after a phase or subtract fifty minutes for each day prior to a new phase. The new moon is invisible because the sun blots it out. One or two days after the date of the new moon, we can see it in the western sky as a thin crescent setting just after sunset.

In following the above rule, care must be taken when using the terms *noon* and *midnight.* These are affected by adjustments for daylight saving time and to a lesser degree by one's longitude in a particular time zone. (Sunrise and sunset, of course, are definite times regardless of people's tamperings with the clock.) Since the moon has no light of its own but merely reflects

**Weather, wind, women, and fortune change like the moon.**

*1942*

sunlight, we see a full moon rise in the east when the sun is setting in the west.

## WHEN WILL HIGH TIDE BE?

With these basics in mind, let's move on to consider the effect the moon has on earthly things such as ocean tides. It has long been known that the moon governs our tides with help from the sun. The perpetual tide calendar in Figure 2, based on the age of the moon, illustrates another interesting phenomenon regarding the effect of the moon on earthly cycles. This chart shows fourteen moon circles around a conventional clock face. Each circle represents two moon shapes, or phases. (This totals twenty-eight moons — about one less than a lunar month. One moon was dropped to make each of the four quarters an even seven days long.)

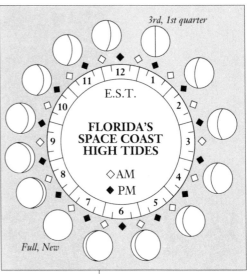

FIGURE 2

The chart indicates that the timing of high tide is the same at the full and new moons. The timing of high tide at the first and third quarters also is the same, as it is at each of the intermediate phases shown around the clock. In other words, a waxing and a waning moon with complementary shapes cause high tide to fall at exactly the same time (Figure 3).

## WHAT EXACTLY IS A GOLDEN NUMBER?

One of the least understood aspects of moon lore involves a lunar cycle that goes beyond monthly phases. In the first century B.C., a Greek astronomer named Meton discovered what became known as the Metonic, or lunar, cycle. Meton found that the moon repeats itself approximately every nineteen solar years. Each year in the cycle has been assigned a Golden Number from 1 to 19, usually expressed in Roman numerals. Almanacs refer to 1992 as Golden Year XVII; our nation's bicentennial year of 1976 was Golden Year I — the beginning of a new Metonic cycle. The dates of moon phases, eclipses, and the like very nearly repeat themselves on the Golden Year numbers. (They may vary one or two days because the cycle is not exactly nineteen years, and leap year throws a curve when we compare two twelve-month periods that are nineteen years apart, only one of which is a leap year.)

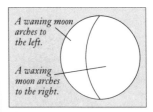

FIGURE 3

I have constructed my own chart, which gives the approximate date of moon phases for checking historic storms or great battles. How do you suppose the moonlight was on the night Paul Revere muffled his oars and rowed to the Charlestown shore? A check of the box on the next page will answer that one more quickly than most people can find an almanac for April 1775. ✦

## WAS THERE EVER A MONTH WITH NO FULL MOON?

YES, AND EVERY one has been a February. The last was February 1980 and the next will be February 1999.

# MOON PHASES: PAST, PRESENT & FUTURE

THIS CHART SHOWS the approximate age of the moon (usually within one day during the twentieth and twenty-first centuries). If used for an eighteenth- or nineteenth-century year, increase the moon's age by one day. An eleven-day adjustment to the calendar in 1752 prevents the chart from being applicable to years prior to 1753. N = new moon; F = full moon. The day after the new moon is numbered 1, and so on. The age of the moon is shown under the appropriate Golden Number column, and the month and day of this phase appear on the left-hand side of the chart.

## HOW TO USE THE CHART

Moon phases occur on the same dates every nineteen years, a fact that is recognized in the concept of the Golden Number. The Golden Number is a particular year's number (1 through 19) within the nineteen-year cycle of the moon. To find the Golden Number of any year, add 1 to that year and divide the result by 19; the remainder is the Golden Number. Where there is no remainder, the Golden Number is 19. Example: What was the age of the moon on July 4, 1776? 1776 + 1 = 1777. 1777 ÷ 19 has a remainder of 10. In line with July 4 and under Golden Number 10, we find 17. Add 1 day to adjust for the eighteenth century, and we discover that on this historic day, the moon was 18 days old and waning, 3 days past full.

*Copyright © 1974 by Robert X. Perry, Cocoa Beach, Florida. All rights reserved.*

| Fb | | | | | SpNv | | | | Golden Number — Lunar Cycle | | | | | | | | | | | | | | | | | | | |
| Jn | Ap | Mr | My | Jn | Ju | Au | Oc | Dc | 1 | 2 | 3 | 4 | 5 | 6 | 7 | 8 | 9 | 10 | 11 | 12 | 13 | 14 | 15 | 16 | 17 | 18 | 19 |
| +Also 31st | | | | | | | | | Age of Moon — Full & New | | | | | | | | | | | | | | | | | | |
| +1 | 29 | 30 | 28 | 27 | 26 | 25 | 23 | 21 | N | 11 | 22 | 3 | 14 | 25 | 6 | 17 | 28 | 9 | 20 | 1 | 12 | 23 | 4 | F | 26 | 7 | 18 |
| 2 | 30 | +1 | 29 | 28 | 27 | 26 | 24 | 22 | 1 | 12 | 23 | 4 | F | 26 | 7 | 18 | 29 | 10 | 21 | 2 | 13 | 24 | 5 | 16 | 27 | 8 | 19 |
| 3 | 1 | 2 | 30 | 29 | 28 | 27 | 25 | 23 | 2 | 13 | 24 | 5 | 16 | 27 | 8 | 19 | N | 11 | 22 | 3 | 14 | 25 | 6 | 17 | 28 | 9 | 20 |
| 4 | 2 | 3 | +1 | 30 | 29 | 28 | 26 | 24 | 3 | 14 | 25 | 6 | 17 | 28 | 9 | 20 | 1 | 12 | 23 | 4 | F | 26 | 7 | 18 | 29 | 10 | 21 |
| 5 | 3 | 4 | 2 | 1 | 30 | 29 | 27 | 25 | 4 | F | 26 | 7 | 18 | 29 | 10 | 21 | 2 | 13 | 24 | 5 | 16 | 27 | 8 | 19 | N | 11 | 22 |
| 6 | 4 | 5 | 3 | 2 | +1 | 30 | 28 | 26 | 5 | 16 | 27 | 8 | 19 | N | 11 | 22 | 3 | 14 | 25 | 6 | 17 | 28 | 9 | 20 | 1 | 12 | 23 |
| 7 | 5 | 6 | 4 | 3 | 2 | +1 | 29 | 27 | 6 | 17 | 28 | 9 | 20 | 1 | 12 | 23 | 4 | F | 26 | 7 | 18 | 29 | 10 | 21 | 2 | 13 | 24 |
| 8 | 6 | 7 | 5 | 4 | 3 | 2 | 30 | 28 | 7 | 18 | 29 | 10 | 21 | 2 | 13 | 24 | 5 | 16 | 27 | 8 | 19 | N | 11 | 22 | 3 | 14 | 25 |
| 9 | 7 | 8 | 6 | 5 | 4 | 3 | +1 | 29 | 8 | 19 | N | 11 | 22 | 3 | 14 | 25 | 6 | 17 | 28 | 9 | 20 | 1 | 12 | 23 | 4 | F | 26 |
| 10 | 8 | 9 | 7 | 6 | 5 | 4 | 2 | 30 | 9 | 20 | 1 | 12 | 23 | 4 | F | 26 | 7 | 18 | 29 | 10 | 21 | 2 | 13 | 24 | 5 | 16 | 27 |
| 11 | 9 | 10 | 8 | 7 | 6 | 5 | 3 | +1 | 10 | 21 | 2 | 13 | 24 | 5 | 16 | 27 | 8 | 19 | N | 11 | 22 | 3 | 14 | 25 | 6 | 17 | 28 |
| 12 | 10 | 11 | 9 | 8 | 7 | 6 | 4 | 2 | 11 | 22 | 3 | 14 | 25 | 6 | 17 | 28 | 9 | 20 | 1 | 12 | 23 | 4 | F | 26 | 7 | 18 | 29 |
| 13 | 11 | 12 | 10 | 9 | 8 | 7 | 5 | 3 | 12 | 23 | 4 | F | 26 | 7 | 18 | 29 | 10 | 21 | 2 | 13 | 24 | 5 | 16 | 27 | 8 | 19 | N |
| 14 | 12 | 13 | 11 | 10 | 9 | 8 | 6 | 4 | 13 | 24 | 5 | 16 | 27 | 8 | 19 | N | 11 | 22 | 3 | 14 | 25 | 6 | 17 | 28 | 9 | 20 | 1 |
| 15 | 13 | 14 | 12 | 11 | 10 | 9 | 7 | 5 | 14 | 25 | 6 | 17 | 28 | 9 | 20 | 1 | 12 | 23 | 4 | F | 26 | 7 | 18 | 29 | 10 | 21 | 2 |
| 16 | 14 | 15 | 13 | 12 | 11 | 10 | 8 | 6 | F | 26 | 7 | 18 | 29 | 10 | 21 | 2 | 13 | 24 | 5 | 16 | 27 | 8 | 19 | N | 11 | 22 | 3 |
| 17 | 15 | 16 | 14 | 13 | 12 | 11 | 9 | 7 | 16 | 27 | 8 | 19 | N | 11 | 22 | 3 | 14 | 25 | 6 | 17 | 28 | 9 | 20 | 1 | 12 | 23 | 4 |
| 18 | 16 | 17 | 15 | 14 | 13 | 12 | 10 | 8 | 17 | 28 | 9 | 20 | 1 | 12 | 23 | 4 | F | 26 | 7 | 18 | 29 | 10 | 21 | 2 | 13 | 24 | 5 |
| 19 | 17 | 18 | 16 | 15 | 14 | 13 | 11 | 9 | 18 | 29 | 10 | 21 | 2 | 13 | 24 | 5 | 16 | 27 | 8 | 19 | N | 11 | 22 | 3 | 14 | 25 | 6 |
| 20 | 18 | 19 | 17 | 16 | 15 | 14 | 12 | 10 | 19 | N | 11 | 22 | 3 | 14 | 25 | 6 | 17 | 28 | 9 | 20 | 1 | 12 | 23 | 4 | F | 26 | 7 |
| 21 | 19 | 20 | 18 | 17 | 16 | 15 | 13 | 11 | 20 | 1 | 12 | 23 | 4 | F | 26 | 7 | 18 | 29 | 10 | 21 | 2 | 13 | 24 | 5 | 16 | 27 | 8 |
| 22 | 20 | 21 | 19 | 18 | 17 | 16 | 14 | 12 | 21 | 2 | 13 | 24 | 5 | 16 | 27 | 8 | 19 | N | 11 | 22 | 3 | 14 | 25 | 6 | 17 | 28 | 9 |
| 23 | 21 | 22 | 20 | 19 | 18 | 17 | 15 | 13 | 22 | 3 | 14 | 25 | 6 | 17 | 28 | 9 | 20 | 1 | 12 | 23 | 4 | F | 26 | 7 | 18 | 29 | 10 |
| 24 | 22 | 23 | 21 | 20 | 19 | 18 | 16 | 14 | 23 | 4 | F | 26 | 7 | 18 | 29 | 10 | 21 | 2 | 13 | 24 | 5 | 16 | 27 | 8 | 19 | N | 11 |
| 25 | 23 | 24 | 22 | 21 | 20 | 19 | 17 | 15 | 24 | 5 | 16 | 27 | 8 | 19 | N | 11 | 22 | 3 | 14 | 25 | 6 | 17 | 28 | 9 | 20 | 1 | 12 |
| 26 | 24 | 25 | 23 | 22 | 21 | 20 | 18 | 16 | 25 | 6 | 17 | 28 | 9 | 20 | 1 | 12 | 23 | 4 | F | 26 | 7 | 18 | 29 | 10 | 21 | 2 | 13 |
| 27 | 25 | 26 | 24 | 23 | 22 | 21 | 19 | 17 | 26 | 7 | 18 | 29 | 10 | 21 | 2 | 13 | 24 | 5 | 16 | 27 | 8 | 19 | N | 11 | 22 | 3 | 14 |
| 28 | 26 | 27 | 25 | 24 | 23 | 22 | 20 | 18 | 27 | 8 | 19 | N | 11 | 22 | 3 | 14 | 25 | 6 | 17 | 28 | 9 | 20 | 1 | 12 | 23 | 4 | F |
| 29 | 27 | 28 | 26 | 25 | 24 | 23 | 21 | 19 | 28 | 9 | 20 | 1 | 12 | 23 | 4 | F | 26 | 7 | 18 | 29 | 10 | 21 | 2 | 13 | 24 | 5 | 16 |
| 30 | 28 | 29 | 27 | 26 | 25 | 24 | 22 | 20 | 29 | 10 | 21 | 2 | 13 | 24 | 5 | 16 | 27 | 8 | 19 | N | 11 | 22 | 3 | 14 | 25 | 6 | 17 |

## Once in a Blue Moon

BECAUSE THERE are always a few days left over in the lunar year, about every six years or so there has to be a thirteenth moon, and thus two full moons in one month to keep the seasons straight. This brings up the term *blue moon*, which has come to denote the second full moon within the same month.

The expression *blue moon* comes from the extremely rare blue-tinged moon caused by atmospheric layers of forest fire smoke or volcanic dust at just the right height and visual angle. "Once in a blue moon," people would say when referring to something that in all likelihood would never happen at all or would take place only far off in the future. In this century, the only real blue moon visible in New England was that of September 26, 1950, caused by forest fire smoke from western Canada. *Courtesy of Andrew Rothovius.*

## The Tide in the Affairs of Men

MANY CLAIM that the moon has an effect on human behavior, and that the wise person will be guided by the appropriate phases of the moon in choosing when to plant crops, when to go fishing, and so on. Police records are said to show an increase in crime during the days of full and new moons. Hospital records likewise are said to show an increase in patients' bleeding during these times. And there is some evidence that great storms have hit our coasts during specific lunar periods.

*Robert X. Perry.*

*If the moon can pull the earth's oceans around every day, says the Almanac, then it probably can also cause some pretty strange phenomena.*

He who keeps company with the wolf will learn to howl.

*1797*

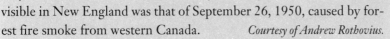

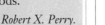

# CHAPTER SEVEN

# UNBELIEVABLE
## *As It May Seem*

*Not only is a telephone serviceable in everyday affairs, but it may be used to help you sell your produce. You can let the dealers in nearby or distant places know what you offer for sale from day to day. You can thus keep in touch with the market quickly and effectively.*

— From the 1905 Almanac

THE ALMANAC HAS HAD AN INCLINATION NOW and then to include stories that deviate from the normal types of situations we encounter in our day-to-day lives. Stories that challenge our capacities to believe in the extraordinary. Stories that, although possibly true, nonetheless give birth to doubts. But even so, surely the best way to enjoy them is temporarily to set aside our cynical responses and open our eyes in awe and wonder. ✦

*Daredevil acts at the 1906 Orange, Connecticut, Fair included high-wire walking with no net.*

# The Curious Case of Holdfast Demeritt

*His head is said to have lived almost six years after
his body was buried!*

THE ASTOUNDING STORY of James T. Anderson of Glenwood, Iowa, made the rounds of the papers a few years back. Mr. Anderson, as discovered by diagnosis, broke his neck but at the time of the reports was still living and promised to live with a dead body attached to his living head.

Astonishing as this story was, it was hardly more remarkable than that of Holdfast Demeritt of Durham, New Hampshire, as told by a friend of ours who was at school there years ago.

It seems that Mr. Demeritt had a taste for chemistry, and had behind his barn a rude laboratory in which he conducted experiments. One day he accidentally seated himself upon a watch crystal filled with fulminate of mercury, the preparation used in the manufacture of percussion caps. When the crystal exploded he was thrown into the air and, falling, broke his neck when it was brought with great force into the fork of a young apple tree.

When found, he was alive, but his physician absolutely forbade his removal from the tree lest "the silver cord" should be thereby loosed and his spirit released from his body. A small but comfortable house was erected over the tree, and there, for five years, eight months, and twenty-three days, Mr. Demeritt kept his vigil, a living head attached to a dead body.

The body soon wasted and, being about some six inches from the ground (the tree having been cut back for grafting), was buried. The head, after it was painted and varnished and the eyes enclosed in glass capsules, showed signs of wasting away. According to the advice of one Dr. Liebig, a friction match was kept constantly burning under his nose, and as the patient retained his senses perfectly, the anticipation of that subtle chemist — that the brain would be sufficiently nourished by the phosphoric acid thus generated — was fully realized. A saturated solution of this acid, poured into the ears, produced all the symptoms of intoxication.

A watchmaker by trade, Mr. Demeritt soon devised a method of communicating his thoughts by means of little feather wings attached to the tips of his ears and worked by the frailest possible levers connecting the wings to his eyelids. It is said that it was from the signals thus devised by him that Professor Morse invented the telegraphic alphabet.

After his accident, Mr. Demeritt was repeatedly chosen one of the selectmen of Durham and proved himself of great use in perambulating the

**Some know
just enough to
excite their pride
but not enough
to cure their
ignorance.**

*1844*

*The BEST of THE OLD FARMER'S ALMANAC*

town lines, the tree to which he was so closely bound being the exact point at which the boundary lines of Durham, Madbury, and Dover intersect.

The gradual growth of the apple tree, by narrowing the fork in which he was held, ultimately terminated his life by strangling him, but his death remained undiscovered for nearly three weeks. The air from a broken pane of glass blowing upon the little wings attached to his ears, and its impulse being communicated to his eyelids through the reflex action of the delicate levers, he was kept winking during the whole period and was supposed by his friends to be talking in the language of the Abnaki, the original Indian tribe of New England, whose tongue he had learned from Longbow Demeritt, who was taken prisoner and carried to Canada during the French and Indian War.

When the ground was opened for the purpose of interring the head, it appeared that by process of natural decay, the body had been separated from the head for probably fifteen months. ✦

*Courtesy of Philip A. Wilcox, Curator, Durham Historic Association.*

*Holdfast Demeritt's experiments in chemistry got him into plenty of trouble — but nothing, according to the Almanac, that he couldn't handle.*

*The* Best *of* The Old Farmer's Almanac

# Frozen Death

*First published in 1943, this is still one of the all-time favorite
(and most-debated) stories among older Almanac readers.*

## By Robert Wilson

**When men speak
ill of thee, live so
as nobody will
believe them.**

*1832*

THE EVENTS DESCRIBED herewith took place within twenty miles
of Montpelier, Vermont. They were first found recorded in a local diary and were verified by an old man who vouched for their
truth — and who said his father was among those operated on. The practice is not common today.

"January 7. I went on the mountain today and witnessed what to me
was a horrible sight. It seems that the dwellers there who are unable either
from age or other reasons to contribute to the support of their families are
disposed of in the winter months.

"I will describe what I saw. Six persons, four men and two women, one
man a cripple about thirty years old and the other five past the age of use-
fulness, lay on the earthy floor of the cabin drugged into insensibility, while
members of the families were gathered about them in apparent indifference.
In a short time, the unconscious bodies were inspected by one man who said,
'They are ready.'

"They were then stripped of all their clothing except a single garment.
The bodies were carried outside and laid on logs exposed to the bitter cold
mountain air.

"Soon the noses, ears, and fingers began to turn white, then the limbs
and faces assumed a tallowy look. I could stand the cold no longer and went
inside, where I found the friends in cheerful conversation. In about an hour,
I went out and looked at the bodies. They were fast freezing.

"Again I went inside, where the men were smoking their clay pipes, but
silence had fallen on them. Perhaps they were thinking that the time would
come when they would be carried out in the same way.

"I could not shut out the sight of the freezing bodies, nor could I bear
to be in darkness, but I piled on the wood in the cavernous fireplace and,
seated on a single block, passed the dreary night, terror stricken by the horrible sights I had witnessed.

"January 8. Day came at length but did not dissipate the terror that filled
me. The frozen bodies became visibly white on the snow that lay in huge drifts
about them. The women gathered about the fire and soon began to prepare
breakfast. The men awoke, and affairs assumed a more cheerful aspect.

"After breakfast the men lighted their pipes and some of them took a

FACING PAGE:
*A typical line drawing
depicting winter, often used
by the Almanac and other
publications during the
nineteenth century. It was
captioned simply, "Snow,
snow, snow!"*

yoke of oxen and went off into the forest, while others proceeded to nail together boards, making a box about ten feet long and half as high and wide. When this was completed, they placed about two feet of straw in the bottom. Then they laid three frozen bodies in the straw. The faces and upper parts of the bodies were covered with a cloth, more straw was put in the box, and the other three bodies were placed on top and covered the same as the first ones, with cloth and straw.

"Boards were then firmly nailed on top to protect the bodies from being injured by carnivorous animals that made their home on these mountains. By this time, the men who had gone off with the ox team returned with a huge load of spruce and hemlock boughs, which they unloaded at the foot of a steep ledge. They then came to the house, loaded the box containing the bodies on the sled, and drew it near the load of boughs.

*The faces and upper bodies were covered with a cloth, more straw was put in the box, and the other three bodies were placed on top . . .*

"These were soon piled on and around the box, and it was left to be covered with snow, which I was told would lie in drifts twenty feet deep over this rude tomb. 'We shall want our men to plant our corn next spring,' said the wife of one of the frozen men. 'If you want to see them resuscitated, you come here about the tenth of next May.'

"With this agreement, I left the mountaineers, living and frozen, to their fate and returned to my home in Boston, where it was weeks before I was fairly myself."

Turning the leaves of the diary, I came to the following entry: "May 10. I arrived here at 10 A.M. after riding about four hours over muddy, unsettled roads. The weather here is warm and pleasant, and most of the snow is gone except where there are drifts in the fence corners and hollows. But nature is not yet dressed in green.

"I found the same parties here I left last January. They were ready to disinter the bodies, but I had no expectations of finding life there. A feeling that I could not resist, however, impelled me to come and see.

"We repaired at once to the well-remembered spot at the ledge. The snow had melted from the top of the brush but still lay deep around the bottom of the pile. The men commenced work at once, some shoveling and others tearing away the brush. Soon the box was visible. The cover was taken off, the layers of straw removed, and the bodies, frozen and apparently lifeless, lifted out and laid on the snow.

"Large troughs made out of hemlock logs were placed nearby and filled with tepid water, into which each body was placed separately with the head slightly raised. Boiling water was then poured into the trough from kettles hung on poles nearby until the water was as hot as I could hold my hand in. Hemlock boughs had been put in the boiling water in such quantities that they had turned the water the color of wine.

"After they lay in the bath about an hour, color began to return to the bodies, when all hands began rubbing and chafing them. This continued about an hour, when a slight twitching of the muscles, followed by audible gasps, showed that vitality was returning.

"Spirits were then given in small quantities and allowed to trickle down their throats. Soon they could swallow, and more was given them when their eyes opened. They began to talk and finally sat up in their bathtubs.

"They were taken out and assisted to the house, where after a hearty meal they seemed as well as ever and in no way injured, but rather refreshed by their long sleep of four months." ✦

## The Night Grandma Disappeared — Completely

ON THE NIGHT OF March 16, 1802, in a town in Massachusetts, the body of an elderly woman disappeared as a result of some internal and unknown cause in the duration of about an hour and a half.

Part of the family had gone to bed, and the rest were abroad. The old woman remained awake to take care of the house. By and by, one of the grandchildren came home and discovered the floor near the hearth to be on fire. An alarm was raised, a light brought, and means taken to extinguish the fire.

While these events were taking place, some singular circumstances were observed on the hearth and the contiguous floor. A sort of greasy soot and ashes were present, along with the remains of a human body and an unusual smell in the room. All the clothes had been consumed, and the grandmother was missing.

It was at first supposed she had, in attempting to light her pipe, fallen into the fire and been burned to death. But considering how small the fire was and that so total a consumption could scarcely have happened if there had been ten times as much heat, there is more reason to conclude that this was another case of the spontaneous decomposition of the human body, of which there are several instances on record. It is regrettable that the particulars of the case were not more carefully noted.

# The Bloodstoppers

*Superstition? Hogwash? Well, the power of the human mind is often underestimated . . .*   By Margo Holden

ONE MUST CATEGORIZE it under "folklore," we believe, this ability that some people have of stopping blood by merely knowing that someone is bleeding badly and needs their help. Bloodstoppers try to get to the patient, or the patient sometimes is brought to them, but usually they do their work after merely receiving word of an accident.

Bloodstoppers were most prevalent in the early lumber camps. These camps were remote, and the only way of taking a victim out was by horse and tote sled or wagon. It usually took several hours to two days to get a wounded person to town, and even then the town might not have a doctor or hospital. Therefore, loggers relied on bloodstoppers to handle the most critical aspect of an accident — the bleeding. The men knew very well about pressure and tourniquets, which they used, but the shout would al-

*Lumberjacks at Camp 3, a remote logging camp somewhere in northern Wisconsin during the winter of 1904–05. The men in such camps often relied on bloodstoppers for emergency treatment of accident victims.*

ways go up for a bloodstopper. The use of bloodstoppers was standard practice all over the North Woods of Maine and Canada.

I saw a bloodstopper work back in 1924 at a lumber camp. A fellow with a deep ax cut in his leg was carried in by the two fellows with whom he had been working. He was very white and weak, and blood kept running down and dripping from the stocking that was over his boot. The cook, who was the bloodstopper, was stooped over, taking cookies out of the oven. When the men entered, they shouted for him. He paused in taking the cookies out, looked at the wounded fellow a long half minute, and then proclaimed, "The bleeding is stopped." The men carried their chum to his bunk in the bunkhouse, cut off his pant leg, removed his clothing, and announced that the bleeding had indeed stopped. In about a week's time, the fellow could stand the trip out and was taken to his home. We heard he was back on the drive that spring.

Another time a friend of mine, Amos, sank an ax into his foot, nearly severing it in two. A bloodstopper was called by camp phone, and about that time the bleeding stopped. When I asked Amos later what it felt like, he said it was as if someone had pressed very firmly on the cut. This led me to ask a bloodstopper once how he did his work. He said that it was nearly impossible to explain but that he forgot everything and concentrated on the person hurt. He imagined himself right there holding the blood back and saying, "It's stopping, it's stopping, it's stopped."

In another case a small child had a severe nosebleed. None of the usual remedies seemed to help. I knew the mother well, and she and I had often talked about the veracity of all these stories of bloodstoppers and how handy they had been in the lumber camps. Of course, we knew that a certain amount of superstition was involved, and although we had seen them stop blood, we ourselves did not wholly believe in their ability. However, after her little boy had had this nosebleed for three days and nights, had been cauterized twice by a doctor to no avail, and was weakening, she began to talk about going to see the bloodstopper. The whole family encouraged her; they were tired of staying up nights with the young fellow, afraid he would choke. I said, "Go ahead. I won't tell anyone."

She drove to the bloodstopper's house. He saw the car drive into the driveway and hobbled out to the porch. He took the scene in at once — the wan little boy at the window holding a bloody rag to his nose, the distraught mother. He raised his hand as if in salute and said, "The bleeding is stopped." So it was. The little fellow did not have another nosebleed for two years.

Because the topic has interested me, I've asked around the state of Maine for more information. I have found that all old people who worked in the woods can tell of times when a bloodstopper helped someone. I also have found that many young people have heard of the practice from older folks and some claim to have bloodstoppers in their own families. One farfetched story concerns a grandmother on whom the family — and, in fact, the neighborhood — depended. She had only recently died when one of the young children cut himself. All efforts to staunch the blood seemed in vain. One of the family lamented, "If only Grandma were here now. How I wish she were here to help us." The bleeding stopped immediately.

Many people still believe in the bloodstoppers' art, although there isn't such a desperate need for them as in the old lumber camps. Today we have radios in most of the camps as well as mobile emergency units. We have planes that can get into even the smallest lakes and better woods roads that allow ambulances to pass. We have put our faith in these newer things. But the urgency of events in the old days, when people mostly took care of one another, led to another kind of solution, the efficacy of which they never doubted. ✦

*After her little boy had had this nosebleed for three days and nights . . . and was weakening, she began to talk about going to see the bloodstopper.*

## A Spooky Story About Angel Wreaths

IN THE MISSOURI AND Arkansas Ozark country, as well as rural southern Illinois, one often hears older residents mention angel wreaths. These mysterious objects supposedly form in the pillows of people who are dying as proof that the person is going to an eternal reward in heaven.

I have read many descriptions of angel wreaths and have even seen two of them with my own eyes. Apparently the majority of the wreaths are simply loosely constructed arrangements of feathers resembling a crudely made bird's nest (as were the two I examined), but some are exquisitely woven works of art resembling, in the words of one folklorist, "a large bun. . .solid enough to be tossed about like a ball, and surprisingly heavy." But how are they formed inside feather pillows?

Every Ozark and southern Illinois folklorist who has dealt with angel wreaths, while conceding that a minute number of crudely made ones might have been faked, is convinced that the overwhelming majority could not possibly have been made by human hands.

One thing is sure: when a person dies, his relatives always search the inside of the pillow for an angel wreath. If one is found, the family rejoices, and the wreath is kept as a treasured relic for years. Although the Missouri and Arkansas Ozarks abound with stories regarding stolen wreaths, shifted pillows, and wreaths turning up in the pillows of people whose lives were hardly exemplary, it should be noted that the possibility of outright fraud in regard to these wreaths is slim because most hill folk are too superstitious to meddle in these matters.

The discovery of angel wreaths is a rare occurrence nowadays. I don't know whether this is a result of the increasing urbanization of the country and the consequent destruction of the old ways and beliefs or just a result of the increased use of foam pillows.

One old-timer I interviewed did offer a third possible explanation for the dearth of angel wreaths: "There jus' ain't as many people that's deservin' 'em these days."

*Courtesy of John Dunphy.*

# He Cried for Everyone

*A strange, tragic story about an occurrence at the former Peoria State Hospital in Bartonville, Illinois — told by the late* Dr. George Zeller, *then superintendent of the hospital.*

WHEN THE GOVERNOR placed me in charge of the big new asylum for the insane that the state had just erected, I recognized that along with the problem of the living, that of the disposal of the dead must also have attention.

The hospital's burial corps consisted of one reliable employee and a half dozen insane men who were handy with the spade and went mechanically through the process of digging a grave and just as mechanically refilling it after the coffin had been lowered. Of these, the most unusual was A. Bookbinder.

Sent to us from one of the poorhouses, he bore mute evidence of the carelessness that is so often shown in the commitment of the insane, especially in large cities. When his malady seized him, he was working in a printing house, and as his mental aberration manifested itself in the loss of coherent speech, the officer who took him into custody merely reported to the court that he was employed as a bookbinder.

The clerk gave as his name that of his calling, and he was committed to us as A. Bookbinder. The perversion of his name extended even further, for the last two syllables were soon dropped, and he became known to us as Old Book. In time, he became a member of the burial corps.

Old Book developed an interesting trait at the first funeral in which he participated. The dead were all strangers to us, and our ceremony was simply a mark of respect rather than an indication of personal attachment. Therefore, it may be imagined how surprised we were when, at the critical moment, Old Book removed his cap, began to wipe his eyes, and finally gave vent to loud lamentations. The first few times he did this, his emotion became contagious, and there were many moist eyes at the graveside. But when at each succeeding burial his feelings overcame him, we realized that Old Book was possessed of a mania that manifested itself in uncontrollable grief.

Book had no favorites among the dead, and he never varied the routine of his mourning. When the grave was opened, he would step back, spade in hand, in an attitude of waiting. First his left and then his right sleeve would be raised to wipe away a furtive tear, but as the coffin began to descend into the grave, he would walk over and lean against the big elm that stood in the center of the lot, giving vent to sobs that convulsed his frame and were heard by the entire assemblage. The tree was known as the "Graveyard Elm."

In the natural order of events, it came Book's turn to be carried to his last resting place. As might be inferred, this was an event that excited more than usual interest. The news spread rapidly that Book had shed his last tear, and through that quick process by which word passes among the employees of an institution, it was agreed that they all would attend his funeral.

It was an impressive sight. The hour was set for noon on a beautiful October day, a time that permitted the greatest attendance, and everyone came. Over against the hillside more than a hundred uniformed nurses were grouped like a great bank of white lilies, while around the grave stood the staff, together with several hundred privileged patients.

As was often the case, I officiated. The coffin rested on two cross beams over the open grave, and four sturdy men stood by, ready to man the ropes

*In the midst of the commotion, a wailing voice was heard, and every eye turned toward the Graveyard Elm.*

by which it was to be lowered. Just as the choir finished the last lines of "Rock of Ages," the men grasped the ropes, stooped forward, and with a powerful muscular effort prepared to lift the coffin, in order to permit the removal of the crossbeams and allow it to descend gently into the grave. At a given signal, they heaved away the ropes. The next instant, all four lay on their backs — for the coffin, instead of offering resistance, bounded into the air like an eggshell, as if it were empty.

In the midst of this commotion, a wailing voice was heard, and every eye turned toward the Graveyard Elm from which it emanated. Every man and woman stood transfixed, for there, just as had always been the case, stood Old Book, weeping and moaning with an earnestness that outrivaled anything he had ever shown before.

No one moved or spoke, and a paralytic fear came over us. Finally, I took the initiative and summoned the helpers to remove the coffin lid. The hands trembled as they loosened the screws. Most of the bystanders turned their faces away. I nerved myself to step forward and to peer into the coffin, but just as they lifted the lid, the wailing sound ceased, and at the identical moment we gazed upon the calm features of our old mourner.

There he lay, cold in death, dressed in his somber shroud, with his hands folded across his breast. Everybody was invited to file by and identify the remains, but I noticed that, after casting a glance at the corpse, every eye wandered over to the Graveyard Elm.

The tree stood there in all its stateliness — the apparition had vanished — and the funeral was completed as if it had not suffered this uncanny interruption, except that many were weeping throughout the ceremony.

It was awful, but it was real. I saw it; one hundred nurses and three hundred other spectators saw it.

Then, believe it or not, a few days later the Graveyard Elm began to wither, and in spite of our best efforts to revive it over the next year, it died. Later, after the dead limbs had dropped, workmen tried to remove the huge stem and forks but reported to me that they discontinued the work after clearly hearing, at the first cut of the ax, an agonized, despairing cry of pain emanating from the heart of the tree. I suggested that they burn it, which they tried. However, as soon as the flames got going around the tree's base, the workers quickly extinguished them, saying to me later that the roar of the flames had become a sobbing, crying sound, as often heard at funerals.

Today Old Book's grave remains without headstone or monument. But if anyone asks where he is, those of us in the know point with a shudder to the remains of the Graveyard Elm. ✦

## The Man Who Performed Brain Surgery on Himself

THE YOUNG MAN, whom we'll call "George," lived in the Vancouver area of British Columbia. Although George was a straight-A high school student, he developed what's known as an intractable obsessive-compulsive disorder, which in his case meant an obsessive fear of germs. He'd wash his hands and take showers hundreds of times a day, which eventually meant he could neither attend school nor hold a job.

According to psychiatrist Michael Jenike of Harvard University, as reported in an article by Thomas H. Maugh II on this case in the *Los Angeles Times*, conventional psychotherapy is "useless" in such victims. As a last resort, if drugs haven't worked, neurosurgeons will occasionally remove part of the left front lobe of the brain, with "mixed results." This procedure is similar to the old-time frontal lobotomies performed in the 1930s to control mental illness, but nowhere near as radical.

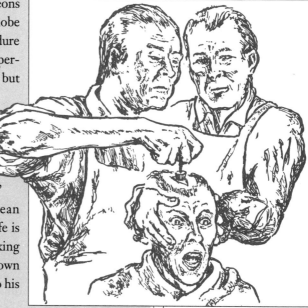

At any rate, according to George's psychiatrist, Dr. Leslie Solym of Shaughnessy Hospital in Vancouver, "George was very depressed, and one day he told his mother that he would like to die."

Apparently George's mother had a mean streak. "Look, George," she said, "if your life is so wretched, just go and shoot yourself." Taking his mother's advice seriously, George went down into the basement, stuck a .22 rifle barrel into his mouth, and blew away part of his head.

Fortunately, it was the part that had been giving him trouble. In fact, the bullet completely destroyed the section of his brain that would ordinarily be removed by surgery in such cases. And yet, miraculously, no other part of his brain was permanently damaged. *Physicians Weekly* referred later to George's suicide attempt as "successful radical surgery." Dr. Solym reported that three weeks after the "operation," George had hardly any compulsions left.

All this happened a few years ago. Last we heard, George was leading a normal life. But we have no way of knowing whether or not he's still inclined to take his mother's advice.

# The Girl Who Struck Out Babe Ruth

*Ruth later swore it was a legitimate strikeout. So did Lou Gehrig
— she struck him out, too!*   BY ROBERT W. PELTON

IT WAS ONLY AN exhibition game, and there are those who still maintain it was a publicity stunt. But a little-known chapter in baseball history was written in Chattanooga, Tennessee, in 1931, when the fabulous New York Yankees played the Chattanooga Lookouts, whose roster included a seventeen-year-old pitcher, Virnie Beatrice "Jackie" Mitchell.

Jackie Mitchell was a left-handed fast-ball pitcher from Fall River, Massachusetts, whose lifetime ambition was to strike out the great Babe Ruth. Promoter Joe Engel, who owned the Lookouts, had signed her up just for that confrontation — and also because sending a girl out to face the Yankees would be a sure-fire way to fill his stadium.

The ploy worked, and a packed house was present when Jackie took the mound midway through the first inning with Babe Ruth coming to bat. Ruth, who was to hit 46 home runs that year and bat .373, tipped his cap to the pretty teen-ager when he stepped into the batter's box. She responded by winding up and throwing the baseball as hard as she could. Ruth took a mighty swing. The crowd went wild as he missed the ball by a foot.

The Babe stepped out of the batter's box and looked out at Jackie. He shook his head as if perplexed, moved back in, and carefully positioned himself for her next pitch. It was wide, as was the third pitch, and his bat never left his shoulder. Ruth requested a new ball from the umpire. Jackie wound up, the ball came blazing in over the plate, Ruth swung — and missed again. But on her final toss, he never moved the bat off his shoulder as the umpire yelled, "Strike three — you're out!" Ruth merely walked back to the Yankee bench, shaking his head. The crowd loved every minute of it.

Next in the line-up was Lou Gehrig, and he looked as if he really meant business. He wasted no time at bat. Gehrig swung at Jackie's first three pitches, missed them all, and quietly walked back to the dugout to sit next to Ruth. Later both Ruth and Gehrig asserted that the strikeouts were strictly on the level.

Joe Engel stood up in the Lookout dugout and motioned for Jackie to come in off the mound. The applause lasted for at least ten minutes.

This escapade was essentially the beginning and the end of Jackie Mitchell's professional baseball career, although Joe Engel kept her around for a while to pitch in a number of other exhibition games for his Lookouts. She was always billed as "The Girl Who Struck Out Babe Ruth." ✦

FACING PAGE:
*The photo of Babe Ruth
was taken about the time
Jackie Mitchell, a teen-age
girl, struck him out (looking) during a 1931 exhibition game in Tennessee.
She struck out Lou Gehrig
(swinging) in the same
game.*

## Unbelievable (but True!) Animal Stories

# Jim, the Wonder Dog

### By Henry N. Ferguson

JIM WAS JUST A plain black and white setter, but among all dogs, there has never been his equal. So unique were this dog's talents that he became a national celebrity: Jim, the Wonder Dog.

I first met Jim one warm summer day in the little town of Warsaw, Missouri, down on what is now the Lake of the Ozarks. Noticing a crowd gathering around some sort of commotion on Main Street, I drifted over.

The dog's master, Sam Van Arsdale, was talking. "What would I do," he asked, "if I had a stomachache?" Jim gave him a sympathetic look, wagged his tail, and trotted over to where Dr. Savage, the town physician, was standing. He nudged the doctor gently.

Sam stroked Jim's ears for a moment. "What made Henry Ford rich?" he asked next. The dog immediately walked over to the curb and stood looking at a Model-T Ford.

*The* BEST *of* THE OLD FARMER'S ALMANAC

"See if you can find me a car," requested Sam, "with this license," and he gave a number. Jim crossed the street, looked up and down, and placed his paws on the running board of the county tax collector's car. The license number was the correct one.

Then someone in the crowd spoke a few words in French. Van Arsdale, who didn't understand the language, looked apprehensive. But Jim slipped through the crowd and began nudging an interested spectator. It was our Methodist minister.

Van Arsdale turned to the questioner. "What did you say to Jim?" he asked.

"I asked if there was a Bible in the crowd," replied the spectator.

The pastor had a quizzical look on his face as he reached into an inside pocket and drew out a Bible.

Jim later acquired a national reputation. Although everyone was amazed, Van Arsdale himself was intensely interested in finding out how

## THE LITTLE PIG THAT SAVED A DROWNING ELEVEN YEAR OLD

CAROL BURK WAS swimming in about five feet of water in Lake Somerville near Houston, Texas, with her friend's two-month-old, twenty-two-pound piglet, Priscilla, when her young son Anthony followed them into the water and began floundering. "I saw him go under, and I screamed at him to grab hold of Priscilla," said Ms. Burk. "They both went under. Seconds later, Priscilla's ears and nose came to the surface. It was like a miracle." The tiny piglet pulled the boy to safety. Priscilla won the American Humane Association's Stillman Award as the most heroic animal of 1984. It was the first time that a pig had won the award.

*From newspaper clippings sent to the Almanac by Bernadine Jurek of Omaha, Nebraska, and Ghita Easter of Fort Worth, Texas.*

or why Jim could perform as he did. Searching for an answer, he arranged for a demonstration at the University of Missouri, with a skeptical Dr. A. J. Durant, head of the School of Veterinary Medicine, conducting the proceedings. Durant was assisted by Dr. Sherman Dickinson of the College of Agriculture.

At the conclusion of the tests, a thoroughly convinced Dr. Durant told the crowd that he was certain Jim possessed an occult power that might never come again to a dog — at least not for many, many generations.

Such were Jim's powers that he could even look into the future and predict events. For seven years in a row, when he was shown a list of entries in the Kentucky Derby, he picked the winner each time in advance of the race. With equal ease, he could predict the sex of babies yet unborn.

In 1936, just before the World Series, Van Arsdale, in the presence of friends, placed before Jim two pieces of paper upon which the names of the competing teams had been written. He explained, "Jim, I have here the names of the two teams that will be playing in the World Series. Will you show us the one that will win?" Jim placed a paw on the slip bearing the word "Yankees." The end of the series proved him correct.

Although Jim could apparently predict the outcome of any event with certainty, Van Arsdale refused to take advantage of his dog's ability by wagering on Jim's predicting, nor would he permit anyone else to reap a profit from the dog's uncanny ability. He rejected all offers with this explanation: "I feel that Jim's powers are beyond my comprehension, and I do not care to commercialize on them in any way."

Jim died on March 18, 1937. He is buried in the Ridge Park Cemetery in Marshall, Missouri. ✦

## THE LONGEST NONFATAL SQUIRREL DROP ON RECORD

IT OCCURRED ON JULY 19, 1934. A MR. and Mrs. Clyde Cooper of Memphis, Tennessee, had just checked into their sixteenth-floor room in New York City's Lincoln Hotel. With them was a pet squirrel they were planning to give to Mrs. Cooper's son Billy. Somewhere in an area adjoining their room, the window to an air shaft that went from the sixteenth to the third floor had been left open, and the squirrel slipped and fell down it. Hotel employees working on the third floor heard a thud in the air shaft. Opening it, they found the squirrel stunned and suffering from a slight nosebleed but very much alive. To this day, it is the longest nonfatal squirrel drop in recorded history.

*Reprinted in the Almanac courtesy of Ralph Jimenez and the* Concord (N.H.) Monitor.

*New York's Lincoln Hotel, site of the world's longest nonfatal squirrel drop — from the sixteenth to the third floor.*

# The Great Stone House Toad Orgy
## By Suzanne Amanda

IN THE SOUTHWEST CORNER of our Connecticut property is a doughnut-shaped depression that in a rainstorm fills with water, making a small pond. The year we moved here to The Stone House, I was delighted to discover toads near the edges of the pond. Little did I know that over the next few years, the toads would be the main characters in a fascinating drama.

That first spring the children and I watched the male toads puff out their white throats to give their shrill mating call (my daughter learned to imitate the sound). In time, the pond was dotted with masses of jellylike eggs. During the next weeks, the children checked the pond daily, entranced as the eggs became polliwogs; then the polliwogs grew little legs, lost their tails, and finally became miniature toads. By this time, the pond was nearly dry, and the toads left. We would see them in the flower garden catching insects or along the foundation of the house.

The following spring, after the ice and snow melted and the heavy rains of April fell, the pond once again was full. The weather grew warm, and one fine moonlit night we heard a lone toad give his high love call. The next night there were two toads, and then a whole population of them. We watched the cycle repeat itself — the mating, the eggs, the polliwogs.

In the succeeding years, there were more and more toads. I did not think much of the increasing numbers until it became difficult to mow the lawn. Robins and bluejays now began to gather at the pond in the spring

# Unbelievable (but True!) Animal Stories

(CONTINUED)

to dine on the polliwogs, but the toads continued to proliferate. Soon we began to notice more and more snakes in the yard, attracted by the prospect of toads for dinner.

Despite the preying of snakes and birds, the toad population continued to increase. Our next-door neighbor walked over to complain of the noise of the mating toads. "You should fill in the pond," he said.

One morning at about eight o'clock, the children, always the first to discover a change in the activities of the pond, came running into the house urging me outside. Arriving at the water's edge, I saw that the pond was literally covered with toads.

"They're drowning each other — look," my daughter said. The toads were mating, the males on the backs of the larger females, ribbons of eggs leaving the females' bodies. We had seen this in previous years. But now there were two males for each female. "An orgy," I thought to myself in disbelief. I sat on the bank and watched for a few minutes. The kids were right: the females were being held under water, and it appeared many of them were drowning.

I looked around the pond. There were hundreds — I want to say thousands — of toads, most of them engaged in mortal threesomes. What was taking place was, I was sure, nature's way of dealing with overpopulation. The orgy went on all day. In amazement, I kept going outside and standing on the banks to watch in horrified fascination.

The following morning I awoke to the gravelly cawing of crows and went out to the pond. Dead toads floated, white bellies up, on the surface of the water. The crows were eyeing the breakfast feast awaiting them.

## A Fact About Three-Colored Cats

Did you know that three-colored cats are almost always female? Years and years ago, P. T. Barnum offered $1,000 for a male three-colored cat. He never got one.

Whether all the toads had died or the males had marched off in a midnight migration, I don't know, but there were few live ones left around the pond that morning. Except for the cleanup work of the crows, the drama of the toads had ended.

We still have toads; there are still eggs and polliwogs in the spring. But the population has never been as great as it was, nor does it appear to be increasing. It is unlikely that we will witness another toad orgy. But then, how many people have witnessed even one? ✦

## WHY A PIGEON HAD A WOODEN LEG

CHER AMI, like almost all pigeons whose acts of bravery have been recorded for posterity, was a military messenger pigeon. He delivered twelve messages from the Verdun front to his loft at Rampont during World War I, but his last flight was by far his most amazing accomplishment.

In October 1918, during a general advance of the Seventy-seventh Division, a number of companies were cut off from support and surrounded by the Germans. The men were being attacked by heavy mortar and machine-gun fire when a French and American artillery barrage began to fall around them. So close was the shelling that the Americans were hit as heavily as the Germans.

One after another, seven carrier pigeons were released with messages, but all of them were shot down by German marksmen. There was but one carrier left, Cher Ami. The message, "For God's sake, lift the fire," was placed in a capsule attached to his leg. Taking off, Cher Ami was almost immediately downed by a piece of shrapnel, but he managed to regain flight. His breast was pierced by a sharpshooter's bullet, but he flew on. A third shot tore off his right leg, leaving the precious message capsule dangling by a tendon, but still the little creature flew on. Twenty-five minutes later, the bird collapsed at his loft in Rampont. The message was relayed, the shelling stopped, and the so-called Lost Battalion was relieved. Cher Ami became a feathered celebrity and even sported a wooden leg carved to replace the one lost in action.

*Cher Ami (or one of his cousins) goes for help in a World War I battle in which friendly fire was falling on American troops. "For God's sake, lift the fire," was the message. The rest is history.*

# CHAPTER EIGHT

## Two Centuries of GOOD EATING

*"Fiddlestock on your butcher's and baker's bills,"* Uncle Jeremy cries again. *"Go down to your own barrels for your meat, and as to bread — patronize and protect your wife's manufacture."*
                                        — From the 1811 Almanac

BECAUSE WE'VE PUBLISHED SO MANY SUPERIOR RECIPES SUBmitted by readers over the years, food is perhaps the most difficult Almanac subject category from which to select "the best." So we handed the task over to the Monadnock Recipe Testing Committee (consisting of about half the Almanac staff, all of whom live in the Monadnock Region of New Hampshire). Here, in their opinion, are the winners. ✦

*Enjoying the food (a lot!) at a picnic near Quonnipaug Lake, Connecticut, in 1911.*

# Holiday Breads for Every Season

*Based, in part, on immigration records from Ellis Island.*

## By Susan Goodman

**M**ANY HOME BAKERS enjoy celebrating special days all year round by baking equally special breads. Luckily, we have scores of holiday loaves to choose from. The immigrants who passed through Ellis Island have provided the basis for a wonderful cookbook of holiday breads: New Year's *vasilopitta* from Greece, Irish soda bread, challah, poppy seed–filled Christmas bread from Hungary, and other ethnic specialties. Here's a sampling.

### For New Year's Day

### VASILOPITTA

*The Greeks wrap coins in foil and place them in the bread when kneading it. Legend has it that anyone who finds them will have luck in the coming year.*

| | |
|---|---|
| 2 tablespoons dry yeast | ½ cup milk |
| ¼ cup warm water | ½ cup butter |
| ½ teaspoon cinnamon | 7 cups unbleached flour |
| ½ teaspoon anise seeds | 1 cup sugar |
| ½ teaspoon orange peel | ½ teaspoon salt |
| 1 bay leaf | 3 eggs |
| 1 ounce ouzo (optional) | 12 walnut halves |
| ½ cup water | |

Dissolve the yeast in ¼ cup warm water and set aside. Place the cinnamon, anise seeds, orange peel, bay leaf, and ouzo, if desired, in a pot with the ½ cup water and bring to a boil. Set the mixture aside to steep and cool. Heat the milk. Remove it from the heat, stir in the butter, and allow the mixture to cool slightly.

Put the flour, sugar, and salt in a large bowl. Remove the bay leaf from the water mixture and add the flavored water, eggs, yeast, and milk mixture to the dry ingredients. Mix until all the flour has been absorbed.

Turn the dough out onto a lightly floured board and knead until smooth (about 20 minutes). Place the dough in a buttered bowl, turning it to grease the top. Cover the bowl with a towel dampened with hot water. Set it in a warm, draft-free place. Let the dough rise until doubled in bulk (about 1½ to 2 hours).

Punch down the dough and knead it for about 5 minutes. Shape it into

one large round loaf and decorate the top with walnut halves. Set the dough aside, uncovered, for about 1 hour to rise once more.

Preheat the oven to 350°F. Bake the bread for 1 hour.

MAKES 1 LOAF.

*Immigrants such as this Hungarian woman and her children arrived at Ellis Island with recipes from home.*

### For St. Patrick's Day

## IRISH SODA BREAD

4 cups unbleached flour
1 teaspoon salt
3 teaspoons baking powder
1 teaspoon baking soda
¼ cup sugar
⅛ teaspoon ground cardamom

¼ cup butter
1 egg, at room temperature
1¾ cups buttermilk, at room
    temperature
1½ cups currants

Preheat the oven to 375°F. In a large bowl, combine the flour, salt, baking powder, soda, sugar, and cardamom. Cut in the butter with a pastry blender or work it in with your fingers. Mix the egg and buttermilk together, then add this mixture to the dry ingredients. Stir until well blended. Add the currants and stir well. Turn out on a floured surface and knead gently for 3 minutes, or until the dough is smooth.

Divide the dough into two pieces, shaping each into a round loaf. Place each in a greased 8-inch cake pan, pressing it down until the dough fills the pan. Use a sharp knife to cut a cross ½ inch deep in the top of each loaf.

Bake for about 40 minutes, or until the bread sounds hollow when you thump the bottom. Turn the loaves out on a wire rack and allow to cool for about 4 hours. Cut in wedges to serve. MAKES 2 LOAVES.

### *For Rosh Hashanah*

## CHALLAH

| | |
|---|---|
| 1 teaspoon sugar | 2 eggs |
| 1 package dry yeast | 3¾ to 4 cups unbleached flour |
| 1 cup warm water | 1 egg yolk beaten with 1 tea- |
| ½ cup corn or vegetable oil | spoon water |
| ¼ cup sugar | Poppy seeds |
| 2 teaspoons salt | |

Dissolve the teaspoon of sugar and the yeast in ½ cup warm water. Let the mixture stand for 10 minutes. Stir in the oil, additional ½ cup warm water, sugar, salt, eggs, and half of the flour. Beat well. Stir in the remaining flour. The dough should be sticky. Cover and let rest for 10 minutes.

Turn the dough out onto a lightly floured board and knead for about 10 minutes, adding flour as necessary. Place in a greased bowl, turning to grease the top. Cover the bowl and let the dough rise in a warm, draft-free place until doubled in bulk (about 1½ to 2 hours).

Punch down the dough, cover, and let rise again until doubled in bulk (about 45 minutes). Divide the dough into 3 pieces. Form a braid on a greased baking sheet, taking care to fasten the ends of the braid securely. Cover the dough with a damp cloth and let rise until doubled in bulk (about 30 minutes).

Preheat the oven to 400°F. Brush the dough with the beaten egg-yolk mixture and sprinkle with poppy seeds. Bake for 30 minutes, or until golden brown. Cool on a wire rack. MAKES 1 LOAF.

## HUNGARIAN CHRISTMAS BREAD

**DOUGH & FILLING**
1 package dry yeast
1 teaspoon sugar
⅔ cup warm water
1 cup butter, at room temperature
1¼ cup sugar
½ teaspoon salt
2 tablespoons grated lemon peel
¼ cup nonfat dry milk

2½ to 3½ cups unbleached flour
1 cup ground poppy seeds
½ cup raisins
½ cup milk

**GLAZE**
1 egg
1 teaspoon water

In a small cup, dissolve the yeast and 1 teaspoon sugar in the water. Let the mixture stand for a few minutes. Meanwhile, combine the butter, ¼ cup sugar, salt, 1 tablespoon lemon peel, and nonfat dry milk in a large mixing bowl. Add 2½ cups of the flour alternately with the yeast mixture. Blend well.

Turn the dough out onto a floured board. Knead for about 10 minutes, or until the dough is smooth and not sticky. Add more flour as necessary. Put the dough into a greased bowl, turning to grease the top. Let the dough rise in a warm, draft-free place until doubled in bulk (about 1 hour).

While the dough is rising, prepare the filling. Combine the poppy seeds, 1 cup sugar, raisins, milk, and 1 tablespoon lemon peel in the top half of a double boiler. Cook over hot water, stirring constantly, until the mixture is of spreading consistency (about 10 minutes). Remove from heat and cool to room temperature.

Punch the dough down, divide it in half, and roll out each piece into a long rectangle about ¼ inch thick. Spread some of the filling on each piece, then roll the dough lengthwise like a jelly roll. Pinch the seams together tightly. Place the rolls on a large greased baking sheet.

To make the glaze, beat the egg with the water. Brush half the mixture on the loaves.

Cover the loaves with wax paper laid across water glasses so the paper doesn't touch the dough. Let them rise for 30 minutes. Apply a second coat of glaze.

Preheat the oven to 325°F. Bake the loaves for about 1 hour. If the tops brown too rapidly, cover the loaves loosely with aluminum foil. When the rolls are done, place them on a wire rack to cool.

MAKES 2 LOAVES. ✦

---

### FOR THOSE WHO LOVE STUFFING BEST

A READER FROM Arkansas, who sounded as if she was telling the truth but who signed her letter simply "Rhonda Plugg," told us that the largest single culinary dish in the world is a Bedouin wedding feast consisting of cooked eggs stuffed in fish stuffed in chickens stuffed in sheep stuffed in a camel.

---

## How to Order Two Bun Halves Filled with Cheese, Meat, Onions, Peppers & Other Stuff

IT'S ALL IN KNOWING what to ask for. For example . . .

In Norfolk, Virginia; Akron, Ohio; Jacksonville, Florida; and Los Angeles: order a "submarine."

In Philadelphia; Ann Arbor, Michigan; Knoxville, Tennessee; Newark, New Jersey, and Providence, Rhode Island: order a "hoagie."

In Des Moines, Iowa; Hartford, Connecticut; Chester, Pennsylvania; and Cleveland, Ohio: order a "grinder."

In Madison, Wisconsin: order a "Garibaldi."

In Norristown, Pennsylvania: order a "zeppelin."

In Mobile, Alabama; Sacramento, California; Houston, Texas; Montgomery, Alabama; and New Orleans, Louisiana: order a "poor boy."

In New Orleans, if "poor boy" doesn't work: order a "Musalatta."

In Gary, Indiana, if "submarine" doesn't work: order a "torpedo."

In Allentown, Pennsylvania, if "hoagie" doesn't work: order an "Italian sandwich."

In Cheyenne, Wyoming; and Cincinnati, Ohio, if neither "hoagie" nor "submarine" works: order a "rocket."

In Buffalo, New York, if neither "submarine" nor "hoagie" works: order a "bomber."

In Dublin, New Hampshire: order "two bun halves filled with cheese, meat, onions, peppers, and other stuff."

*Adapted for the Almanac from a study by Edwin Eames and Howard Robboy.*

*Italian grocer Benedetto Cataldo invented the grinder/submarine/hoagie, which he sold to hungry sailors at the Groton–New London submarine base in Connecticut. As those sailors moved on to new ports, so did the delicious new invention — but rarely did it go by the same name in more than one town.*

## How to Cook an Ostrich

CLEAN AND PUT in a tub an ostrich from 60 to 100 pounds. Put the bird in a cool place, cover tightly for 4 or 5 days, then dress and put in a pan with about 6 quarts water. Place in a baker's oven — not too hot — basting occasionally on all sides with the marinade.

Add 6 pounds sliced onions, 5 pounds sliced carrots, 3 bunches parsley, ¼ pound peppercorns, 24 bay leaves, 30 cloves, 12 whole allspice, 3 cloves garlic (crushed), 4 quarts claret, 2 quarts amontillado, 1 quart vinegar, 1 pint good brandy, 2 pounds brown sugar, and ¼ pound juniper berries. Mix all together. Cook for 4 to 6 hours, or until the bird is browned.

Skim and strain the gravy. Add 2 to 4 pounds currant jelly or pounded almonds, a little grated fresh horseradish, 4 pounds glazed cherries, a little grated orange peel, and the pulp of 12 oranges (diced). Season with salt and pepper if desired. Boil for 15 to 20 minutes. Serve sauce separately.

## Fortune Cookies Are Chinese — Right? Wong.

ACCORDING TO THE National Geographic News Service, the fortune cookie was invented by an unknown genius who introduced the cookies at a California restaurant around 1920. The recipe called for butter, flour, egg whites, sugar, a little salt, vanilla extract, tea for seasoning, and a slip of paper on which was written a prophecy or tidbit of wisdom. Believe not from whence come some things.

# Oh, There's Nothing So Fine as Dandelion Wine

*It's definitely one of our ancestors' better inventions.*

## By Marilyn Kluger

D IS FOR DANDELION, a beautiful, useful plant whose virtues were much praised in earlier times by country people who ate salads of its leaves in the spring and drank tonics made from its roots to purify their blood. Dandelion wine has long been considered good for the liver and digestion. But it is also a delicious intoxicant to be drunk simply for its own sake. Like Keats's winter wine, "it maketh glad the heart of man."

## PINK DANDELION WINE

2 quarts dandelion blossoms (stems and calyxes removed)
2 quarts boiling water
Strained juice of 3 lemons
1 package (10 ounces) frozen sweetened red raspberries, thawed
3½ cups sugar
1 cake yeast

Pick the dandelion blossoms early in the morning. Rinse them thoroughly in cool water, then remove the green parts. Put the petals in a one-gallon stoneware jar and pour the boiling water over them. Let them stand overnight.

In the morning, strain the liquid through cheesecloth, squeezing the flowers to remove all of the juice. In a large enameled pan, combine the dandelion juice with the strained lemon juice, raspberries, and sugar. Bring the mixture to a boil, then reduce heat and simmer for 20 minutes.

Pour the mixture back into the jar, cool to lukewarm, and add the yeast. Stir until the yeast dissolves, cover the jar loosely, and let the mixture ferment for about 10 days, or until it stops hissing.

Using filter paper or a double layer of cheesecloth, strain the liquid into a scalded cider jug and let it stand for about 3 days. Strain the liquid again and put it into clean wine bottles with screw-on caps. Do not tighten the caps. Let the wine stand until it is still before capping the bottles tightly. Age the wine in the cellar.

FILLS 3 WINE BOTTLES. ✦

**If you eat and drink to excess in this hot weather . . . your brains will lie in your belly.** *1807*

FACING PAGE:
*A little dandelion wine after a swim at a park outside Philadelphia "maketh glad the heart of man."*

# Anyone Can Make
# a Perfect Cup of Coffee

*All it takes is the perfect water at the perfect temperature, poured
over the perfect beans freshly roasted and ground to perfection.*

## BY LESLIE LAND

THE MELANCHOLY TRUTH is that the two most common ways to
make coffee in the United States result in the worst coffee in existence. You'd think the main villain was instant coffee, for which
1,175,000 bags of green coffee (enough to make 4,272,727,200 cups) were
imported into the United States in one recent year. But the real offender is
perked coffee, made in a percolator — glub-a-glub-a-glub — the inescapable
sound of morning for several wholly misguided generations. Mostly it's awful because it is boiled, the one thing that coffee should never be. Boiling
disperses the fragile, rich aromas that are so important to flavor, while it con-
centrates acids, extracts extra tannin, and intensifies bitterness.

For *absolutely* the best coffee, you would have to start by roasting your
own beans. Fragrance and flavor deteriorate quickly after green coffee is
roasted, and from its ancient Middle Eastern beginnings to the turn of the
century, almost everyone everywhere who made coffee roasted the beans as
needed. This is, however, a modest proposal, so we will simply insist that
the coffee be as freshly roasted as possible and ground at the last minute.

Although the beans are obviously crucial, water is the main ingredient
in coffee. If the water doesn't taste good, the coffee won't taste good. Avoid
using very hard water or water that has been artificially softened, heavily
chlorinated, or otherwise made to taste bad. In some places, this means using bottled water.

Draw fresh cold water (hot might pick up impurities from the pipes)
and put it on to boil. Use hot water to rinse the china, earthenware, stain-
less steel, glass, enamel, silver, or gold (but *not* tin or aluminum) coffeepot
so that it will be warmed up. Do the same with the cups. If you intend to
use milk, put it in a double boiler to heat up gradually. Cream should be allowed to come to room temperature.

Decide which kind of coffee you want to make. Filtered coffee is light
in body and aftertaste but very clear, refreshing, and sediment-free. Steeped
coffee is heavier and richer because none of the superfine flavoring compounds have been trapped and filtered out.

**Filtered coffee.** Put the pot where it will keep warm — in a larger pan of simmering water, on a heat spreader, or on the side of the wood stove. When you hear the water about to boil, grind the coffee fairly fine — not quite to powder. Put the filter holder over the pot, line it with filter paper, and for each cup of coffee insert 1½ to 2 tablespoons ground beans. Tamp down lightly so the water will take more time to filter through. When the water boils, turn off the heat and let its temperature fall back a few degrees, then pour on only enough water to dampen the coffee. Allow the grounds to swell for about 2 minutes, then add the rest of the water, in batches if necessary. Serve as soon as filtering is complete. (*Note:* Filter papers are pretty

*The perfect cup of coffee as envisioned by Norman Rockwell in this ad for Maxwell House, the brand of coffee always served at Nashville, Tennessee's old Maxwell House Hotel.*

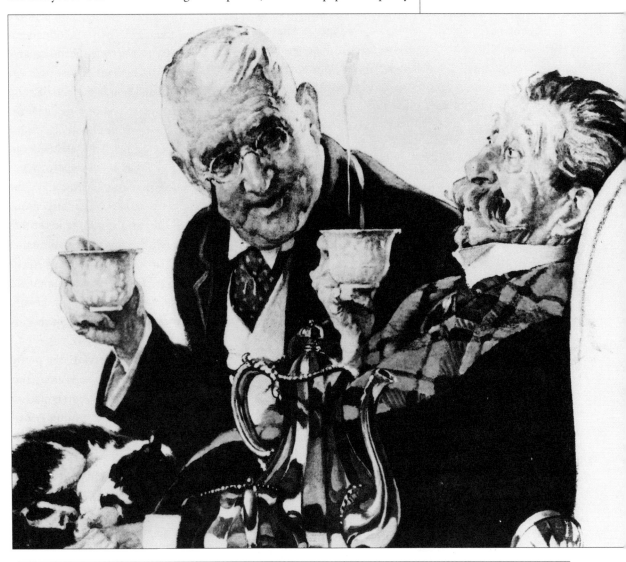

## How the Doughnut Was Invented — for Sure

Hanson Crockett Gregory was born in Clam Cove, Maine, then a part of the township of Camden. One day in 1847, when he was a lad of fifteen, he was watching his mother make dough cakes in a large kettle of fat on the iron stove. "Why doesn't the center cook up?" Hanson asked, after eating one. "They taste so soggy." When his mother did not reply, he said, "I have an idea. Why not poke a hole through the center?" Having said this, he picked up a fork and poked it through the center of the dough cake, and the hole in the doughnut was born.

Hanson Crockett Gregory went on to become one of the youngest sea captains to sail out of Maine, being given command of his own ship at age nineteen. He died in Quincy, Massachusetts, in 1921 at age eighty-nine.

*Courtesy of Fred E. Crockett.*

close to tasteless when they leave the factory but will pick up strong odors — garlic, cheese, tobacco smoke — if exposed to them. Store accordingly.)

**Steeped coffee.** Follow the instructions for filtered coffee, except:

1. Be sure to use a wide-bottomed, high-spouted pot so the grounds have a good chance to sink to the bottom and stay sunk at pouring time.

2. Grind the coffee (2 tablespoons per cup) only to the texture of rough cornmeal. Put it in the pot, pour on the not-quite-boiling water, and stir.

3. Let the coffee infuse for 4 minutes, stir again briefly, and let steep for 2 to 5 minutes more, depending on how strong (and clear) you want the coffee to be. Dash in a few drops of cold water, which will sink through the hot coffee and carry stray particles to the bottom. Serve at once. Don't let the liquid sit around on the grounds for very long.

**About that egg.** Many recipes call for an eggshell, an egg white and shell, or an entire egg to be added at the end of the process. The idea is to have the albumen in the egg bond with the floating coffee particles, carrying them out of the liquid. It isn't really necessary, and it certainly isn't very tasty.

And there you have it — all the ingredients for a flavorful, aromatic, bracing, *perfect* cup of coffee. ✦

*The Best of The Old Farmer's Almanac*

## Which Burns More Calories, Riding a Bicycle or Making Your Bed?

FOR THOSE interested in exercising to lose weight, it's useful to know which activities are the most effective in terms of calories burned per hour — how dancing, for instance, compares with scrubbing floors. . . .

| | |
|---|---|
| Bicycling (5 miles per hour) | 150–250 |
| Bowling | 200–250 |
| Cooking | 125–200 |
| Dancing | 250–450 |
| Gardening | 250–325 |
| Jogging (5 miles per hour) | 450–500 |
| Making beds | 200–250 |
| Reading | 75–125 |
| Scrubbing floors | 200–250 |
| Skiing (downhill) | 350–500 |
| Swimming | 230–325 |
| Television watching | 75–125 |
| Tennis (doubles) | 250–350 |
| Typing | 75–125 |
| Walking (3 miles per hour) | 200–250 |
| Washing dishes | 125–200 |

If you cut down on your intake of sweets and fats, of course, your weight will decrease. Every pound taken off is equivalent to 3,500 calories burned.

*Dancing burns anywhere from 250 to 450 calories per hour (slightly more for jitterbugging, as shown here). Cooking — even before you eat the results — is considerably less effective.*

## Recipes from More Than 100 Years Ago

*The Shakers, who invented many great recipes, believed rhythmic movement would shake off their sins.*

**Hope is a good breakfast but a bad supper.**

*1857*

## Favorites of the Shakers

MOTHER ANN LEE, founder of the Shakers in the United States, settled near Albany, New York, shortly before 1782. By 1882 there were about eighteen "families" of Shakers numbering roughly one hundred each. Celibates, they did not marry but vowed to perform some sort of honest labor each day — and to owe no one. Outsiders were universally struck by the excellence of what the Shakers produced. About 1888 the Shaker community at Mount Lebanon, New York, was destroyed by fire. A calendar was produced to help them rebuild and to sell a certain "Extract of Roots" that they prepared. These recipes, published in the Almanac over the years, are taken from that calendar.

### CABBAGE SALAD

One small head cabbage, one-half bunch celery, one-quarter cup vinegar, one tablespoon dry mustard, one egg well beaten, one tablespoon sugar, salt and pepper. Take a little of the vinegar to wet the mustard, then put the rest of the vinegar over the fire. When boiling, stir in the celery, mustard,

## YE FINEST RECIPE FOR COOKING YE FISHES
### (CIRCA 1800)

TAKE THE FISH while still alive and scour and run him clean with water and salt, but do not scale him. Open him and put him with his blood and liver in a small kettle. Add a handful each of Sweet Marjoram, Thyme, and Parsley, and a sprig each of Rosemary and Savory. Bind the herbs in two or three small bundles and put them into the fish with four or five whole onions, twenty pickled oysters, and three anchovies. Pour on your fish as much Claret Wine as will cover him and season well with salt, cloves, mace, and orange and lemon rind. Cover the pot and put on a quick fire till it be sufficiently boiled. Then take out the fish and lay it with the broth in a dish. Pour upon him a quarter of a pound of fresh melted butter beaten with six spoonfuls of the broth, the yolks of two or three eggs, and some of the herbs, shredded. Garnish with lemons and serve it up.

egg, sugar, pepper, and salt. Pour this over the cabbage while hot and mix it well. When cold, it is ready for the table. The same sauce will do for lettuce.

## DELIGHTFUL PUDDING

Butter a dish, sprinkle the bottom with finely minced candied peel and a very little shredded suet, then add a thin layer of light bread. Continue layering until the dish is full. For a pint dish, make a liquid custard of one egg and one-half pint milk. Sweeten, pour over the pudding, and bake as slowly as possible for two hours.

## BROILED PARTRIDGES

Partridges, gravy, butter, pepper, salt, cayenne. Thoroughly pick and draw the partridges, divide each through the back and breast, and wipe the insides. Season them highly with pepper, salt, and a very little cayenne, then place them over a clear, bright fire to broil for fifteen to twenty minutes. When done, rub a piece of fresh butter over them and serve them up hot with brown gravy. ✦

# From *The Woman Suffrage Cook Book*

IN 1886 HATTIE A. BURR edited *The Woman Suffrage Cook Book*. The book included recipes from women teachers, lecturers, physicians, ministers, and authors known to favor suffrage. Mrs. Burr stated in her preface, "I believe . . . our messenger will go forth a blessing to housekeepers, and an advocate for the elevation and enfranchisement of woman." The following recipe, reproduced in the 1968 edition of the Almanac, comes from that book.

### OLD-TIME BAKED INDIAN PUDDING

Three pints of sweet milk, two large iron spoonfuls of yellow cornmeal, one small egg, one iron spoonful of molasses, three-quarters cup of sugar, heaped teaspoonful of ginger, level teaspoonful of cinnamon, one-third of a small nutmeg, and one-half a teacupful of thick, sour cream. Put half the milk over the fire with a sprinkling of salt; as soon as it comes to a boil, scatter the meal quickly and evenly in by hand.

Remove immediately from the fire to a dish; stir in the cold milk, the well-beaten egg, the spices, the sweetening, and the sour cream. Bake three hours, having a hot oven the first half hour and a moderate one the remainder of the time. Eat with sweet cream. If rightly made and rightly baked, this pudding is delicious, but four things must be remembered as requisite: First, the pudding must be thin enough to run when put in the oven. Second, the egg must be small, or if large, but two-thirds used for a pudding of the above size. Third, the sour cream must not be omitted (but in case one has no cream, the same quantity of sour milk with a piece of butter the size of a small butternut can be substituted). Fourth, the baking must be especially attended to. Many a good receipt is ruined in the cooking, but if the directions are carefully followed, this pudding will be quavery when done and, if any is left, a jelly when cold. Use no sauce, but sweet cream or butter. ✦

*Matilda Joslyn Gage, Fayetteville, New York.*

*Susan B. Anthony (1820–1906), shown here with glasses, and Elizabeth C. Stanton (1815–1902) worked together on women's suffrage issues for some forty years and helped pave the way for the 1920 adoption of the Nineteenth Amendment to the U.S. Constitution.*

# The Best of Old Cape Cod

B Y CUSTOM, FOOD of the first English settlers at Plymouth and on Cape Cod was intended not to differ much from that of Old England's meat, fish, and produce. But Squanto, a native Plymouth Indian and the last survivor of a 1617 smallpox epidemic, introduced changes. After attaching himself to Plymouth Colony in 1620, Squanto showed the colonists how to plant Indian corn, how to fish, how to dig for shellfish along tidal shores, where to find lobsters, and how to procure and prepare other local foodstuffs.

Since then, the Cape's developing orchards, wild fowl and game, and shellfish and ocean fish have stood the population in good stead. Eventually,

*Clambakes have long been a tradition on Cape Cod, though the dress code for such occasions has changed considerably over the years. The back of the old print states that this photo was taken "after the Decoration Day parade."*

West Indies traders introduced molasses, raw sugar, ginger, and other spices that contributed to many savory dishes peculiar to the Cape. Many of these have survived, almost unchanged, to the present.

Through the courtesy of Albert E. Snow of Orleans, Massachusetts, who shares a common ancestor with Fred H. Snow of the F. H. Snow Canning Company (purveyors of Snow's Clam Chowder), we present several Snow family favorites — genuine, original recipes from old Cape Cod.

### SCALLOPED OYSTERS

1½ cups cracker crumbs
¾ cup bread crumbs
¾ cup melted butter
2 tablespoons finely chopped parsley

2 tablespoons chopped chives
1½ pints oysters
Salt and freshly ground pepper
⅓ cup oyster liquor
3 tablespoons heavy cream

Preheat the oven to 425°F. Mix the cracker and bread crumbs with the butter, parsley, and chives. Pick over the oysters. Drain them, reserving their liquor. Butter a shallow 6-cup baking dish, then sprinkle a thin layer of the crumb mixture over the bottom.

Arrange half the oysters over the crumbs and season with salt and pepper to taste. Combine the oyster liquor and cream and sprinkle half over the oysters. Cover with half the remaining crumbs. Add one more layer each of oysters, salt and pepper, liquor, and crumbs. (No more than two layers should be attempted.) Bake for 25 to 30 minutes, or until browned.

SERVES 6 TO 8.

### BAKED SEA CLAMS

2 sea clams per person (reserve the liquor.)
Cracker and/or bread crumbs

Chopped onion
Chopped celery
Bacon strips

Preheat the oven to 450°F. Shuck the clams and cut off their heads. Remove the black parts from their stomachs. Grind the clams fine in a food grinder. In a large bowl, combine the ground clams, cracker and/or bread crumbs, onion, and celery. Moisten the mixture with clam liquor. Press the mix into clean shells. Lay a strip of bacon atop each. Bake for 15 minutes, or until browned.

### BOILED DINNER — CAPE COD FASHION

3 to 4 pounds corned beef
6 medium onions
6 carrots, cut in half lengthwise

6 potatoes, cut in half lengthwise
6 turnips, cut in quarters
1 medium cabbage

For pickling beef, for 100 pounds, take 16 pounds fine salt, 2 pounds brown sugar, 4½ gallons water, and 6 ounces saltpeter.

*1826*

Place the corned beef in a large pot and cover with cold water. Bring the water to a boil to remove any excess salt. Drain the meat, then cover it with 4 quarts water. Let simmer until tender (3 to 3½ hours). If the liquid is still too salty, pour off part of it and add more water to make at least 3 pints of broth.

Add the onions, carrots, potatoes, and turnips to the pot; cook about 20 minutes. Cut the cabbage into sections through the center so the pieces will keep their shape; add these to the pot. Cook about 15 minutes more or until all vegetables are tender. Serve on a large platter with the meat in the center and the drained vegetables around it. Grated horseradish may be served on the side. SERVES 8 TO 10.

## FRIED HERRING

Pour boiling water over herring. Let stand 5 minutes, then drain. Put a small piece of butter in a hot skillet. Place the herring in this and cook 8 to 10 minutes, turning frequently. Serve with shirred eggs. ✦

### TWO GOODIES FROM THE 1885 ALMANAC

CORN MUFFINS **for breakfast.** Pour one quart of boiling milk over one pint of fine cornmeal. While the mixture is still hot, add one tablespoonful of butter and a little salt, stirring the batter thoroughly. Let it stand until cool, then add a small cup of wheat flour and two well-beaten eggs. When mixed sufficiently, put the batter into well-greased shallow tins (or, better yet, into gem pans) and bake in a brisk oven for one-half hour, or until richly browned. Serve hot.

**Potato pie.** Boil one-quarter pound potatoes until soft, then peel them and rub them through a sieve. Add one quart of milk, three teaspoonfuls of melted butter, four beaten eggs, and sugar and nutmeg to taste. Bake as you would a custard pie.

# CHAPTER NINE

# *The* TRUE STORIES *Behind the* HISTORY STORIES

*"A man's reputation is like his shadow: sometimes it follows and sometimes it precedes him; and at times it is longer and at other times shorter than he is."* — 1910 *Old Farmer's Almanac*

AN ALMANAC HISTORY STORY USUALLY COMMEMORATES AN ANNIVERSARY. Anniversaries divisible by one hundred are obviously preferred. Fifty and twenty-five are fine, too. But sometimes anniversaries divisible by only five or ten have to do — as in the case of the story that begins this chapter. The first step in choosing subjects for the next *Old Farmer's Almanac* is to compile a list of next year's anniversaries. It sorta gets us in an Almanac mood. ✦

---

*While their parents seek entry into the U.S., immigrant children practice waving their American flags on the roof garden at Ellis Island.*

# Lest We Forget the Passenger Pigeon

*The introduction to this story in the 1974* Old Farmer's Almanac *read as follows: "Exactly sixty years ago, the earth's last passenger pigeon trembled quietly, slowly closed her eyes . . . and fell from her perch, dead at twenty-nine years of age. Less than one hundred years ago, the passenger pigeon composed almost 40 percent of the total U.S. bird population! What happened? It's a story to be remembered. . . ."*

## By George W. Pothier

*Alexander Wilson, father of American ornithology, once sighted a flock of passenger pigeons he estimated to be 240 miles long and a mile wide, and containing 2,230,272,000 birds. This statue of Wilson is in Paisley, Scotland.*

IT WAS THE AUTUMN OF 1813. Myriad tiny sunbeams sifted through the branches and remaining leaves of the tall beech trees common to this Ohio River area. Small puffs of billowy clouds hung motionless in the pale blue sky. The stillness of the day was interrupted only by the occasional thud of dropping beechnuts.

Then the quiet was broken by the sound of a distant movement of air coming from the northeast. About three miles away, dark clouds could be seen moving southwestward at a startling rate. Faint but almost constant rumblings of thunder announced the threat of an approaching storm. The clouds wavered, and before long the sun was almost totally eclipsed. The clouds, which were of abnormal length and breadth, rolled furiously forward as they neared the great beech forest.

As the faint thunder became a roar, a great vibration of air caused the ground to tremble. The clouds were alive, propelled by a billion wings flapping in unison. The passenger pigeons, on their annual flight southwest for the winter, were coming.

The famous ornithologist John James Audubon estimated that this flock represented no fewer than 1,000,136,000 pigeons — and those were only a fraction of the number in the total flight, which took three days to pass over the area.

These are startling but well-documented figures. At the turn of the nineteenth century, it was estimated that passenger pigeons accounted for almost 40 percent of the total bird population in the United States.

The passenger thrived in the wild. One pair was capable of producing three broods in less than four months, and the adult life span averaged around twenty-five years. Everyone thought that these birds would be around in massive numbers forever.

The passengers were communal in their roosting habits. In one reported roosting, the birds covered a 150,000-acre area with fifty to one hundred

nests in every sizable beech or hemlock. Often trees two feet in diameter toppled to the ground from the weight of so many birds and nests. Branches the size of a man's thigh would snap from the dead weight put upon them. Such huge flocks consumed a calculated 17,424,000 bushels of mast a day — and dung from the propagating pigeons averaged two inches thick on the forest floor.

Then the hunting began.

People discovered that the passenger pigeon's flesh, especially that of the young squabs, made good eating. The feathers were used in pillows. Dried gizzards stewed in milk were believed to be a sure cure for gallstones. And pigeon's blood, mixed with a proportionate amount of water, was guaranteed to ease eyestrain, halt sties, and even improve failing eyesight. The dung was invaluable. It was rich in saltpeter, used in explosives, fertilizers, and some patent medicines. Migraine headaches, stomachaches, pleurisy, colic, dysentery, and apoplexy almost always disappeared after taking a spoonful or two of crushed saltpeter mixed with molasses.

*Shooting passenger pigeons in northern Louisiana in the late nineteenth century. In Grand Traverse, Michigan, a handful of men once became wealthy in three weeks by shooting or snaring five million pigeons for a dealer.*

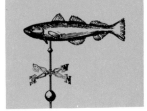

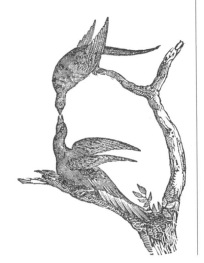

Both amateur and professional hunters recognized a growing market when they saw one. In the early 1800s, professional pigeon hunters numbered in the hundreds. By 1880, their ranks had swelled into the thousands, thanks mainly to the increased market for passenger pigeons. And the value of the birds kept inching upward. In the mid-1800s, a man could earn a year's wages in five weeks by hunting pigeons. In Grand Traverse, Michigan, a handful of men became wealthy in three weeks by supplying a total of five million pigeons to a dealer. More than half of these birds were young squabs.

Huge seine nets, some one hundred yards long, were strung along the banks of the Ohio River near Cincinnati, where the birds flew low. Men and boys using clubs, poles, and oars swung wildly, killing thousands of the confused and frantic birds entangled in their nets. Those birds that were fortunate enough to get through or avoid the nets were rewarded with blasts from shotguns. A single blast frequently brought down 130 pigeons.

The purse net also was effective. With a wide opening at one end and closed at the other end, it resembled a huge windsock. When strung in line across treeless avenues in roosting areas, where the birds liked to skim six to eight feet above the ground, it trapped thousands of pigeons. Once the purse was full, the end was closed. Then, with the dazed and bewildered birds irretrievably trapped, a group of boys wielding blacksmith pincers would snip off the heads that protruded through the net.

But the greatest carnage was yet to come. In the city of Petoskey, Michigan, in 1881, hunters using the aforementioned methods and a few innovations killed or captured alive an estimated one billion birds, according to a report by Professor H. B. Roney in the *Chicago Field Magazine*. After the choice birds had been picked out, hogs were brought in to feed on the leftover carcasses.

Reports of probable extinction were scoffed at. Attempts at passing legislation to preserve the passenger pigeon were usually futile, and in areas where laws eventually were passed, the lack of enforcement rendered them useless. After all, folks believed, it was ridiculous to think that a bird that reproduced so readily could ever be extinct. The slaughter continued.

In 1896, however, it became more noticeable that the number of passenger pigeons was diminishing. Less than a decade earlier, the already-below-average migrating flock had taken ten to twelve hours to pass over Louisiana; in 1896 the entire flock passed over the same territory in less than two minutes.

Prior to the last sighting of wild pigeons — reported on March 24, 1900, near Saragents, Ohio — thirty-six squabs had been crated and shipped to the Cincinnati Zoological Gardens in an attempt to preserve the species. On September 1, 1914, the last survivor of the thirty-six trembled quietly, slowly closed her eyes, nestled her head into her shoulder cavity, and fell from her perch, dead at twenty-nine years of age. She now rests permanently perched in the Smithsonian Institution.

To this day, an aggregate reward of $1,500 for a pair of living passenger pigeons remains unclaimed. ✦

## How Did Shooting a Pigeon Save the Washington Monument?

*By Lucille J. Goodyear*

THE IDEA OF a lasting memorial to George Washington took hold as early as 1783, but political wrangling, money raising, and design hassles held up construction until 1848. In the next six years, the monument rose to a height of over 150 feet. Then donations began to dwindle, and work stopped. Throughout the Civil War, the unfinished "stump," as it was generally called, remained an eyesore on the Washington scene.

As the nation's centennial celebration approached in 1876, the project was resumed. But when the engineers arrived on the scene, they discovered that all the scaffolding and ropes within the unfinished tower of blocks had rotted beyond use. There seemed to be no way of getting up the 153 feet of completed wall to the top. (The final plan called for a 550-foot height.)

So here's where one solitary pigeon comes into the story to save the day — and the monument! Following an on-the-spot plan put forth by one of the engineers, the construction workers managed to capture a pigeon and attach several hundred feet of threadlike wire to one of its legs. The bird was then taken inside the base of the monument and, after all the entrances were blocked, released. As soon as it began to fly, a pistol was fired, which so startled the pigeon that it soared upward and out the open top of the shaft. Once outside, it was immediately shot down by an engineer. The wire attached to its leg was recovered, to be used to haul progressively heavier ropes, until a thick cable was in place on which scaffolding could be mounted.

Thereafter, the work proceeded continuously until it was completed, and in February 1885, the monument was finally dedicated.

Mules make a
great fuss about
their ancestors
having been
horses.

*1881*

## Was a Pig Really Responsible for Starting the War of 1812?

*By Steve Yankee*

ONE OF THE most intriguing tales of animals in history is an undocumented story circulated during the early 1800s. It seems that a certain pig in Providence, Rhode Island, was constantly breaking through fences and eating the contents of a neighbor's garden. Now the neighbor in this case was a Federalist candidate for Congress who became so enraged one day at the sight of the pig eating his garden that he killed the pig on the spot — with a three-tined pitchfork!

This, in turn, enraged the late pig's owner who, on Election Day shortly thereafter, naturally cast his vote for his neighbor's opponent — who, as it turns out, won the election by one vote.

So the winner went to Congress, and presumably the loser stayed home tending his garden — and no doubt spent some time wishing he'd delayed his revenge upon the pig at least until after all the votes had been cast.

Some time later, when the question of war with England came to a vote before the U.S. Senate, the measure passed by only one vote — that of the senator who had defeated the Federalist gardener. The outcome, of course, was the War of 1812 and our eventual economic liberation from England.

This story might be a lot of hogwash — but then again, it might not!

# He Saw Lincoln Shot

*The story of an obscure captain in the Union Army who was both a witness to and a part of a historic tragedy . . .*

## By Charles E. Greenwood

H E WAS SEATED IN the second row on the left side of the theater in back of the orchestra — with a command view of President Abraham Lincoln watching the play. Because the audience was laughing at the antics on stage at the time, few heard the shot that came suddenly during the performance. Edwin Bedee, a captain in the Twelfth Regiment, New Hampshire Volunteers, stared in disbelief as a man vaulted from the president's box onto the stage.

When Captain Bedee saw the man jump from the president's box, his first reaction was to pursue the fleeing gunman. Instead, Bedee, like the rest, listened as John Wilkes Booth boldly uttered the incredible words, "Revenge for the South!" Little did the captain know that he had just witnessed the murder of one of America's great presidents.

Recognizing a catastrophe, Captain Bedee sprang from his chair, climbed over some rows, bolted past the orchestra and footlights, and crossed the stage in the direction in which Booth had disappeared.

A scream shattered the mounting noise: "They've got him!" Bedee presumed the assassin was caught. Another scream, this time from Mrs. Lincoln: "My husband is shot!" A doctor was called for. Captain Bedee reeled around and bounded across the stage toward the box. As he was scaling the box, another man appeared and stated he was a physician. Captain Bedee stepped aside, pushed the doctor up to the railing, and followed directly behind.

When Bedee and the surgeon reached the box, President Lincoln lay reclined in his chair, his head tilted back as though he were asleep. The doctor searched for the wound. Seeking some evidence of blood or torn clothing, he started to remove Lincoln's coat and unbutton his vest. Meanwhile, Captain Bedee was holding the president's head. Suddenly he felt a warm wetness trickling into his hand. "Here is the wound, doctor," Captain Bedee

*This is the last known portrait of Lincoln, taken two months before his death. Ironically, the original glass negative became cracked in processing, so all subsequent reproductions are flawed.*

said, as one of his fingers slid into the hole in the back of Lincoln's head where the ball had only moments before forced an entry.

During the removal of some of the president's clothing, papers fell from his pocket. Mrs. Lincoln, apparently rational in spite of the shock, is said to have handed the packet to Captain Bedee, requesting, "You are an officer. Won't you take charge of these papers?"

By now others had gained entrance to the box through the door. One was a surgeon, who proceeded to work with his colleague on the president. When Lincoln was removed to the house across the street from the theater, Captain Bedee helped carry the dying man; he waited at the house until Secretary of War Edwin Stanton arrived soon afterward. Then Captain Bedee delivered the papers to the secretary, writing his own name and regiment upon the wrapper that Stanton placed around the documents. Secretary Stanton gave the captain two assignments: first, to go to the War Department with a message, and second, to contact the officer in command at Chain Bridge on matters dealing with the escaping assassin.

When the missions were completed, Captain Bedee returned to Stanton. The secretary thanked him for his diligence in handling the duties assigned him and also for caring for the president's papers. He was then told to return to his post of duty.

Captain Bedee spent the following day with his regiment, but that evening an officer brought an order for the captain's arrest. Apparently a misunderstanding of the connections between Bedee, Lincoln's papers, and the assassination had made him a suspect within the War Department. Captain Bedee was so distraught that he telegraphed the department, explaining the situation.

For two days Captain Bedee was kept under arrest. Finally his release came, with an explanation of the confusion. Immediately the captain wrote Secretary Stanton a personal letter stating that his honorable record during the war would have a very serious blemish if the details were not clarified. The secretary wrote back, explaining the error and giving proper acknowledgment to Captain Bedee for his commendable acts in handling Lincoln's papers. Thus the good captain was completely exonerated from any suspicious association with the murder of President Lincoln.

How did Captain Bedee happen upon this sorrowful moment of American history?

Edwin Bedee was born in Sandwich, New Hampshire, and grew up in the area. Prior to the war, he was a printer by trade. At twenty-four he enlisted and spent three months in a New York regiment, but upon his release,

*John Wilkes Booth, an actor who sympathized with the southern cause. After shooting Lincoln at Ford's Theater on April 14, 1865, he was pursued for twelve days before being shot in a barn near Bowling Green, Virginia.*

*The Best of The Old Farmer's Almanac*

he hastily returned to his home state to join the Twelfth Volunteers, wanting to be with fellow New Hampshirites.

Mustered in as a sergeant major of the regiment, Bedee was soon promoted to the rank of first lieutenant. At the Battle of Chancellorsville, though wounded, he assumed command of his regiment when those higher in rank were either killed or unable to lead. His actions at Chancellorsville led to his promotion to captain.

A year later, at Cold Harbor, Virginia, Captain Bedee was severely wounded. He was still recovering when he went back into action. This time he was captured at Bermuda Front, Virginia. Paroled in February 1865 and selected to serve on the staff of General Potter shortly thereafter, Captain Bedee went to Washington on special duty. On Friday evening, April 14, 1865, he decided to attend Ford's Theater.

A month after this tragic and involved affair, Captain Bedee was promoted to the rank of major. Soon he was mustered out of the army along with his regiment. He died in Plymouth, New Hampshire, on January 13, 1908, just five days after his seventy-first birthday. ✦

*The funeral train carrying Lincoln's body stopped at almost every town on the long, sad journey from Washington to Springfield, Illinois.*

# The Death of Sitting Bull

*During his later years, the Wild West Show billed Sitting Bull as the "Killer of Custer." Then, on December 15, 1890, the cavalry came to get him.* By Christine Schultz

ON A CHILLY DECEMBER NIGHT IN 1890, a Sioux chief sat smoking kinnikinnick in his log cabin at Standing Rock in South Dakota. His friends kept watch because just that afternoon the Indian Bureau had ordered his arrest, and soon forty-three Indian police officers and two troops of cavalry would come to get him. His name was Sitting Bull. He was the most famous Indian chief in American history, a leader in the attack on General George Armstrong Custer. That night he seemed untroubled as he talked of old times. He spoke of his first buffalo hunt at age ten and of the battle against the Crow that earned him his name at fourteen. Perhaps he told again the story of Custer's last stand, of the sun dance when a hundred pieces of skin were cut from his arms, of seeing soldiers on horseback falling upside-down like grasshoppers from the sky.

His reservation days had not been so glorious, but he told with pride of his welcoming speech to the white men when the last spike was driven in the Northern Pacific Railroad. They had sent a young bluecoat to prepare a polite speech for Sitting Bull to deliver. But when the chief stood upon the platform, he replaced the flowery words with his own bitter ones: "I hate all the white people. You are thieves and liars. You have taken away our land and made us outcasts." He had paused occasionally for applause, bowing and smiling at the crowd, who could not understand his insults. How the interpreter had squirmed, translating his harsh attack into sweet platitudes.

So great was Sitting Bull's popularity that the Indian agents had booked him for a speaking tour of fifteen cities the summer after that episode. Then, in 1885, he joined William "Buffalo Bill" Cody in the Wild West Show. For a year he traveled through the United States and Canada, drawing large crowds. Although the audiences heckled the "Killer of Custer," they eagerly pressed around him after the show to exchange their coins for his autograph. When the season closed, Buffalo Bill gave him two gifts: one, a white sombrero, the other, a gray circus horse that danced to the sound of gunshots.

BUFFALO BILL'S WILD WEST

"THE MAZE"
THE MOST ANIMATED EQUESTRIAN SPECTACLE EVER SEEN. A GORGEOUS MOVING PICTURE IN WHICH OVER 300 HEROIC HORSEMEN PARTICIPATE

For many years Sitting Bull had persuaded his people not to sell their land to the government, but in 1889 he could resist no longer; the reservation was divided. It was then that the Indians embraced with desperate hope the ghost dance. During the Drying Grass Moon in the autumn of 1890, Sitting Bull's people danced long into the night. They wore ghost shirts marked with magic symbols said to protect them from the white man's bullets. Often they fainted and saw before them the ghosts of their ancestors. The old men said that in the spring, the dance would bring the Indian messiah, leading wild horses and buffalo back to the plains. Sitting Bull did not believe in the dance, but he did not dissuade his people from its practice.

By mid-November the dancing had superseded all other activity on the Sioux reservation: farm work had stopped, trading stores were empty, and the schoolhouse was deserted. The Indians dancing in the snow frightened the agents, who sent a message to the Indian Bureau in Washington: the Sioux are beyond control; send a thousand soldiers. The most dangerous Indian, they decided, must be eliminated.

And so came the early morning of December 15, two days after the night of quiet talk. As Sitting Bull's men were sleeping and the chief lay on a pallet alongside his wife, pounding hoofbeats broke the stillness of the chill predawn. A rifle butt banged open the door, and several hands pulled the

*Posters like this one advertised "Buffalo Bill" Cody's Wild West Show featuring Sitting Bull. After the season ended, Buffalo Bill gave Sitting Bull the gray circus horse that was with the chief the night of his death.*

As in a game of cards, so in the game of life we must play what is dealt to us; and the glory consists not so much in winning, as in playing a poor hand well.

*1907*
*Josh Billings*

chief unclad from bed. A match flared; the kerosene lamp caught. Ironically, it was Indian agents who grabbed Sitting Bull's carbine, knife, and revolver from beneath the bed cover.

"Brother, we have come for you," said one Indian policeman.

"If you fight, you will be killed here," said another. Three men who had once stood with Sitting Bull held him. They wore the ill-fitting blue uniforms and metal badges of the police. They were nervous, trying to hurry Sitting Bull into his clothes. He did not refuse to go. He told them to saddle his horse and struggled to walk alone as they dragged him toward the door. "Let me go. I'll go without help."

Still they held him, so he spread his arms and legs across the doorway, defying them. Fear seemed to lie less with the prisoner than with his captors. One policeman later said, "Sitting Bull was not afraid; we were afraid." No Indian before had been so bold as to carry off a chief from within the camp of his seasoned warriors.

The men pulled the chief outside, while others shoved him from behind with a revolver. A crowd of ghost dancers gathered, shouting insults at the police. Some women wailed.

Suddenly Catch-the-Bear, commander of Sitting Bull's bodyguards and chief soldier of his camp, emerged from the crowd and threw off his gray blanket. He raised his Winchester. "Let him go!" he called out to Bull Head, who held the chief.

The call shook Sitting Bull, and he decided then to resist. "Take action!" he cried. "I am not going!"

Just then, Catch-the-Bear fired at the chief's captor. As the policeman fell, he shot upward, and his bullet lodged in Sitting Bull's back. Red Tomahawk, another policeman, fired next. His bullet pierced Sitting Bull's skull. Both shots were fatal; either one alone would have ended the life of the great Sioux leader.

In the midst of the bloody fighting that followed, fourteen men were killed. Some Indians watching believed that the chief's spirit entered his old mare, for when the shots rang out, the horse that had been trained to dance to gunshots raised her front hoof as if in farewell.

Following the death of Sitting Bull, the Sioux people fled to Wounded Knee Creek, where some three hundred were massacred in their final battle two weeks later. Sitting Bull's body was buried in the northwest corner of the Post Cemetery at Fort Yates, North Dakota. In 1953 it was moved across the Missouri River to Mobridge, South Dakota. In the end, the Indian messiah never led the buffalo and the ghost of Sitting Bull back to the plains. ✦

# President Garfield's Two Months of Agony

*Over the years, all Americans have vicariously experienced, through exhaustive media coverage, horrendous national tragedies. But this was perhaps the longest.*

SHORTLY BEFORE HIS assassination, Abraham Lincoln dreamed that he saw a casket in the White House, guarded by soldiers. When he asked one of them who was dead, the soldier said, "The president."

Sixteen years later, on June 30, 1881, President James A. Garfield was winding up the last cabinet meeting before his vacation trip to New England. For some reason, he asked Secretary of War Robert Todd Lincoln to tell the story of his father's dream. Two days later, at 9:30 in the morning of July 2, Garfield was shot in a Washington railroad station. For the next eighty days, the nation seemed to hold its collective breath as the president struggled to live.

The desperate attempt to save Garfield's life enlisted the best efforts that nineteenth-century medicine and science could offer. It caused a po-

*The President James A. Garfield family, including his mother (second from right) and his wife (second from left). The Currier & Ives print was published in 1882, the year after Garfield's assassination.*

litical and constitutional crisis such as the nation had never experienced and led in time to reforms that changed the face of American government.

Garfield had been a surprise choice as the nominee of the Republican party in 1880. The convention had become deadlocked between the "Stalwarts," who wanted to renominate Ulysses S. Grant, and the reform-minded "Half-Breeds," who favored James G. Blaine. Garfield was a compromise, with Stalwart Chester A. Arthur as his running mate.

Once elected, Garfield angered the Stalwarts by refusing to name their men to his cabinet. A bizarre character named Charles Guiteau, who had been making a pest of himself seeking a diplomatic post, decided that God had chosen him to set things right. He bought a pistol and started stalking the president.

On the morning of July 2, he fired at Garfield, then immediately dropped his weapon. Surrendering to a stunned policeman, he said, "I did it and want to be arrested. I am a Stalwart, and Arthur is president. Take me to the police station."

Garfield was alive but grievously wounded. The assassin had fired two shots from close range; one merely grazed the president's shoulder, but the other smashed into his lower back a few inches to the right of his spine.

*In planning Garfield's murder, Charles Guiteau, below, spent an extra dollar for a bone-handled pistol he thought would look good in a museum. Then he practiced marksmanship on the banks of the Potomac, within earshot of the White House. In stalking Garfield, he once walked away from an opportunity because Garfield's wife was present.*

But the president, a powerfully built six-footer who had been turning handsprings with his teen-age sons the morning of the shooting, rallied. Out of a swarm of doctors, Garfield chose a boyhood friend, Dr. Willard Bliss, to supervise his treatment. Dr. Bliss in turn chose three physicians to assist him.

Unsolicited medical advice came from all over the country. One man proposed that the president's body be "inverted for some hours in order that the bullet might gravitate downwards." Another outlined a plan to run a rubber tube into the wound until it made contact with the bullet, which could then be sucked out by an air pump. An Irish maid in the White House surreptitiously sprinkled holy water on the invalid's oatmeal.

Garfield's doctors were obsessed with locating the bullet, and one or another of them seemed to be poking an unsterile finger or probe into the open wound every day.

On July 26 Alexander Graham Bell and an assistant showed up at the White House with a new invention, a precursor of the metal detector, that Bell hoped would locate the bullet. A large group of spectators, including the conscious president and his wife, watched in fascination as Bell moved the contraption around Garfield's body, listening through earphones for a telltale click. He got no results that day but came back on August 1 for another try and announced that he had found it, in the president's groin. That was where Bliss and the others had believed it to be all along. But the risk of exploratory surgery was too great.

Meanwhile, as the doctors dithered, politicians wondered who was in charge of the country. Chester Arthur, after one courtesy call on the White House, tactfully remained in New York. Fortunately for the nation, July, August, and the first part of September passed without any external threat or internal disorder.

The president died on the night of September 19. Curiously, his body was embalmed before an autopsy took place, adding fuel to a fiery medical controversy over his treatment and over the cause of his death that has hardly died out to this day. The official verdict of the autopsy was that Garfield died of a hemorrhage of his splenic artery, presumably nicked by the bullet, which was found nowhere near the place his doctors had predicted. Critics questioned why the artery should have waited eighty days to begin bleeding. The word bacteria does not appear in the report, although the evidence is strong that it was a raging infection that killed the president.

Charles Guiteau went to the gallows insisting that it was not he but the doctors who killed James Garfield, and some medical men agreed. Many doctors, however, objected to the second-guessing. One recommended sarcastically that someone "gather into one volume — or a dozen volumes — all the plans of treatment which would, beyond question, have saved the life of our late president."

For the second time in a generation, thousands of Americans lined railroad tracks to see a president's body borne home for burial. Although he had been in office only four months, Garfield's death caused an outpouring of grief that exceeded that following Lincoln's assassination. "There is no longer any South, North, East, or West," wrote William Balch in a biography of Garfield. "Guiteau's bullet will accomplish much to better our political life, to make purer our political purposes."

And, in fact, it did. Chester A. Arthur, to the surprise of all, pushed through a willing Congress a civil service reform bill that largely ended the frantic office seeking that had corrupted earlier administrations. ✦

*Courtesy of John Robinson.*

*Robert Todd Lincoln witnessed three of America's four presidential assassinations: those of his father, Garfield, and McKinley.*

**Every man should profit by his mistakes, but most of us would prefer to profit by the mistakes of others.**

*1911*

# CHAPTER TEN

# STILL LAUGHING
## *After All These Years*

*A little time for laughter*
*A little time to sing*
*A little time to kiss and cling,*
*And no more kissing after.*
— Philip Bourke Marston

IN THE 1829 ALMANAC, ROBERT B. THOMAS told his readers that "our main endeavor is to be useful, but with a pleasant degree of humour." The eleven editors who have served after Thomas have attempted, with varying degrees of success, to follow suit — sometimes without bothering to be "useful." ✦

*How cold was it in Pennsylvania during the winter of 1933? Well, cold enough to freeze your long johns.*

# Why My Great-Uncle Gave Up the Ministry

*When the following was published in the 1984* Old Farmer's Almanac, *many readers wrote to say that it was the funniest Almanac story they'd ever read . . .* By Marcia Barnard Chandler

THE FOLLOWING SAD but true tale concerns my great-uncle, a wonderful, jolly, beloved man who was over six feet four and probably weighed close to three hundred pounds. He was also very well educated (Colgate University, Doctor of Divinity) and in the early 1900s became a full-time Baptist minister. A kindly, gentle man despite his size, Uncle Alden Bentley's only real fault seemed to be that he was terribly clumsy. As a young minister, he was paying a pastoral call one day on a woman in Dillon, South Carolina, when he inadvertently sat on her Chihuahua, Twinkie, and killed it. As the lady searched and called for her dog throughout the house, Uncle Alden felt underneath his hip and, realizing what he had done, panicked and slipped the dead dog into his coat pocket. Although he was devastated, he could not bring himself to tell the woman what had happened.

Five years later, he returned to the same home for an overnight visit and resolved to unburden himself by finally telling the woman exactly what had happened to Twinkie. She had just had the guest room repapered and had hung brand-new curtains. To make Uncle feel welcome, she had placed on the bedside table a large pitcher of ice water and a glass, as well as a pen and bottle of ink so he could work on his sermon before retiring.

Uncle liked to sleep with the window open and got up in the night to open it. As he did, he knocked over what he assumed to be a full glass of water. Then, groping along the walls in an unsuccessful search for the light switch, he retraced his steps several times before raising the window and settling back on the bed for the night. When he opened his eyes

*Actress Norma Shearer with her dog, Pedro — a Chihuahua exactly like poor Twinkie.*

the next morning, he was horrified. The fresh wallpaper on two walls was covered with great black blobs. The crisp white curtains were thoroughly smudged with the prints of Uncle's huge paws. It had not been the water glass he'd overturned during the night — it had been the ink bottle.

In a shaken state of mind and knowing he must face his hostess, Uncle dressed hurriedly and started down the stairs outside the guest room. As he approached the landing, his foot slipped. Reaching wildly for support, he grabbed the nearest object, which happened to be a beautiful electric brass candelabra mounted on the stairwell wall. The fixture was hissing and smoking as he ripped it from the wall and toppled down to the landing below, still clutching it in his hand.

"Are you hurt?" his hostess cried as she rushed to Uncle's side.

"No," said Uncle as he rose to his feet, "but I have demolished your home." With that he quickly walked out the front door and, at the end of the walk, turned and said to his hostess with deep reverence, "Twinkie had a Christian burial."

He then retired from the ministry and became a teacher of philosophy for many years at a private preparatory school in Massachusetts. ✦

**A joyous smile adds an hour to one's life; a heartfelt laugh, a day; a grin, not a moment.**

*1895*

## CASES OF ACCIDENTAL REPORTING

THE FOLLOWING ARE actual quotes from accident reports submitted to insurance companies by hapless policyholders, as collected by the United Services Automobile Association:

• "Coming home, I drove into the wrong house and collided with a tree I don't have."

• "The guy was all over the road. I had to swerve a number of times before I hit him."

• "I pulled away from the side of the road, glanced at my mother-in-law, and headed over the embankment."

• "I had been driving for forty years when I fell asleep at the wheel and had the accident."

• "I was sure the old fellow would never make it to the other side of the road when I struck him."

• "The pedestrian had no idea which direction to run, so I ran over him."

• "The telephone pole was approaching. I was attempting to swerve out of its way when it struck my front end."

# Great (But Nearly Forgotten) Moments in American History

### BY DON BOUSQUET

*We laugh most at those we most respect and love.*
— Robert B. Thomas

## 1789
President Washington is accompanied to his inauguration by his teeth.

## 1620
Indigenous Americans greet the *Mayflower* Pilgrims at Plymouth Rock.

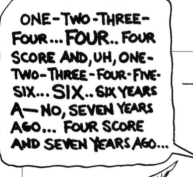

## 1863
Abraham Lincoln writes his Gettysburg Address.

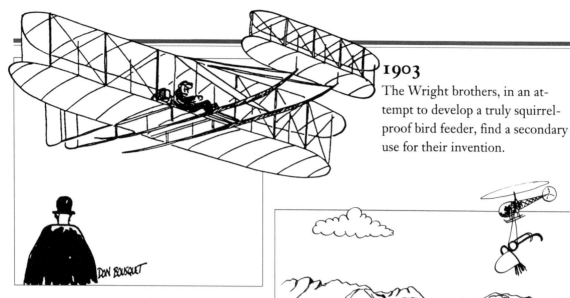

## 1903

The Wright brothers, in an attempt to develop a truly squirrel-proof bird feeder, find a secondary use for their invention.

## 1954

In what was then termed "The Crime of the Century," airborne Albanian extremists defaced the majestic countenances of Mount Rushmore.

## 1916

Irving Berlin writes, "Oh, How I Hate to Get Up in the Morning."

## 1968

The secret diaries of Calvin Coolidge are discovered in a hayloft in Plymouth, Vermont. The two-volume set discloses the president's innermost thoughts of the period 1897–1932 and contains eight pages.

# Mardon Me, Padam, But Do You Know Any Spoonerisms?

*People sometimes become famous for the silliest reasons . . .*

## By John I. White

*The man who inadvertently invented "spoonerisms," Reverend William Archibald Spooner.*

THE REVEREND William Archibald Spooner was for many years warden of New College at England's great Oxford University. Believe it or not, it was a mere slip of the tongue that started this dignified British clergyman on the road to eternal renown.

Spooner was highly regarded as a scholar, with a number of published classical and religious works to his credit. But his claim to fame rests on something almost akin to folklore. One day in chapel, when announcing the name of a hymn, Spooner intended to say "Conquering Kings Their Titles Take." But what came out was "Kinquering Kongs Their Titles Take."

Although the members of the congregation probably maintained their composure, no doubt with considerable difficulty, from then on Spooner was a marked man. Oxford students quickly proceeded to manufacture other topsy-turvy expressions and hang them on the warden of New College. There is evidence, too, that Spooner went along with the joke and contributed some sterling examples of his own making. By about 1900, the word *spoonerism* had entered the language.

When Spooner died in 1930 at the age of eighty-six, *The New York Times* allotted his obituary nearly a full column crammed with choice examples of the literary curiosity bearing his name. At the time of Queen Victoria's Jubilee, said the *Times*, he was credited with calling for "three cheers for our queer old dean." On a visit to the British fleet at Portsmouth, he was quoted as asking to go out and see the "cattleships and bruisers." At a meeting of farm laborers, he was reputed to have referred to members of the assemblage as "tons of soil." A student once noted that he had been rebuked by the warden for "fighting liars in the quadrangle," and an entire class was scolded severely for "hissing my mystery lectures." ✦

## OFTEN-QUOTED SPOONERISMS

- "It is kistomary to cuss the bride."
- "A blushing crow."
- "Those girls are sin twisters."
- "I was hocked and shorrified."
- "We each had tee martoonies."
- "The enemy quickly fled from the ears and sparrows."
- "She joins this club over my bed doddy."
- "He rode off on his well-boiled icicle."
- "The old revival hymn 'Shall We Rather at the Giver?'"
- "Mardon me, padam, you're occupewing the wrong pie; let me sew you to another sheet."

## May Harold Be with Us Always

FAMILIAR AND MUCH-recited prayers, songs, and sayings are often innocently altered by those too young to attach much meaning to the words. For instance, the seven-year-old son of one of this Almanac's editors was heard to begin the Pledge of Allegiance with "I led the pigeons to the flag. . ." and end with "The Republicans for Richard stands. . . ." Children reciting the Lord's Prayer have been heard to say, "Lead me not into Penn Station," and some have been baptized "in the name of the Father and the Son and in the hole he goes." One person we know remembers, as a little girl, the old familiar hymn "The Cross I Bear" as being "The Cross-Eyed Bear," while scores of people from the cities of Boston, Milwaukee, and Atlanta remember singing about "the land of the free and the home of the Braves."

When we asked Almanac readers to send us their own examples of such tortured turns of phrase, these were some of the best we received:

"Thou shalt not kick a duckery" (Seventh Commandment).
— *Mrs. H.D. Sheldon, McLean, Virginia*

"One nation on the windowsill, with liberty and just for us all." — *Jack Barnes, LaForte, Indiana*

"I pray the Lord to sew a cake."
— *Mrs. Gordon Schmal, Olivia, Minnesota*

"Our Father, Who art in heaven, Harold be thy name."
— *Mrs. Albert Jenkins, Chicago, Illinois*

## Actual Excerpts from Church Bulletins

- "Sunday being Easter, will Mrs. Johnson please come forward and lay an egg on the altar?"
- "Tuesday at 7 P.M. there will be an ice cream social. All ladies giving milk please come early."
- "Wednesday the Ladies Aid Society will meet and Mrs. Johnson will sing 'Put Me in My Little Bed' accompanied by the minister."
- "Thursday at 7 P.M. there will be a meeting of the Mothers' Club. All those wishing to become little mothers please meet with the minister at 7 P.M."
- "This evening there will be a meeting in the north and south end of this church. The children may be baptized at both ends."

*From Lewis Robinson.*

# Alan Ferguson's Historical Footnotes

*Certain moments in history that, generally, have been overlooked by less thorough scholars than cartoonist FERGUSON.*

"Yes, I still remember the *Maine*, but I forget what for."

"I didn't realize we had to be ready the very FIRST minute!"

"Captain, if you mean it when you say you have not yet begun to fight, I sure as hell could use a little help here!"

"Sure — HE says he never told a lie, but what does THAT prove?"

"You and your 'Damn the torpedoes — full speed ahead!'"

## A New Story of Lincoln

WHEN ABRAHAM LINCOLN was a young lawyer practicing in the courts of Illinois, he was once engaged in a case in which the lawyer on the other side made a speech to the jury full of wild statements. Lincoln opened his reply by saying, "My friend who has just spoken to you would be all right if it were not for one thing, and I don't know that you ought to blame him for that, for he can't help it. What I refer to is his reckless statements, without any ground of truth. You have seen instances of this in his speech to you. Now, the reason of this lies in the constitution of his mind. The moment he begins to talk, all his mental operations cease, and he is not responsible. He is, in fact, much like a little steamboat that I saw on the Sangamon River when I was engaged in boating there. This little steamer had a five-foot boiler and a seven-foot whistle, and every time it whistled, the engine stopped."

## Moreau's Mistake

GENERAL JEAN MOREAU was known for forsaking the colors of Napoleon and later being killed in Germany fighting against his former commander. When the general was in the city of Boston, he was much courted and sought after as a lion of the first quality. On one occasion, he was invited to Cambridge to attend the Harvard commencement exercises. In the course of the day, a musical society of undergraduates sang a then very popular song, the chorus of which was "Tomorrow, tomorrow, tomorrow." Moreau, who was imperfectly acquainted with the English language, fancied that they were complimenting him, and at every recurrence of the chorus, which he interpreted, "To Moreau, to Moreau, to Moreau," he rose and bowed gracefully to the singers' gallery, pressing his laced chapeau to his heart. The Frenchman was very much mortified when he discovered his mistake.

# Typical Almanac "Jokes"

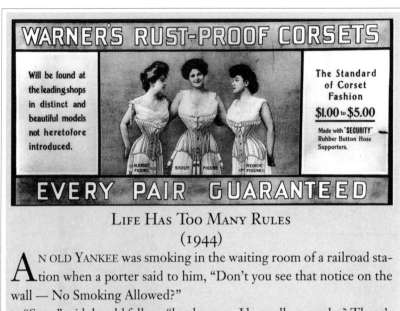

**WARNER'S RUST-PROOF CORSETS**

Will be found at the leading shops in distinct and beautiful models not heretofore introduced.

The Standard of Corset Fashion $1.00 to $5.00

Made with "SECURITY" Rubber Button Hose Supporters.

SLENDER FIGURE   STOUT FIGURE   MEDIUM FIGURE

**EVERY PAIR GUARANTEED**

### LIFE HAS TOO MANY RULES
### (1944)

AN OLD YANKEE was smoking in the waiting room of a railroad station when a porter said to him, "Don't you see that notice on the wall — No Smoking Allowed?"

"Sure," said the old fellow, "but how can I keep all your rules? There's another on the wall over there that says 'Wear Felicia Corsets.'"

### THE FRUSTRATED LOVER
### (1834)

I AM AFRAID of the lightning," murmured the pretty young woman during a thunderstorm.

"Well you may be," sighed her despairing adorer, "when your heart is steel."

### THE MATE'S REVENGE
### (1945)

PONDER THEN upon this story of the mate, who, after a day's shore leave had left him somewhat befuddled, forgot or was unable to write up the day's log. The next morning he found that his captain had attended to that duty, adding at the end of the record, "Mate drunk today." The mate said nothing, but at the close of the next day's record, he wrote, "Captain sober today."

## An Easterner's Letter to Her Son
### (1977)

Dear Stanley,

I write to let you know I am still alive. I am writing slowly, as I know you don't read fast.

You won't know the house when you come home — we moved. We had trouble moving, especially the bed — the man wouldn't let us take it in the taxi, and we were afraid we might wake your father.

Your father has a nice new job and very responsible. He has about five hundred people under him — he cuts the grass at the cemetery.

Our neighbors, the Browns, started keeping pigs — we got wind of it yesterday.

I got my appendix out and a dishwasher put in. There is a washing machine in the new house here, but it don't work too good. Last week I put fourteen shirts in the washer and pulled that chain. They whirled around real good but then disappeared. I think something is wrong with the machine.

Your uncle Dick drowned last week in a whiskey vat at the distillery. Four of his work mates dived in to save him, but he fought them off bravely. We cremated his body the next day and just got the fire out this morning.

It rained only twice last week — once for three days and once for four days. Monday was so windy that our chicken laid the same egg four times.

I got a letter from the undertaker this morning. He said if we don't make up the installments on your grandmother's grave, up she comes.

Your loving mother,
Stella

P.S. I was going to send you $10, but I had already sealed the envelope.

*Condensed in* The Old Farmer's Almanac *from an article in the* Union County Advocate, *Morganville, Kentucky.*

**There is one thing about hens that looks like wisdom: they don't cackle much till they've laid their eggs.**

*1878*
*Josh Billings*

# CHAPTER ELEVEN

# When's Easter Sunday? And Other Matters of Time and the Calendar

*"We live in deeds, not years; in thoughts, not breaths; in feelings, not figures on a dial. We should count time by heart throbs. He most lives who thinks most, feels the noblest, acts the best."*

— Festus, quoted in the
1974 *Old Farmer's Almanac*

ANCIENT ALMANACS WERE OFTEN described as "calendars of the heavens," a definition that has always neatly expressed the basic function of *The Old Farmer's Almanac*. In fact, the traditional hole punched into the upper left-hand corner is there so readers can hang the Almanac on a wall as they would a calendar. ✦

*In March, 1923, old-time comedian Harold Lloyd demonstrates for the camera how time flies.*

# So When IS Easter?

*Most holidays fall on the same date year after year. But not Easter.*

## By Charles O. Roth

THANKSGIVING IS always the fourth Thursday in November; Christmas always comes on the 25th of December; the Fourth of July is always on . . . well . . . the fourth of July. But Easter's not so easy. We know that some years we celebrate Easter in March, but more often it comes in April. All we know for sure is that Easter will be on a Sunday and that its timing has something to do with the vernal equinox.

Let's go back a bit. When Sosigenes fashioned the Julian calendar (about 57 B.C.), he established the length of the year by saying that all years divisible by four (leap years) would have 366 days while all other years (common years) would have 365 days. This arrangement resulted in the average length of the year being 365¼ days, or 365 days and 6 hours. This length, of course, is too long by 11 minutes and 14 seconds. What appears to be an insignificant error actually accumulates to 1 day every 128 years.

About the middle of the sixteenth century, this error of 11 minutes and 14 seconds per year had accumulated to an error of 10 days. What this means is that the vernal equinox was occurring, on the average, on March 11 instead of March 21. If this error had been ignored, the seasons would have shifted around the calendar year, with, for example, the summer season occurring during the winter months.

To solve the problem, in March 1582, Pope Gregory XIII issued a brief that abolished the use of the Julian calendar and substituted one that has since been recognized in all Christian countries as the Gregorian calendar.

The Gregorian calendar's reckoning of time differs from that of the Julian calendar only in the way it uses leap years. In the Julian calendar, all years divisible by four are leap

## A General Rule for Finding Easter

EASTER IS THE first Sunday following the full moon on or after the vernal equinox — unless that Sunday coincides with the beginning of Passover, in which case Easter is the following Sunday. The time of the vernal equinox varies somewhat from year to year, from March 20 to March 22. However, there are relatively few times when the rule is in error.

## Formula for Determining the Date of Easter for Any Year in the Gregorian Calendar

| Step | N = Numerator | Denominator | Equation | Quotient | Remainder |
|---|---|---|---|---|---|
| 1. | N = The year | 19 | N / 19 | Discard | a |
|  | *Example*, N = 1992 |  | 1992 / 19 |  | a = 16 |
| 2. | N = The year | 100 | N / 100 | b | c |
|  | N = 1992 |  | 1992 / 100 | b = 19 | c = 92 |
| 3. | N = b | 4 | N / 4 | d | e |
|  | N = 19 |  | 19 / 4 | d = 4 | e = 3 |
| 4. | N = (b + 8) | 25 | N / 25 | Discard | f |
|  | N = 27 |  | 27 / 25 | — | f = 2 |
| 5. | N = (b - f + 1) | 3 | N / 3 | g | Discard |
|  | N = 18 |  | 18 / 3 | g = 6 | — |
| 6. | N = (19a + b - d - g + 15) | 30 | N / 30 | Discard | h |
|  | N = 328 |  | 328 / 30 | — | h = 28 |
| 7. | N = c | 4 | N / 4 | i | j |
|  | N = 92 |  | 92 / 4 | i = 2 | j = 0 |
| 8. | N = (32 + 2e + 2i - h - j) | 7 | N / 7 | Discard | k |
|  | N = 56 |  | 56 / 7 | — | k = 0 |
| 9. | N = (a + 11h + 22k) | 451 | N / 451 | L | Discard |
|  | N = 324 |  | 324 / 451 | L = 0 | — |
| 10. | N = (h + k - 7L + 114) | 31 | N / 31 | m | n |
|  | N = 142 |  | 142 / 31 | m = 4 | n = 18 |

m = Month in which Easter occurs: m = 4 = April.
n + 1 = Day of month on which Easter occurs: n + 1 = 19, hence Easter 1992 occurs on April 19.

years. In the Gregorian calendar, the century years (1200, 1300, and so on) are leap years only if they are divisible by four hundred; hence 1700, 1800, and 1900 were not leap years.

The change from Old Style to New Style was accomplished by reckoning the day that followed October 4, 1582, to be October 15, 1582, thereby dropping ten days — except in Great Britain, which did not recognize Pope Gregory's decree but continued to use the Julian calendar until 1752.

In considering how to determine when Easter will fall on the Gregorian calendar in any particular year, it's useful to understand some of the early thinking that has made the computation so complex. The Jews celebrated their Passover on the fourteenth day of the "first month" — that is, the lunar month in which the fourteenth day falls on or is the day after the vernal equinox. Most Christian sects agreed that Easter should be celebrated on a

### How Early Can Easter Be?

MARCH 22 IS the earliest possible date for Easter. It has not been celebrated that early since March 22, 1818, and will not be again until 2285. The latest date on which Easter can fall is April 25, on which it was celebrated last in 1943 and will be next in 2038.

*When's Easter Sunday? And Other Matters of Time and the Calendar*

171

Sunday. But when a minority of Christians followed the example of the Jews in the timing of their holiday, the result was both scandal and schism in the early church.

To put an end to the problem, in A.D. 325 the Council of Nicaea ordained that the celebration of Easter should henceforth always take place on the Sunday that immediately follows the full moon on or after the vernal equinox. Should the fourteenth day of the moon, which was regarded as the day of the full moon, fall on a Sunday, then the celebration of Easter was deferred to the following Sunday (to avoid concurrence with the Jews' celebration of Passover). This rule has been followed ever since. ✦

## DAY FINDER
*A computation to find the day of the week for any given date.*

To FIND THE DAY of the week for any given date as far back as the mid-eighteenth century, proceed as follows:

Add the last two digits of the year to one-quarter of the last two digits (discard any remainder if it doesn't come out even), the given date, and the month key from the left-hand column of the key below. Divide the sum by seven; the number left over is the day of the week (one is Sunday, two is Monday, and so on). If it comes out even, the day is Saturday. If you go back before 1900, add two to the sum before dividing; before 1800, add four; and so on. Don't go back before 1753.

**EXAMPLE:** The Dayton Flood was on Tuesday, March 25, 1913.

| | |
|---|---|
| Last two digits of year: | 13 |
| One-quarter of these two digits: | 3 |
| Given day of month: | 25 |
| Key number for March: | 4 |
| | 45 |

45÷7 = 6, with a remainder of 3. The flood took place on Tuesday, the third day of the week.

| KEY | | | |
|---|---|---|---|
| Jan. | 1 | June | 5 |
| *(leap yr.)* | *0* | July | 0 |
| Feb. | 4 | Aug. | 3 |
| *(leap yr.)* | *3* | Sept. | 6 |
| Mar. | 4 | Oct. | 1 |
| Apr. | 0 | Nov. | 4 |
| May | 2 | Dec. | 6 |

## Wanna Fool Around with the Calendar — Again?

I F YOU ARE one of the many people who have trouble remembering what comes after "Thirty days hath September," then you might be interested in calendar reform. There is a movement afoot to simplify the calendar by making a year consist of thirteen months, with each month exactly twenty-eight days long. The extra month would be called Sol (after our sun) and would fall between June and July, thus giving those of us in the northern hemisphere an extra month of summer.

Among the advantages of this system, called the international fixed calendar, is the fact that we wouldn't need a new calendar every year (bad news for calendar makers but good news for the rest of us). Every month would begin on a Sunday and end on a Saturday, and every date would fall on the same day of the week every year. For those of you who have been doing some quick calculating, you are right — the international fixed calendar has only 364 days in the year. The extra day would be stuck in between December 28 and January 1 and would be designated a world holiday, identified with no month or day of the week. In leap years, there would be a second world holiday wedged in between June 28 and Sol 1.

One of the disadvantages of the international fixed calendar is that thirteen months can't be easily divided into quarters for business purposes. This has led to a counterproposal — the world calendar, made up of four 91-day quarters, each consisting of a 31-day month followed by two 30-day months. Once again, it adds up to 364 days, and so one day would be set aside for general hoopla.

But perhaps you are a traditionalist. "Why fool around with the calendar?" you ask. "It was good enough for Moses, and it's good enough for me." In fact, people have been fooling around with the calendar for as long as calendars have existed. But that's another story for another time. . .

*Courtesy of Tim Clark.*

**'Feared of dying? Were you 'feared of being born?**

*1943*

# The Real Reason Why the Week Has Seven Days

*No more logic supports seven days than, say, eight or five, but the seven-day week has resisted all attempts at change.*

IT HAS BEEN PRAISED AS the "most ancient monument of astronomical knowledge" and damned as an illogical arrangement, but the seven-day week appears to be here to stay.

The year and the month correspond, respectively, to the movements of the earth around the sun and the moon around the earth. The week, however, has no astronomical analogue. It is roughly the same as the length of a phase of the moon — seven days, nine hours — but any system of time-keeping based on the moon's phases quickly falls apart as those extra hours pile up. The seven-day week is artificial, the first truly manmade unit of time.

Though the seven-day week was officially adopted by the Roman emperor Constantine in A.D. 321, its origins go back thousands of years before that to the first civilizations of the Middle East. Mesopotamian astrologers

*The seven-day week was officially adopted by the Roman emperor Constantine in A.D. 321.*

designated one day for each of the seven most prominent objects in the sky — the sun, the moon, and the five major planets visible to the naked eye. The Jews also adopted a seven-day cycle, based on the time it took the Lord to create the universe as reported in Genesis. A new wrinkle in their week was the Sabbath, a day set aside for rest. According to sociologist Eviatar Zerubavel, author of *The Seven Day Cycle: The History and Meaning of the Week*, no other culture had yet invented a holiday that occurred on a regular basis, unrelated to natural phenomena. "This was one of the great breakthroughs of human civilization," Zerubavel maintains.

But other cultures adopted different weeks, probably for business reasons. The Romans thought of a week as the eight days between market days. West African societies preferred a four-day market cycle. In Assyria six days was the rule, in Egypt ten, in China fifteen.

The ancient Germans used a five-day cycle named for their primary gods, which is how our week ended up honoring Norse deities such as Tyr (Tuesday), Odin (Wednesday), Thor (Thursday), and Frigg (Friday). They borrowed Saturn from the Romans to make Saturday. (Sunday and Monday, of course, honor the sun and the moon.) In fact, our word *week* probably comes from the Old Norse word *vikja*, which means "to turn."

Atheistic revolutionaries have tried, unsuccessfully, to get rid of the seven-day week. In 1793 the leaders of the French Revolution produced a new calendar with each month divided into three 10-day "decades." It never caught on, and Napoleon abandoned it in 1805. In 1929 the Soviet Union tried a five-day week, with one day of rest. Instead of the traditional day names, the days were assigned colors: yellow, orange, red, purple, and green. To keep mass production going, each Soviet citizen was assigned a different day of rest, so that a husband might have a yellow day off, while his wife took her leisure on a green. This produced mass confusion. In 1932 the plan was revised to a six-day week, with numbers replacing the colors. That didn't work either, and by 1940 the Russians were back on the familiar seven-day cycle.

*In 1793, the leaders of the French Revolution (shown here storming the Bastille) produced a new calendar in which each month was divided into three ten-day "decades." It never caught on.*

There is no doubt that the seven-day week is illogical. It doesn't divide evenly into 365- or 366-day years, so holidays fall on different days of the week from year to year, creating problems determining the dates of important holidays. But human beings are not logical creatures. Who can imagine saying, "What are you doing next purple?" And as a member of the British Parliament remarked in a 1944 debate on calendar reform, "It is bad enough to be born on April 1, but to have one's birthday always on a Monday would be perfectly intolerable." ✦

# Friday the 13th: The Luckiest or Unluckiest Day of All

*Trouble is, both Friday and the number 13 are unlucky — and if you believe that, you may have a case of triskaidekaphobia.*

## By Rick Horowitz

TRISKAIDEKAPHOBIA is the fear of the number 13. If you've got it, you're not alone — and you're probably at your worst on a 13th that's also a Friday.

Why all the fuss? What's made 13 such a worrisome number and Friday such a troublesome day? The people who claim to know such things say there were 13 people at the Last Supper, and the Crucifixion of Christ occurred on a Friday. *Are* 13ths particularly unlucky?

Well, as with so many things, where you stand depends on where you sit. For example, on Friday the 13th of July 1900, Teddy Roosevelt laid the cornerstone for a new county courthouse in New York and spoke of the need for honesty in government. "During the exercises," a newspaper reported the next day, "Nathaniel Ketcham, who was on the platform, had his pockets picked of $140, another man lost $103, and several watches were stolen." It was a good day for Roosevelt, who in a year's time would become president. It was a pretty good day for pickpockets. But not so good a day for Nathaniel Ketcham.

On July 13, 1865, Horace Greeley said, "Go west, young man." On July 13, 1881, Billy the Kid, who did, was shot dead in New Mexico. Ludwig II, the insane king of Bavaria, drowned on June 13, 1886, and Alexander the Great died of fever in Babylon on the same date in 323 B.C.

Richard Nixon nominated Gerald Ford to replace the recently departed Spiro Agnew as vice president on October 13, 1973. That was a lucky break for Mr. Ford but perhaps not so lucky, as it turned out, for Mr. Nixon.

Then there are those who consider the number 13 quite lucky, like some theatrical people of old, who tried to sign all their contracts on that day. Or the British, whose tradition once held that eating Christmas pudding in 13 different houses before January 1 would bring prosperity in the new year.

The U.S.A. is so full of lucky 13ths that even normally superstitious types should be able to put their minds at ease. There were 13 original colonies, of course, and the Great Seal of the United States contains 13 stars, 13 bars, and an eagle with 13 tail feathers, holding 13 arrows and 13 olive branches. "E Pluribus Unum" even has 13 letters. You'd think all that would calm at least the American triskaidekaphobes, but no such luck. ✦

*One of the unluckiest days for New York City garbage collectors came when 750,000 pounds of paper fluttered down on "Lucky Lindy" during his ticker-tape parade — on June 13, 1927.*

# The Man Who Unraveled a Tangle in Time

*Until 1883, a traveler going from Maine to California had to adjust his watch twenty times to match local variations in time-keeping. Then along came Charles Ferdinand Dowd and his invention: standard time.* By H. I. Miller

*It took thirteen years for Dowd, above, to convince apathetic railroad officials to give his plan a try.*

UNTIL LATE IN THE nineteenth century, things were in a sorry state of confusion among American railroads: no one agreed on what time it was. It was not until November 18, 1883, that U.S. railroads, in desperation, finally put the country on standard time. As the nation synchronized its watches, it ended a welter of confusion across the land and forever enshrined in history the name of Charles Ferdinand Dowd.

Prior to the adoption of standard time, many communities based their time on the position of the sun over city hall. The result was no end of chaos. Railroad timetables, lacking a nationally synchronized master time system, gave arrival and departure times in terms of the time of each city. A traveler going from Maine to California had to adjust his watch twenty times to match local variations in timekeeping. Moreover, a traveler coming in to the city of Buffalo from Portland, Maine, might find the New York Central clock indicating noon, the Lake Shore clock pointing to 11:25 A.M., the Buffalo city clock showing 11:40, and his own watch indicating 12:15 P.M.

But then along came Charles Ferdinand Dowd, an 1853 graduate of Yale University, classmate of railroad executive Chauncey Depew, and principal of a female seminary in Saratoga, New York. Dowd, a man of meticulous methodology, found timetables a mess of confusion. It took him less than a year to work out a basic formula that would unravel the snarled skeins of time. But it took him thirteen years to convince apathetic public officials and railroad executives to give his plan a try.

Dowd proposed his idea of hourly divisions at each annual convention of the railroad trunk lines. The system called for the establishment of four geographic zones, each fourteen degrees of longitude wide. While each zone would observe a uniform time, the time would vary exactly one hour from zone to zone. The zones were Eastern, Central, Mountain, and Pacific. This meant that if it were four o'clock in the Eastern zone, it would be three o'clock in the Central zone, two o'clock in the Mountain zone, and one o'clock in the Pacific zone.

In 1869 one of Dowd's plans was finally given the nod when railroad convention delegates expressed a desire to see it worked out in detail. In response, after much time and expense, Dowd published a pamphlet titled *A System of National Time for Railroads*.

But it wasn't until 1883 that the delegates to the annual railroad convention pledged their officers to run all trains "by the standards agreed upon [in Dowd's plan]. . .and to adopt same. . .at 12 o'clock noon, Sunday, November 18." From *Harper's Weekly*, a leading periodical of the day, comes this description of the historic event: "On the last day under the old system, when the sun reached the 75th meridian, the clocks began their jangle for the hour of noon and kept it up in a drift across the country for four hours, like incoherent cowbells in a wildwood.

"But on Monday the 19th, no clock struck for this hour until the sun reached the 75th meridian. Then all the clocks on the continent struck together, those in the Eastern Belt striking 12; the Central Belt 11, in the Mountain Belt 10 and in the Pacific Belt 9.

"Timetables everywhere became intelligent."

Although the railroads benefited from the improvement to a degree too prodigious to determine, they gave scant recognition to Dowd, never even naming a Pullman car after him. And in a final irony, it was a railroad train that killed the inventor — at a Saratoga railroad crossing twenty-one years after his proposal was finally adopted. ✦

*Before the adoption of standard time, trying to interpret the times in railroad promotions was often an exercise in confusion and frustration. Every town had its own timekeeping system.*

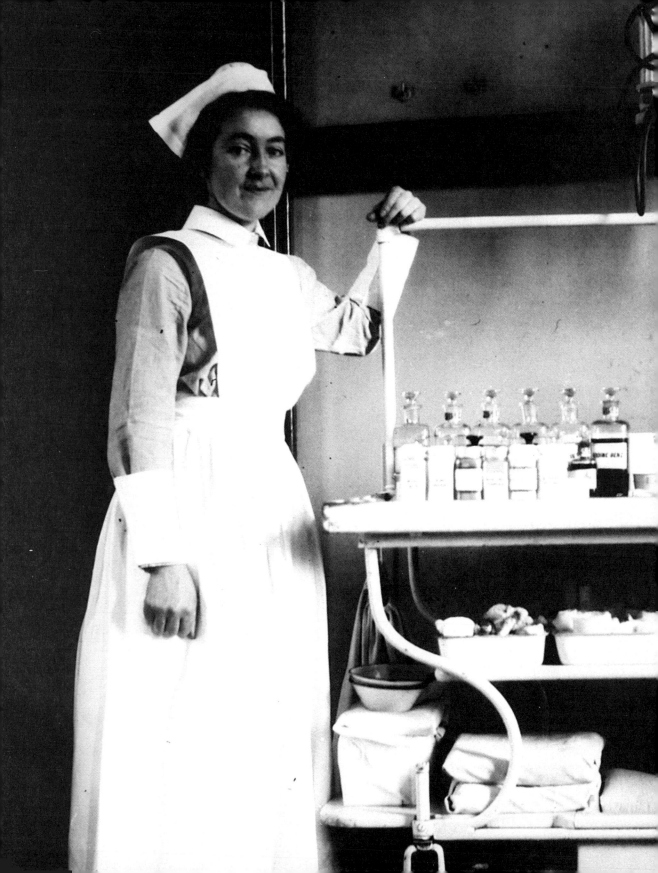

## CHAPTER TWELVE

# HOW TO CURE
## *Whatever Ails You*

*"At Antwerp, a countryman coming into a perfumer's shop fell immediately into a swoon and could not be brought to himself but by applying horse dung to his nose."*
— 1796 *Old Farmer's Almanac*

DEEP IN THE DUSTY BOWELS OF THE WIDENER LIBRARY AT Harvard University are hundreds of volumes on American folklore that contain the wisdom — and the superstitions — of the past two centuries. *The Old Farmer's Almanac,* as you might imagine, is well represented, particularly in the category of cures. So during the 1980s, Almanac executive editor Tim Clark, who was once briefly a folklore and mythology major at Harvard, began mining this mother lode of information for a series of articles. This entire chapter is taken from that ongoing series. ✦

*A nurse at the New Haven (Connecticut) Hospital displays some of the "cures" available in 1928.*

# Cures for the Common Cold

*There are plenty of them — from standing on one's head under water to wearing a bag of onions . . .*

CASE HISTORY: THE PATIENT, a vigorous man in his late sixties, went out riding on December 12, 1799, a day of cold rain, sleet, and strong winds. Arriving at home late for dinner, he sat down to eat before changing his clothes. The next day he complained of a sore throat and stayed indoors for the morning. In the afternoon, he went out to mark some trees to be cut down. That same evening he was hoarse but refused suggestions to take medicine. "You know I never take anything for a cold," he said. "Let it go as it came."

At about 3 A.M., the patient awakened his wife to complain of chills. He was having trouble speaking and breathing. Near dawn, he was offered a mixture of molasses, vinegar, and butter but was unable to swallow it.

A doctor was summoned, and he took one pint of blood from the patient. The patient then soaked his feet in hot water and had a piece of flannel soaked in salve wrapped around his neck. Hot compresses and mustard packs also were applied, along with various gargles and inhalations. More blood was taken. On December 14, the patient died.

What killed George Washington? Was it pneumonia or a strep infection, as some historians believe? Or was it, as others have suggested, the common cold, aided by "remedies" such as bleeding?

Washington himself believed he had a cold, and the remedies he and his doctor applied were considered the normal treatment for a cold in those days. They may sound quaint, but after nearly two hundred years, modern science is not much closer than it was then to a cure for the common cold.

The very word *cold* refers to what was commonly believed to be the cause of the illness — becoming chilled by exposure to cold, or overexertion followed by rapid cooling off. But one of the few things that scientists can say with any certainty about the common cold is that it is *not* a result of such chilling. Volunteers have spent many hours attesting to this fact by standing in drafty hallways wearing wet clothing. They were chilly and uncomfortable, but they caught no more colds than other volunteers who were kept warm and dry. Similarly, Eskimo communities were free of colds until they were visited by ships from warmer climates.

Statistics on the common cold are hard to gather, both because

*During World War I, military doctors noticed that men who slept in wet trenches during the winter had fewer colds than those who lived in comfortable barracks behind the lines.*

it resembles many other illnesses and because often it is not considered important enough to report. Some authorities think that Americans suffer from as many as 1 billion colds a year. The National Center for Health Statistics announced in 1978 that Americans annually reported almost 100 million colds, resulting in the loss of 30 million work days and 30 million school days, as well as 276 million days of "restricted activity." One out of five acute illnesses in the United States is a common cold.

Other studies provide a wealth of information about who gets colds and how often. One found that 75 percent of all people have at least one cold a year, while 25 percent have four or more. At Cornell University, 25 percent of all the students had 75 percent of all the reported colds. Children under age four average eight colds a year, but the number declines with increasing age, so that adults average only two colds a year.

The costs of colds, in terms of work time lost, have been estimated in the billions of dollars. And Americans spend more than half a billion dol-

*Sufferers often feel a greater sensitivity to temperature changes during the early stages of a cold. So when you start shivering and think, "I'd better put on a sweater, or I'll catch cold," you may already have one.*

*As recently as 1978, Dr. Marvin Sackner, acting chief of medicine at Mount Sinai Medical Center in Miami Beach, reported that chicken soup cleared mucus from sinus passages faster than other hot beverages. Dr. Sackner's findings were published in the medical journal* Chest.

lars a year on drugs aimed at fighting colds, though so far there is no pharmaceutical cure. Antibiotics do not affect the viruses that cause colds, and although vaccines can be developed to combat them, the large number of different cold viruses (more than 100) makes that approach impractical.

Folk remedies for colds, however, are legion. They may be based on conceptions about colds that are outdated by scientific research, but people still believe in them, and some research indicates that belief may be the most important element in fighting a cold. In one five-year experiment, a variety of cold vaccines were tested, while a control group, which had been told it was receiving a vaccine, was actually injected with distilled water. More than one third of those in the control group reported that their "medication" had cured or improved their colds.

A look through history provides a representative sampling of popular folk remedies for colds, which seem to fall into several distinct categories.

**Diet.** A wide variety of herbal teas are recommended for colds, including teas made from coltsfoot, peppermint, yarrow, boneset, mint, catnip, verbena, horehound, and sage. Garlic is frequently recommended, as are licorice and lemon in many forms. A Vermont doctor prescribed chewing on a honeycomb to clear sinus passages.

Onions figure in many cold cures from early days in this country. A mixture of onions and butter was placed on the throat and chest. Cooked onions were put in a muslin bag and worn around the neck. To protect children, it was agreed that a large red onion should be tied around the bedpost.

According to *Grannie's Remedies* by Mai Thomas (1965), "In some country districts [in England] there are still many folk who believe that swallowing a spider will cure them."

**The nose.** People have suggested washing out the nose with hot water, soap, sodium bicarbonate, ammonium bicarbonate, cod-liver oil, cream, salt water, vapors of ammonia, eucalyptus oil, iodine, and formalin. Sniffing aspirin, pepper, snuff, and cinnamon has been tried. Several authorities recommend that cold sufferers can reduce the length of their illness and avoid more serious sinus and ear infections by refraining from blowing the nose. Some colonial Americans rolled up orange peels inside out and stuffed them into their nostrils.

**Alcohol.** A traditional cure known to some as the Hungarian Hat Trick is performed as follows: Place a hat on a bedpost. Get into bed and start drinking. When you see two hats, stop drinking.

Actually, alcohol has been found to dilate small blood vessels in the skin and help reestablish circulation in the mucous membranes of the nose, along with raising the temperature of those membranes to help neutralize viruses. It also produces a feeling of comfort and drowsiness.

Curing the common cold has become a sort of Holy Grail to some researchers, an ideal at once infinitely desirable and seemingly unattainable. The person who achieves it should be able to accept the Nobel Prize as his or her just deserts. Indeed, one famous Nobel laureate, Dr. James D. Watson, accepted his prize with these words: "It is an important thing we have accomplished, but we have not done away with the common cold — which I now have." ✦

## CURES OF A MORE DRASTIC NATURE

SIR CHRISTOPHER ANDREWES became head of England's Common Cold Research Unit in 1946. In his book *The Common Cold* (1965), Sir Christopher cataloged the one hundred remedies for colds that had been sent to him by helpful laypersons. Most of them could be included under general categories such as drugs, diet, and treatment for the nose, but a number of them defied pigeonholing:

"Under miscellaneous remedies these occurred: . . . rubbing methylated spirit into a bald head, rubbing the body with Vaseline, transient exposure to tear gas or other war gas (two letters), wearing a gas mask for an hour, . . . taking up fencing, avoiding people with poisonous auras, mental concentration (especially on mathematics), growing a mustache right up to the nostrils, sweeping chimneys, standing on one's head under water, or wearing on the back between the kidneys a bag containing onions. Cure of colds was reported to have followed an electric shock, a car smash, and destruction of one's home by a V-2 missile. Finally, several letters pointed out the value of attention to psychology, a subject that probably had considerable relevance to the prescriptions of the other ninety-odd of our correspondents."

*The toughest cure: a V-2 missile explosion.*

# Favorite Ways to Ease
# the Pain of a Toothache

*Some are really quite simple, others a little weird, and a few
probably worse than the toothache itself.*

THE EXQUISITE PAIN of a toothache has been part of the human condition for as long as humans have had teeth. Stone Age skulls show evidence of tooth decay, and the oldest known medical document, the Papyrus Ebers (dating from before the birth of Christ), suggests the use of ground incense or cloves to relieve the pain of a toothache.

Most toothaches are caused by an infection of the tooth pulp — the nerves, lymph, blood vessels, and other tissues inside the hard enamel and dentine casing of the tooth. That casing begins to decay when carbohydrates, especially sugars, are taken into the mouth. Microorganisms in the mouth combine with saliva to transform the sugars into acids that, if undisturbed, dissolve calcium, which is the main ingredient of the dentine and enamel.

The most common treatment of diseased teeth once was extraction, a hideous procedure that was accomplished in one of three ways. One was to loosen the tooth by the application of caustics — the drawback was that the caustics tended to loosen adjoining teeth as well. Another approach was to insert a dry peppercorn into the cavity, which would soon swell so large as to break the tooth into pieces that were more easily extracted. Most common of all was the use of dental forceps, or tongs. The patient lay on his back, his head between the physician's knees, while the tooth was shaken back and forth until it came loose or the patient's jaw was dislocated or broken. It's no wonder that most people preferred rotting teeth.

Those who suffered from toothaches used a variety of folk remedies or prayed to the patron saint of toothaches, St. Apollonia, "a virgin of advanced age," according to authorities, who was martyred in A.D. 249 for professing Christianity. She refused to deny her faith even while Roman soldiers pulled out all her teeth. Prayers uttered on her feast day, February 9, are regarded as especially effective, and many churches in Europe treasure relics of the saint, including some of her teeth.

*The* BEST *of* THE OLD FARMER'S ALMANAC

Today toothaches as a result of decay may be on the verge of extinction in this country. Better eating habits, preventive hygiene, and most of all fluoridation of water supplies and toothpaste have dramatically reduced the incidence of tooth decay in Americans. According to the National Institute of Dental Research, nearly 40 percent of all children between the ages of five and seventeen have no cavities at all, and the use of resin sealants on children's teeth is expected to eliminate cavities entirely.

However, dentistry is not an endangered profession. This can be proved, according to an old story, by wrapping a bandage around your jaw and complaining of a toothache. Every person you meet will suggest a remedy. The box below lists some of the more exotic methods used throughout human history to prevent or cure toothaches. Take them, as the Talmud suggests for toothaches, with a grain of salt.✦

---

## Remedies to Be Taken with a Grain of Salt

### The Simple but Disgusting Methods

- Eat grasshopper eggs.
- Place fresh cow manure on the side of the face where the ache occurs.
- Hold a live frog against the aching cheek.
- Apply a crushed ladybug to the aching tooth.
- Never wash on a Tuesday.

### The Weird & Complicated Methods

- Take the tooth of a murdered man or, better still, an executed criminal and apply it to the aching tooth in a graveyard at midnight under a full moon.
- On Good Friday, comb your hair and collect the hair that falls out. Burn it and inhale the fumes.
- Pick your teeth with the nail of the middle toe of an owl.

### Better to Have the Toothache

- Eat the eyes of a vulture.
- Bite off the head of a live mouse, put it in a bag, and suspend it from your neck. The ribbon or thread must not have a knot in it.
- Press the finger of a corpse against the aching tooth.
- If all else fails, an ancient Chinese physician recommended a pill of arsenic, which the patient should "put close to aching tooth, then sleep. Cure certain." And final.

*Famous insomniacs Napoleon, Charles Dickens, and Winston Churchill.*

# How to Fall Fast Asleep

*One way, research shows, is to try as hard as you can to stay awake...*

NAPOLEON BONAPARTE could not do it. Winston Churchill had problems. Charles Dickens and Franz Kafka had to get into unusual positions to achieve it. The Earl of Rosebery had to resign as prime minister of England because he couldn't do it. And Thomas Edison hardly did it at all.

What these famous people and up to fifty million modern-day Americans have found difficult or impossible to accomplish is the simple, natural act of falling asleep. Insomnia, an ailment as old as humankind, is little understood even today, after three decades of vigorous and groundbreaking research into the nature of sleep.

Insomnia is defined by most researchers as an inability to sleep that interferes with efficient daytime functioning. In other words, it's not how much you sleep that makes you an insomniac, but how well you function when you're awake. Some people can get along very nicely on as little as three or four hours of sleep a night. They may even complain of needing more sleep because we've all heard that we need eight hours a night. It's just not true for everyone.

But we can't all be like Edison, who performed very efficiently on a few naps, and chronic insomnia can be devastating. An insomniac understands too well why sleep deprivation is a favorite form of torture. This explains why sleeping pills are, after aspirin, the most commonly used drugs in the United States, with an estimated thirty million tablets swallowed before bed every night.

Though misfortune may make a man unhappy, she can never make him completely and inseparably miserable without his own consent.

*1800*

*The BEST of THE OLD FARMER'S ALMANAC*

And yet, paradoxically, misuse of sleeping pills is a leading cause of insomnia, in addition to a variety of other ills, including drug dependence.

It is comforting, however, to learn that the latest scientific methods for inducing sleep are not so different from the tried and true. Indeed, the recommendations of modern sleep experts for improved "sleep hygiene" — or how to fall asleep — have a familiar ring to them.

Take counting sheep, for example. This ancient and reliable method — some old-timers prefer to imagine crows circling in the sky — draws support from current-day sleep researchers who cite recent discoveries about the nature of the brain to explain the success of counting sheep. The human brain is divided into two hemispheres whose functions are different. The right side of the brain is chiefly concerned with visual images, the left side with speech and counting. Counting sheep puts both sides of the brain to work, providing enough distraction from worries or other intrusions to allow sleep to sneak up on our consciousness.

Another unusual approach is called "paradoxical intention." People who have trouble sleeping are instructed to try as hard as they can to stay awake at night (without using drugs or caffeine). In laboratory experiments where insomniacs were ordered to stay awake for thirty minutes, many of them fell asleep almost immediately. Conversely, when the sleeping subjects were called over an intercom at the end of the thirty minutes and told it was all right to go to sleep now, many of them woke up and were unable to go back to sleep.

A psychologist named Richard Bootzin developed a therapy called stimulus control for people who have grown to associate insomnia with being in bed. It is a demanding process, requiring the patient to stay out of bed except when sleepy. That means no read-

*Thomas Edison, who rarely got what we call "a good night's sleep," performed efficiently on a few naps, especially after a particularly difficult problem had been solved.*

ing, knitting, watching television, or any other nonsleeping behavior (except sex). If the patient can't fall asleep within ten minutes of getting into bed, he has to get up and go to another room until he feels sleepy. Then he goes back to bed and, if necessary, repeats the process until he falls asleep within the allotted ten minutes. Regardless of how many times he has to get up, he must rise for the day at exactly the same time every morning, avoid daytime naps, and keep a careful written record of the number of times he had to get up before falling asleep.

With most patients, the immediate effects have been horrible — the sleeper gets out of bed as many as ten times the first night. But the long-term effects are impressive: within six weeks, most patients, even insomniacs who haven't had a full night's sleep in ten years, are sleeping through the night.

A number of herbal teas have been put forward as sleep inducing, including chamomile, boneset, passion flower, and catnip, which the late Euell Gibbons claimed would prevent nightmares. An English herbalist of the seventeenth century recommended tying the dried root of the peony around one's neck to ward off "the Incubus which we call the Mare." In those days people thought nightmares were caused by goblins that sat on a sleeper's chest, threatening him with suffocation. An old New England folk cure for nightmares was to smell your socks after taking them off before bed. Some might prefer suffocation.

Eating before bedtime has long been associated with bad dreams and troubled sleep. "Those who indulge in late suppers, or eat heartily before retiring, are usually troubled with unpleasant dreams and nightmares, and are often found dead in the morning," a nineteenth-century herbalist warned gravely. But modern researchers agree that it is better to have a light snack before bedtime than to go to bed hungry. Laboratory rats deprived of food sleep less, and in humans severe dieting and loss of sleep seem to go hand in hand. One English folk remedy for insomnia recommends eating onions, preferably raw, though consuming them stewed or made into soup or jelly also is believed to work.

All authorities agree that you should stay away from caffeine, a stimulant found in coffee, tea, chocolate, cola drinks, and many over-the-counter pain relievers. Caffeine is the most widely used stimulant in the country, and studies have shown that it will disturb sleep even in persons who believe that it does not affect them. Nicotine has a similar effect.

Alcohol in moderation tends to promote drowsiness. Heavy drinking, however, has the unpleasant consequence of canceling out the normal periods of dreaming. When the drinking stops, the dreaming comes back for longer, more intense periods, often in the form of nightmares.

The French author Alexandre Dumas was ordered by his doctor to eat an apple under the Arc de Triomphe every morning at 7 A.M. exactly. This was a scheme to make Dumas observe regular hours, which scientists today agree will help one sleep. Dumas's sleeping problems might have had something to do with his estimated five hundred illegitimate children, however.

Between walking to the Arc de Triomphe in the morning and hiking up the French population growth in the evening, it would seem that Dumas got plenty of exercise. But he got it at the wrong times. The latest studies indicate that regular exercise, while helping one sleep well, is most beneficial in the afternoon or early evening, and violent exertions at bedtime are more likely to keep one awake.

That's why the authorities agree that one should avoid too much mental or emotional stimulation just before bedtime. Reading or watching television is fine, but not if the subject matter is likely to get your heart pounding and adrenaline pumping. Don't do your income taxes or talk about your in-laws. And if you don't fall asleep right away and feel yourself getting tense and frustrated, get up and do something else. Ben Franklin advocated a brisk walk around the bedroom, as well as a thorough airing of the bedclothes, shaking them at least twenty times. He did not mention the effect of this on his bed partner.

"These are the rules of the art," Franklin concluded in a letter to a lady who had asked him how to avoid unpleasant dreams. "But, though they will generally prove effectual. . .there is a case in which the most punctual observance of them will be totally fruitless. The case is when the person who desires to have pleasant dreams has not taken care to preserve what is necessary above all things, A Good Conscience." ✦

> **In youth the absence of pleasure is pain; in old age the absence of pain is pleasure.**
>
> *1892*

# Causes & Cures (?) for the Common Headache

*More time is lost to business and industry from headaches than from heart disease, stroke, and cancer combined.*

**You are not alone.** In the United States, more than forty million people annually consult physicians for relief of headache pain. A research organization called the International Headache Registry estimates that 20 percent of the world's population suffers chronic and disabling headaches. Americans spend more than $700 million annually on aspirin and acetaminophen. More time is lost to business and industry from headaches than from heart disease, stroke, and cancer combined.

**Take two Kolbes and call me in the morning.** Adolf Wilhelm Hermann Kolbe was a great nineteenth-century chemist whose work has made life bearable for uncounted billions of people. What? You've never heard of Adolf Wilhelm Hermann Kolbe?

Such are the vagaries of fortune. Kolbe, who was the first scientist to synthesize organic compounds from inorganic materials, also found a cheap way to produce salicylic acid, the key ingredient in acetylsalicylic acid — better known as aspirin.

**It's not all in your head.** Psychological factors play a role in producing headaches by causing actual changes in tissue and blood. Some experts believe there is a headache-prone personality, often described as perfectionist, hard working, inflexible, and likely to set unrealistically high standards for himself and others. Evidence to support this theory is disputed, however.

**My head feels better, but now my nail polish is melting.** In experiments with biofeedback, test subjects have reported relief from headache pain by concentrating on making their hands feel warm. Scientists believe such concentration can increase blood flow to the hands, thus relieving headache-producing pressure on blood vessels in the head.

## 16 Folk Remedies for Headaches

- Put leeches on your forehead.
- Rub cow dung and molasses on your temples.
- Tie a buzzard's head around your neck.
- Use powdered moss as snuff.
- Have someone else rub your head; the headache will be transferred to that person, but it will be less severe.
- Have a relative read chapters of the Bible to you.
- Stand on your head or spin around until you are dizzy.
- Soak your feet in hot water to draw blood from your head.
- Run around the house three times.
- Ask a seventh child to blow in your ear.
- Put a buckwheat cake on your head.
- Rub your head with a piece of stone containing iron ore.
- Wrap damp cloths around your head and burn scented wood.
- Plait a handful of hair very tightly on top of your head.
- Lean your head against a tree and have someone else drive a nail into the opposite side of the tree.
- Tie a leather thong tightly around your head. (If this fails, you may tell your friends, "The thong is over, but the malady lingers on," which will give *them* headaches.)

WHERE DOES IT HURT?

**Because it feels so bad when I stop.** Cluster headaches, so known because they seem to occur in clusters around one eye or the other, are among the most painful of all headaches, described by some sufferers as feeling like "a knife in the eye." They are twenty times more common among men than women, especially among heavy smokers. Most remedies are ineffective, and patients with cluster headaches have been known to beat their heads against walls because of the agonizing pain.

**Not tonight, dear. I'll get a headache.** Headaches may be caused by the sudden contraction of head and neck muscles just before orgasm, excessive pressure on the spine, or a sudden increase in blood pressure during sexual activity.

**An hour later, your head hurts.** Food prepared with monosodium glutamate (MSG), common in Chinese food in America, can trigger headaches in persons susceptible to migraines. ✦

HAMMOND

# Home Remedies for the Hiccups

*If nothing else works, stick your head under water while you count to twenty-five . . .*

H ICCUP, HICKE UP, hikup, hickop, hickhop, hecup, hiccop, hickup, hicket, hickok — it sounds like a bad attack of a condition that has plagued or amused humanity (depending on your point of view) since the dawn of time. In reality, it is a list of the different ways people have spelled the word in English, dating back as far as 1544, when the accepted medical practice was "to cast colde water in the face of him that hath the hicket."

Hiccups have nothing to do with coughing, nor are they, as some have supposed, unsuccessful efforts to inhale or vomit. In fact, according to the world's leading authority on the biology of hiccups, the muscle spasm in the diaphragm that causes a sudden intake of air, ending with a "hic" as the glottis snaps shut, may be one of the most ancient behaviors in the animal kingdom, with links to breathing, digestion, and even reproduction.

Dr. Terence Anthoney, a specialist in animal behavior at Southern Illinois University, believes the hiccup originated millions of years ago as a gasp, a primitive form of breathing. Even now, he points out, some dying patients with respiratory problems begin to hiccup in the last moments of their lives, as if reverting to this primitive behavior. Eventually, more efficient forms of respiration evolved, but when such improvements occur, Anthoney says, "nature doesn't throw the old behavior away." It persists, held in reserve, perhaps adapting to some new function. In the case of hiccups, Anthoney believes that the new function was regurgitation of food to feed the young, a behavior still found in many mammals. Along with the new behavior evolved the ability to close the glottis, to prevent food from being sucked into the lungs, and thus was heard the primal "hic!"

Although human beings today do not regurgitate digested food for their young to eat (at least not in polite circles), Anthoney cautions against assuming that hiccups have no function. In years of study, he has found clues linking hiccups in infants to improved digestion, and his discovery that women, as a rule, have much more frequent bouts with hiccups than men has led him to investigate the possibility that hiccups may be connected with the human reproductive cycle. "The belief that hiccups have no purpose is a lot of hooey," says Anthoney. "It's just so common we don't look closely at it." ✦

> **To avoid dysentery, eat moderately, drink sparingly, lie not down on the damp earth, nor overheat yourself; but change your clothes as the weather changes.**
>
> *1802*

---

### TIME-TESTED CURES FOR HICCUPS

- Pant like a dog. Bite your thumbs and blow hard against them for a minute.
- Drink nine swallows of water from your grandfather's cup without taking a breath.
- Drink water through a folded handkerchief.
- Take a mouthful of water and swallow it in three gulps. Repeat this three times while standing perfectly still and breathing through your nose.
- Stand on your head for five minutes.
- Lie over a chair on your stomach and drink a glass of water.
- Put the head of a burnt match in your ear.
- Lay a broom on the floor, bristles to the right, and jump over it seven times.
- Hold your left elbow for seven minutes.
- Wet a piece of red thread with your tongue, stick it to your forehead, and look at it.
- Stand in the middle of the road and say, "Hiccup, stickup, not for me, hiccup, stickup." (*Editor's note:* Keep an eye on the traffic while practicing this one, or the cure is likely to be permanent.)

# CHAPTER THIRTEEN

# GARDEN WISDOM *That Has Stood the* TEST OF TIME

*And thanks that from our daily need*
*The joy of simple faith is born;*
*That he who smites the summer weed*
*May trust thee for the autumn corn.*
— John Greenleaf Whittier

"LOOK WELL TO YOUR GARDENS," ROBERT B. THOMAS ADVISED his readers in the 1793 Almanac. In those early days, Thomas actually devoted far more space to advice for full-fledged farmers than to tips for backyard gardeners. But as the years went by and fewer and fewer readers lived on farms, gardening developed into a dominant Almanac subject. Here, from dozens of past gardening articles, are the ones we've found to be the most useful. ✦

*In the rose garden at Elizabeth Park, Hartford, Connecticut, about 1906.*

# When Is It Ripe? When Is It Ready?

*Ralph Waldo Emerson once observed that there are but ten minutes in the life of a pear when it is perfect to eat.* BY GEORGIA ORCUTT

NO MATTER WHETHER we plant, weed, nurture, and wait for the perfect moment to harvest, or we press and pinch in supermarkets, we all face the same questions about produce: Is it ripe? Is it ready?

To help in your quest for the perfect harvest, we present three different approaches:

## THE BOTANICAL APPROACH

**Flowers** (broccoli and cauliflower). Foods in this family are really only strange-looking roses that you can eat. Their maturity is controlled by a time clock. When enough time has gone by, and when the amount of daylight (photoperiod) is right, they flower. We pick that flower and eat it.

**Fruits** (apples, pears, cherries, and so on, plus string beans, cucumbers, eggplant, peas, peppers, pumpkins, and squash). Think about that peach, pear, or tomato as a living thing, just like you. During its life cycle, it goes through many changes. At a certain stage (thirteen to fifteen years for you), it becomes capable of reproduction. Its flesh changes, fills out, becomes sweeter. It ripens. Matters of taste and culinary tradition define desirability throughout the ripening process. But it is simply a matter of time until the fruit loses its reproductive capacity, its flesh loses its tone, and the once living thing withers and dies.

**Leaves** (spinach, kale, lettuce, and cabbage). You can let leaves get bigger and bigger or start cutting them as soon as you like their size. You also can harvest selectively, leaf by leaf.

**Roots** (beets, carrots, onions, and parsnips). These are the least touchy parts of the plant in terms of having a "right" time to harvest. A few weeks make little difference, and in many parts of the country, these crops can stay in the ground through hard frost and even winter without losing their vigor.

## THE TACTILE APPROACH

Use your hands and eyes to determine ripeness and readiness, according to these guidelines.

**Asparagus.** Skinny little stalks have very little flesh, which is the delectable part of asparagus. Seek spears six to eight inches high that are at least one-half inch thick.

**Beans.** Snap or string beans are ready when they are as thick as a pencil and before the seeds swell and become visible through the pods. Lima

FACING PAGE:
*Movie actress and dancer Carmen Miranda tests the ripeness of the fruit on her head.*

beans are ready when their pods take on a good green color and feel full; don't wait for those pods to turn white.

**Broccoli.** Harvest when the buds (treetops) are dark blue-green and tightly closed. If the tops turn yellow, you've waited too long.

**Cantaloupe.** Squeeze it gently. If it gives slightly and smells sweet, it's ripe.

**Chili peppers.** If you want the pods to be very hot, let the ground dry out before you pick them. If you want milder pods, pick them right after you water them.

**Chives.** Cut before the purple blossoms form on the ends.

**Corn.** Ripe corn will have a tight husk, and its silks will have dried and turned brown. Open an ear and stab a kernel with your fingernail. If the kernel contains milk, the corn is ripe; if it contains water, it isn't; if it is tough and dry, it's overripe.

**Leeks.** Harvest when the white portions are about one and a half inches in diameter.

**Okra.** Pick the pods when they are two to two and a half inches long, or about four to five days old.

**Onions (green).** Harvest when the bulbs are one to two inches.

**Onions (to store).** Wait for their tops to fall over and turn brown.

**Parsnips.** The best ones will be two to three inches in diameter and will have gone through a frost.

**Peaches.** Pick when there is no green showing. Let them ripen on the tree for the best flavor.

**Pears.** A ripe pear will have a faint yellow blush but still be greenish. Don't let pears ripen on the tree, or they'll be mealy.

**Peas.** Pick when plump but before the pods wrinkle on the stem.

**Potatoes.** Harvest the first delectable little potatoes when they look as if a chicken could have laid them. For the more mature potatoes, which will be the best keepers, wait until the foliage has died down.

**Pumpkins.** When they turn orange and you can't penetrate their flesh with your thumbnail, they're ready.

**Raspberries.** Pick berries when they loosen easily from the core. When the berries are fully ripe, the core will stay on the plant when you remove the fruit.

**Rutabagas.** They'll taste best at three to four inches in diameter.

**Scallions.** Pull when the tops are six to eight inches long.

**Squash (summer).** Yellow squash and zucchini are at their best when they're four inches long.

**Squash (winter).** This group is ready to eat when their skin has hardened. Press your fingernail through the flesh; if you have to work at it, the squash is ripe. If it's very easy to pierce, it is immature.

**Sweet potatoes.** Dig when the vines turn yellow.

**Swiss chard.** Cut the first leaves when they're four to six inches long. Then let the leaves grow to six to ten inches before cutting again. If you forget, that's O.K. Big leaves taste good, too.

**Turnips.** For the best flavor, eat when they're the size of golf balls.

**Watermelons.** When the stem curls and turns brown and the place where the melon touches the ground turns yellow, it should be ready. Rap it with your knuckles and listen for a dull, hollow sound.

## THE SURVIVALIST APPROACH

Get as much as you can as fast as you can.

**Bananas.** Buy bunches of very green bananas, right off the boat. They're cheapest when they're very hard and green. Put the entire bunch in a large paper bag along with an apple. Wait five days, and they should all be yellow and ready to eat.

**Corn.** The experience of only one growing season will teach you that corn reaches perfection the day after the raccoons have stolen it. Start harvesting ears as soon as they are filled out — that is, when you can grab on to something that feels like a cob. Slathered with butter and salt, even the whole young cob will taste fine.

**Tomatoes.** Growing tomatoes will sharpen your skills at a popular backyard game, Beat the Frost. Study recipes for using green tomatoes in novel ways — jams, jellies, chutneys, and breads — and listen to weather reports as you read. You may discover that hard, greenish white tomatoes are plenty ripe.

**Watermelon.** These words of wisdom come from a friend skilled in midnight raids on the neighbor's patch: pick as many melons as you can as fast as you can. Later, when no one is around, decide which ones to eat.

**Zucchini.** This garden favorite first appears fully grown and has an uncanny ability to reproduce on the pantry shelf. Those who study squash behavior also note that zucchini tends to reappear, even after it has been eaten, in its whole form. Here's what you can do with your bountiful harvest: Get some good, sturdy boxes — the kind with lids. Stuff as many zucchini as you can into the boxes, gift wrap them, and add colorful ribbons. Drive the boxes to your nearest metropolitan area. When no one is looking, leave them in places such as movie theaters, restaurants, and dark alleys. ✦

*In the 1890s, the Menominee River Boom Company of Wisconsin supplied homegrown vegetables for its employees. Here the company gardener, along with his wife and child, proudly displays the fruits of his labor.*

Seed Time and Harvest,
*a 1937 Grant Wood*
*lithograph.*

# The Seeds Your Grandfather Used to Grow

*After being discontinued by seed suppliers for so many years,*
*they're now becoming available again . . .* BY GORDON PEERY

YOU'RE SITTING BY the warm fire some February evening, browsing through the seed catalogs, and suddenly you realize that the tomatoes you've grown for the past twenty years are no longer available. Or perhaps you remember those tasty beets that Grandfather used to grow, or the pumpkins that Grandmother made into the most scrumptious of pies. Where have they gone?

In the name of progress, seed suppliers have discontinued many of the old vegetable varieties. In many cases, large corporations have bought out seed companies that prospered under two or three generations of family management. With more of an eye to profits, the new owners have let the less popular varieties go and have developed new varieties primarily for commercial growers. These are usually vegetables that have great shelf life and cosmetic appeal, often at the expense of flavor.

What may be of greater concern is that until recently very little effort was being made to retain the old varieties at any level. Many of them have become extinct because no one bothered to save even a few seeds. Because of this, the genetic diversity that is fundamental to long-term successful agriculture has been significantly reduced. But there is hope.

\* \* \*

It might seem self-defeating, but Rob Johnston, president of Johnny's Selected Seeds, encourages his customers to save their own seeds. While he concedes that he might have lost a few sales over the years, this approach has earned the respect of those who subscribe to the seed-saving philosophy but still need to make some seed purchases every year. Some of the types Johnston sells now are old family heirloom varieties that he has rescued from obscurity and possible extinction.

Johnston may be one of the few commercial seedsmen taking this approach today, but other individuals are getting involved in saving the old varieties. A key figure in the preservation of heirloom seeds is Kent Whealy, founder and director of the Seed Savers Exchange. Kent tells the story of how it started: "My involvement with heirloom seeds began quite by chance. In the early 1970s, my wife and I had just moved to the northeast corner of Iowa. It's a beautiful area of limestone bluffs and clear streams and dairy farms near the Mississippi River where Iowa, Wisconsin, and Minnesota meet. We were newly married and were planting our first garden together. Diane's grandfather, an old fellow named Baptist Ott, took a liking to us and taught us some of his gardening techniques.

"That fall he gave me the seeds of three garden plants that his family had brought with them from Bavaria four generations before. He gave me the seed of a large pink German tomato, a potato-leaf type; the seed of a small, delicately beautiful morning glory, which was purple and had a red star in its throat; and the seed of a strong-climbing prolific little pole bean. Well, the old man didn't make it through the winter. I realized that if his seeds were going to survive, it was up to me."

Whealy decided to contact other gardeners who were growing vegetables passed down through the generations. At the end of the first year, his efforts had yielded only five names. But he kept at it, and today the Seed Savers Exchange has about nine hundred members. The exchange encourages people who are saving seeds of old varieties to trade them. When a sufficient surplus is generated, the seeds are made available to others who are interested in joining the project but have no seeds of their own to swap.

The Seed Savers Exchange publishes an annual yearbook listing members and available seeds, and an annual Harvest Edition, which contains transcripts of lectures from seed-saving seminars and a wealth of other information.

> **Let your flowers and rosebushes be protected against the frost by straw and coarse dung.**
>
> *1801*

Whealy also has compiled *The Garden Seed Inventory*, a 488-page listing of the 5,785 nonhybrid varieties of seeds being offered today in the United States and Canada. The only precedent to this was a study published by the U.S. Department of Agriculture in 1903. In addition to listing the variety name, range of date to maturity, and all the known sources of these seeds, *The Garden Seed Inventory* indicates which varieties are in the greatest danger of being dropped by commercial seed companies. This book has been heralded by gardeners and scientists as a landmark study.

\* \* \*

## Sources for Seed Savers

To receive information about any of the following, write to the address listed and enclose $1.

Kent Whealy
Seed Savers Exchange
R.R. 3, Box 239
Decorah, IA 52101

Alex Caron
R.R. 3
King City, Ontario
L0G 1K0, Canada

Canadian Organic Growers
46 Lorindale
Toronto, Ontario
M5M 3C2, Canada

Alex Caron is a gardener in Ontario who became interested in seed saving five or six years ago, sort of by accident. He had let someone use a portion of his land to grow potatoes, but when harvest time came, the planter was nowhere to be found. Caron harvested the crop himself, finding an excellent yellow-skinned potato he calls the Austrian Crescent. At about this time, he became aware of the work Kent Whealy was doing with the Seed Savers Exchange, and it sparked his interest. He now has about 150 potato varieties, several hundred beans, and 50 or 60 tomatoes. He makes these available to other gardeners, preferably through trade for other varieties. Caron also is a founding member of the Canadian Organic Growers, which has developed a Canadian equivalent of the Seed Savers Exchange called Heritage Seeds.

\* \* \*

Perhaps part of the reason for the current popularity of seed saving is that gardeners are learning that it is not very difficult to maintain a few strains of favored vegetables. Seeds from annuals such as beans and tomatoes, which are self-pollinating, are easily saved. Slightly more complicated are plants such as corn and cucumbers, which can cross-pollinate and therefore require some degree of isolation. Biennials, which include carrots, cabbage, Brussels sprouts, and beets, must be wintered over to produce seeds. Many gardeners are finding that seed saving opens up a whole new aspect of gardening, and after all, how many gardeners are afraid of a little extra work?

Thomas Jefferson once said, "The greatest service which can be rendered to any country is to add a useful plant to its culture." Two hundred years later, we might say that the greatest service would be to preserve those plants. ✦

Set cabbages
in the middle
of the day, first
putting the top
into very cold
water. Hoe your
cabbages in the
morning.

*1805*

## Tips on Saving Seeds

- Save the seeds from plants that display the characteristics you most want to encourage. A strong, healthy plant is as important as large, well-formed fruit, and early bearing is usually a desirable quality as well.
- Wash the seeds clean of any vegetable matter and then dry them thoroughly. If you use an artificial heat source, it should be kept at around 90°F. Setting the seeds out in the sun is usually the best method for drying, provided you can get the seeds indoors if it starts to rain.
- Allow the seeds to dry for several days (larger seeds take longer than smaller ones). Before they regain any moisture, put each variety in an envelope labeled with the seed type. Put the envelopes in tightly sealed glass jars.
- Store the jars in a dry location between 32°F. and 40°F.
- Peas and beans require less work. Just take the seeds from the dried pods and store them in labeled bags.

# The Secrets of Championship Vegetable Showing

*A few tips from an established prize winner.* BY ROGER B. SWAIN

IT'S ONE THING TO BE AN expert gardener but quite another to win blue ribbons for your efforts at the county fair. If you're ready to add a little showmanship to your gardening expertise, here are some points to consider.

There are two types of vegetable exhibits: one contains a specified number of a single variety of vegetables; the other displays many different vegetables together. The single-variety exhibit is more common and a good starting point. In such an exhibit, the judge looks for five things.

**1. Uniformity.** Ask for a copy of the fair catalog for prospective exhibitors. When it arrives, look under the vegetable division to find out how many samples of each vegetable are required. You may need two pumpkins or watermelons, but you will probably need five peppers or tomatoes and ten string beans or pea pods. This is where uniformity comes in.

First, all the vegetables in the same exhibit must be the same variety; you cannot put an Early Jersey Wakefield cabbage in the same exhibit with an Early Flat Dutch cabbage. Some fairs lump all cabbage varieties together as "cabbage," but such fairs are victims of the supermarket mentality and should be avoided by aspiring purists.

Of course, all the vegetables in an exhibit must look as much alike as possible. It is useless to exhibit a hundred-pound Blue Hubbard squash unless you have another the same size. Even though it hurts your soul to leave your biggest at home, you are much more likely to win with a matched pair of forty pounders.

In selecting uniform vegetables, you should consider size, shape, color, and maturity. With some vegetables, this is not so easy; selecting identical pole beans is like selecting identical snowflakes. Pole beans curve dextrally, sinistrally, helically, or terminally. They are uniform only in their departure from straightness. Ideally, you are a truck gardener and have five acres of each vegetable variety from which to select five identical individuals. But if you can find five identical two-pound onions in a backyard row of half pounders, then you have earned the right of implying that all your onions were like these this year.

**2. Freedom from disease or injury.** I never read the pest or disease section of gardening manuals because they make it sound as though your

Copyright 1905.
By S.D. Butcher &
Son.
Kearney, Neb.

Nebraska Potatoes.

*This "tall-tale" postcard from the early 1900s shows a wagonload of "Nebraska potatoes."*

garden has a life expectancy of several milliseconds before being sacked by the Huns and Tartars of the insect world. But you should learn to recognize the pitted rough spots that indicate scab infection on potatoes (try growing them in a more acid soil) and the tunnels left by wireworms in turnips. The presence of disease or insect injury will disqualify an exhibit.

Harvesting injury also disqualifies an exhibit. It is impossible to harvest a row of potatoes without wounding at least one, but to show a spud that has been run through by a spading fork implies that you have the same attitude toward them as an army cook. We will discuss later how to harvest and prepare vegetables for show, but for now suffice it to say that they should arrive at the exhibit table without glaring touches from the human hand.

**3. Trueness to type.** The judge, often a county agent or professor of vegetables (olericulturist) knows how to tell a Chantenay carrot from a Danvers. If your sweet potatoes never thickened up or your zucchini look like a snake that just swallowed a rabbit, don't exhibit them. Whenever you're in doubt as to how your produce should look, try to find specimens that match the pictures in your seed catalogs.

**4. Quality.** This is a trait closely related to edibility. Perhaps the most common error of new exhibitors is to show summer squash that are over-ripe. Zucchini squash should still have fine hairs on them. (If you never suspected that zucchini had hairs, go out to your garden and examine one that is less than eight inches long.) Cooks know that bigger has nothing to do with better (except for tomatoes and melons). The same is true for quality vegetables. Don't show five great gnarled soccer ball–like turnips, turnips that would indeed keep all winter — or two winters for that matter. Instead, your exhibit should look like the ingredients for turnip soufflé, delicate and delicious.

**5. Display.** This is important even if you are showing only one exhibit. There are 120 different ways to arrange five beets on a paper plate and there will always be one way that makes them look more uniform and of higher quality than they really are. You don't need to try all the permutations. Just shift them around a bit until you have given them the artistry that will carry them on to victory.

N OW THAT YOU KNOW the rules, you need to decide where you are going to exhibit. Fairs in late August and early September are best because your garden will be in full production by then. However, if your horticultural triumph is ripe tomatoes by the Fourth of July, enter in a July fair. You will certainly win first prize, admiration, and tomato green envy.

You've already requested a catalog from the fair commission. As soon as it arrives, start planning what you will enter. All members of the squash family should be cut with some stem left on the vegetable. Carrots, beets, parsnips, and turnips should have one and a half inches of tip left on them. Wash the carrots and beets gently in tap water, but let the potatoes air dry and gently whisk off the dry dirt, as the skin of new potatoes is very delicate.

Corn should be exhibited with only one side of the husk removed. Cabbage should have a few of the outer leaves removed. Don't even start peeling onions, however; you'll invariably go too deep. Tomatoes should be uniformly ripe and free from growth cracks. Leave the stems on or take them off, but be consistent. Green tomatoes are surprisingly difficult to select because they must be full size but free from any touch of ripe color. Since they often turn pink overnight, pick them at the last minute. Other last-

The most effective method of ridding your garden of bugs is to visit your vines several times a day and destroy the bugs with your fingers.

*1805*

minute vegetables are leaf crops such as lettuce and endive. They should be pulled as late as possible, with their roots left on, and should be exhibited with their roots in jars of water to prevent wilting.

When you have selected all your vegetables for exhibition, wrap them individually in newspaper and put them in boxes. Country roads are guaranteed to bruise a choice tomato unless it is packed with the same care as Steuben cut glass. You can usually take your vegetables to the fair the night before it opens or, if not, early in the morning. They will be judged the first day, so you don't need to worry about their being at their freshest for more than a day.

Always take along a few extras. One of the green tomatoes will turn pink just before the judge arrives, and children

### A Contest Winner Tells How
### She "Vanquishes Varmints from My Vegetable Patch without Violence"

I SOAK CIGAR butts in a gallon jug for weeks at a time and spray this liquid around my garden and shrubbery to keep animals from lifting a leg on my plants. When bugs are bad, I make pyramid tents over susceptible plants using netting and wire hangers. Dried blood scattered along the edge of my garden keeps wild animals away; two pounds lasts a whole growing season.

*Courtesy of Mary H. Smith, Hagerstown, Maryland.*

who never eat vegetables at meals are sure to carry them off from fair exhibits. At those fairs that have not yet resorted to barricades of wire fencing, thus depriving the public of their inalienable right to fondle the vegetables after judging, you may lose a vegetable or two. Judges, however, are sympathetic about missing vegetables and vegetables with teeth marks in them — as long as they are from human teeth.

For an exhibitor, fairs are a chance to talk with other gardeners. But they are also a chance to talk to the public. Perhaps not surprisingly, an increasing number of people don't know what an eggplant looks like. And whether your gourmet tastes run to sno-cones or fried bread, the culinary delights of a county fair always taste better when you are purchasing them with prize money. ✦

# Flower Planting Table for the Northern United States

| Variety | When to Start Under Glass | When to Start Outdoors | Thin or Transplant to (inches) | Season of Bloom | Miscellaneous Information |
|---|---|---|---|---|---|
| Aquilegia columbine | | July–Aug. | 8 | June–Sept. | Perennial. Start and winter in cold frame. Transplant in April. |
| Aster (China) | Mar.–Apr. | May | 12 | July–Oct. | Bedding plant. If possible, avoid planting twice in the same place. |
| Aster (New England) | | June | 12 | Sept.–Oct. | Perennial. *A. novae-angliae* is the best blue fall flower. Plant for mass effect. |
| Calendula (pot marigold) | March | May | 6 | June–Sept. | Grow in clumps in border or beds. Self-sows. A useful plant to fill vacant spaces. |
| California poppy | | May | 4 | July–Sept. | Plant in masses. Good edging. Keep seedpods picked off. |
| Canterbury bells | | June–July | 12 | June–Aug. | Biennial. Grow in clumps in border. Protect young plants over winter. |
| Chrysanthemum | | June | 8 | Sept.–Nov. | Perennial. Divide every spring. Keep well watered. |
| Cosmos | April | May | 30 | July–Sept. | Cut back when half-grown to induce flowering. Early varieties preferable. |
| Dahlia | | May–June | 36 | Aug. to frost | Separate clumps and plant tubers flat with eye up. |
| Delphinium | | July–Aug. | 30 | June–July | Perennial. Seed must be fresh. Spray with Bordeaux mixture as soon as up. |
| Forget-me-not | | July–Aug. | 6 | June–Aug. | Plant in moist, partially shaded places. Blooms the second season. |
| Foxglove | | June–July | 12 | July–Aug. | Biennial. Plant clumps near back of border. Protect seedlings over winter. |
| Gaillardia | | June–July | 18 | July to frost | Perennial. Plant for mass effect. Insists upon a dry location. |
| Gladiolus | | April–June | 5 | July–Sept. | Plant corms in double rows, six inches apart. Take up when tops begin to die. |
| Hollyhock | | July–Aug. | 15 | July–Aug. | Perennial. Spray with Bordeaux mixture for rust. Destroy all leaves that drop. |
| Iris (bearded) | | July–Sept. | 24 | May–June | Perennial. Divide every three years. Set almost on surface in a dry, sunny spot. |
| Iris (Japanese) | | Aug.–Sept. | 24 | July | Perennial. Divide every 3 or 4 years. Set 2 inches deep and keep well watered. |
| Larkspur | Mar.–Apr. | May | 6 | June–Sept. | Annual. Seeds sprout slowly. Remove old flowers. Excellent cut flowers. |
| Lupine | | May | 18 | June–Aug. | Perennial. Sow seeds where plants are to stand. Grow in clumps in border. |
| Marigold | April | May | 10 | July to frost | Good for beds or as a filler in border. Guinea Gold is the finest variety. |

| Variety | When to Start Under Glass | Outdoors | Thin or Transplant to (inches) | Season of Bloom | Miscellaneous Information |
|---|---|---|---|---|---|
| Mignonette | | May–July | 6 | July to frost | Plant seed where plants are to grow. Runs out quickly. Sow two or three times. |
| Morning glory | April | May | 6 | July to frost | Train over porches and trellises. Needs a rich soil and abundant moisture. |
| Nasturtium | | May | 6 | July to frost | Dwarf for edging. Tall for trellises or fences. Needs rather poor soil. |
| Petunia | Mar.–April | May | 6 | July to frost | Easy to grow. Good for bedding, edging borders, and window boxes. |
| Phlox (drummondi) | April | May | 12 | July to frost | For edging or beds; remove old flowers to lengthen blooming. Needs good soil. |
| Portulaca | | May | 6 | July to frost | For beds in dry, sunny places. Flowers open only on bright days. Self-sows. |
| Salvia | Feb.–Apr. | | 18 | Aug. to frost | The best scarlet flower for late fall and summer. Good bedding plant. |
| Snapdragon | March | | 6–12 | July to frost | Good bedding plant; must be started early. |
| Sweet pea | | Mar.–Apr. | 6 | July–Sept. | Plant early. Syringe with water to deter red spiders. Needs rich soil. |
| Sweet William | | July–Sept. | 12 | June–July | Biennial. Grow in clumps in border. Remove old flowers to prolong blooming. |
| Verbena | Feb.–April | | 12 | June to frost | Good for bedding and cut flowers. Perpetuate by cutting. Spray for mites. |
| Zinnia | April | May | 12 | June–Oct. | May be used as a bedding plant or in border. Flowers will last after frost. |

*E. I. Farrington, Secretary, Massachusetts Horticultural Society.*

## CHAPTER FOURTEEN

# *Good* COMMON-SENSE *Advice*

*"Though we may give advice, we cannot give conduct."*
— *The Old Farmer's Almanac,* 1802

DON'T BE IDLE, PLAN YOUR DAILY ACTIVITIES, SEND YOUR CHILDREN to school, stay on the farm, avoid hard liquor, watch every penny, mend your fences, and be good to your wife. The Almanac bombarded its readers with this sort of advice throughout its first 150 years. In the past half century, from which most (but not all) of the following is gleaned, the emphasis shifted slightly to more practical matters. ✦

*A kerosene salesman from Titusville, Pennsylvania, in 1885.*
*Such men were quick to advise using "coal oil."*

## The Forgotten Art of Building a Long-Lasting Fire

*You surely have your own advice to give on this subject — but do try to keep an open mind.*  By RAYMOND W. DYER

THE FIRE ON THE hearth is one of the very few things that has been passed down all the way from primitive cave dwellers to modern man. The fireplace warms all — the room, the conversation, and the people about. However, we often have many fireplaces and all too few fires burning in them — probably because we have lost the art of building a long-lasting fire without constant and bothersome attention.

Most people begin with no ashes in the fireplace and proceed to build the fire with paper and dry kindling wood laid directly on top of the andirons. This explodes into a large, scary blaze. As soon as it dies down, so that one can get close to it, larger logs are thrown on top, and another large, uncontrollable blaze quickly burns and dies out.

All of this results in a fire constantly needing attention and always either too hot or too cold, too large or too small. It also can result in a scorched mantle or a second good fire up in the chimney.

All of this amateur nonsense is the result of too much draft — which in turn results from the improper use of the andirons. You should not think of the andirons as a grate but simply as uprights to prevent the logs from rolling out of the fireplace.

To build a fire of good steady heat with a small blaze and minimum use of wood, the fireplace should be covered with a bed of ashes about one or two inches above the andirons' legs. If ashes are not available, sand may be used.

Now choose a log eight to ten inches in diameter. Place this, called the back log, against the brick back of the fireplace, with a slightly smaller log balanced on top of it. Then place a log four to six inches in diameter in the front of the fireplace, just in back of the andirons. This is called the fore log. It is essential that these logs be well bedded down in the ashes as the point is to keep the flames and draft out from under the logs so only their tops and faces burn.

Build the fire between the back and fore logs, starting with paper and kindling and gradually building up to four- and six-inch logs. Once the fire is lit, the fore and back logs eventually will burn through. As this happens, move them into the center of the fire and replace them with new logs, once more well bedded in ashes.

This results in a fire that burns with a hot blue flame and red-hot coals. The face of the back log burns red-hot and reflects the heat of the fire. The fore log holds the fire in and prevents air from passing under it.

If you want less fire, you can dampen this arrangement by putting a shovel of ashes on it. If you prefer more blaze, a few small sticks of kindling can be added to the top of the fire.

If a good fire remains when you retire for the night, cover it with ashes from the side of the fireplace. This will hold all night, and when you uncover it the next day, or even the next evening, you will find a bed of red-hot coals upon which to build a new fire.

This is how heat and fire were maintained from day to day in colonial homes, when such fires were a hard necessity.

It goes almost without saying that a hardwood such as oak, maple, cherry, or birch is the best to burn. This must be cut in late winter or early spring so that it can dry and cure in the hot summer sun. A drying and curing period of at least six months is necessary.

Even if you learn how to build a hot, economical fire, I am not sure you will be out of the woods. You still must hope that your favorite ecologist will forgive and forget the little smoke that curls from your chimney. ✦

**Do not permit a servant to carry a candle to his bedroom if he sleeps in an unplastered garret.**

*1797*

# Expert Advice on Catching, Keeping, Measuring & Cooking Your Favorite Fish

*Useful tips a pro has gleaned from a lifetime of angling.* By Bud Leavitt

THERE'S NO PLACE TOO FAR to go fishing," says Bud Leavitt, sportswriter, member of the Fishing Hall of Fame, and avid freshwater and saltwater fisherman. His fishing trips, which have taken him to Honduras and Mexico, across the United States and Canada, and into Alaska, have included famous sportsmen such as Ted Williams, Sam Snead, Prince Rainier, Curt Gowdy, and John Havlicek. Six days a week for more than forty years, Bud Leavitt has written about his fishing exploits in a column for the *Bangor* (Maine) *Daily News.* His favorite fishing tips, drawn from a lifetime of angling, are listed here.

• Spinning reels need only infrequent attention if used exclusively in fresh water. Reels that see saltwater service should be rinsed in fresh water and allowed to dry before storage. The easiest and surest method is to bring the entire outfit into the shower stall. A hot, soapy shower revives the fisherman after a hard day on the ocean and works wonders with a rod and reel.

• Next time your children insist on chewing bubble gum when fishing, ask them to chew red gum. After the youngsters have chewed it a while, roll it into small worm-like shapes. Hook these in the middle to catch perch, bass, bluegills, and occasionally a wise old brook trout. You have to strike fast when you feel a nibble.

• Did you ever try to find a swivel in a tackle box with anywhere from one to one thousand items in storage? Here's how you can do it in a hurry. String a dozen or so on a large safety pin and fasten the pin to the underside of your shirt pocket flap.

• When cooking over an open fire, you can save yourself a lot of work scouring the outside of pots and pans if you smear a thin coating of mud over them before cooking. The soot collects on the mud. After you are finished cooking, tap the pans, and off comes the mud, soot and all.

• Empty cardboard milk cartons make excellent fire starters. You can carry your supply easily by cutting off the ends of the cartons, slitting down one corner, and folding them flat. The paraffin-soaked cardboard will light when wet wood will sputter and refuse to burn.

• You will always have a ruler with which to measure the length of your fish if you paint dots one inch apart on your fly or casting rod. Paint every fifth dot red. Paint as far as the biggest fish you would like to catch.

• When fishing in a pond or lake, never pass up a half-sunken boat or a boat that is tied up offshore. Fish often lie in the shade of boats.

• Fish belonging to the sunfish family — bass, bluegills, and others — can be dressed by removing scales and skin with a pair of pliers. Start behind the head and keep pulling off the skin.

• A bicycle tire laid on the lawn can help you improve your fishing technique. For either fly casting or bait casting, try landing your lure in the center of the tire. When you can put three out of four in the center, you are ready to talk to the trout — or the salmon, bass, or saltwater species such as striped bass and weakfish.

• For fish to be at its best on the table, it must be properly frozen. One method is to put the fish in an empty milk carton, fill the carton with water, and then freeze it. The meat is encased in ice, and the heavy carton helps prevent freezer burn.

• You can prevent hooks from becoming part of your thumb or from scattering all over your tackle box. Stop at the hardware store and pick up a small magnet. Put the magnet in the compartment where you store your hooks. I know what I'm talking about. Nothing's funnier than a 245-pound outdoor writer walking into the local emergency center wearing a four-inch bass plug with one of the treble hooks in his fat thumb.

• The really smart and sharp fishermen I know usually carry a tube of liquid cement in that already 101-pound pack that stores their fishing gear. The cement comes into play for plugging boat leaks, patching canoes and torn waders, and tightening a loose rod ferrule. It can even be used as a quick fire starter on a rainy day.

• Here's a salute to the man who invented Vaseline. Every fisherman should have a jar in his or her tackle box. It can be used as a lubricant, rust preventative, medication for insect bites, water repellent, and even a float- for fly lines and dry flies. Here's to you, Mr. Vaseline.✦

**We must look out for the devil, for if he finds anyone idle, he will set him at work, and who wants to do the *devil's* work?**

*1854*

FACING PAGE:
*Trout fishing in New Hampshire's White Mountains around the turn of the century.*

*The* BEST *of* THE OLD FARMER'S ALMANAC

# The Best & Cheapest Way to Get Rid of Fleas

*Knowing a thing or two about fleas' habits may help you outwit them . . .*

FACING PAGE:
*Through the miracle of old-time photography, a good-sized flea weighs in at a little over three pounds.*

YOU KNOW YOU'RE IN trouble when (1) certain areas of your carpet seem to hop; (2) sitting on the couch becomes an experience in acupuncture; and (3) your dog and cat act like animal contortionists in their efforts to scratch and bite six itches at once. In other words, your house has become a giant flea bag.

What's worse, commercial insecticides are often not only smelly and poisonous to other life but also ineffective. Fleas, highly specialized blood-sucking parasites with the evolutionary hardiness of cockroaches, have become resistant to the pesticides commonly found in insect bombs and flea collars. In fact, many veterinarians advise pet owners not to waste their money on flea collars.

But there's more than one way to flummox a flea, and we are pleased to offer a few suggestions:

• Vacuum rugs and upholstered furniture daily to remove fleas, eggs, and larvae. Fleas spend most of their time away from their hosts and can survive for several weeks without feeding, so keep up the vacuuming diligently for at least a month. Be sure to block up any exits from the vacuum cleaner after vacuuming lest the fleas hop back out. Vacuum your pets if they will let you (some love it; some would sooner die a horrible death).

• Add minced fresh garlic and a sprinkling of brewer's yeast to your pet's food to repel fleas.

• Your veterinarian can supply you with a nonaerosol spray for pets (Sectrol is one brand) based on the chemical pyrethrum, which is extracted from the dried heads of certain varieties of chrysanthemums. Another veterinary product that is safe for indoor use is a nonaerosol rug and upholstery spray called Duratrol that contains tiny drops of an effective insecticide.

• Many pets are made miserable not only by the flea bites themselves but also by an allergic reaction to flea saliva, a persistent condition that is often treated with cortisone-related medication.

• For the most effective control of fleas, start early in the spring and be diligent. With any luck, your fleas will flee. ✦

## A FEW FACTS ABOUT THE INFAMOUS FLEA

• Fleas can jump 150 times their own length, vertically or horizontally. This is equivalent to a human jumping approximately one thousand feet.

• Flea bodies can withstand tremendous pressure, their secret to surviving the scratches and bites of the flea-ridden host.

• Fleas are covered with bristles and spines that point backward. That's why it's so difficult to pick a flea from your pet's fur.

• As carriers of plague, transmitted from infected rats to humans, fleas have killed more people than all the wars ever fought.

# More Tricky Pieces of Almanac Advice

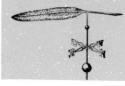

## THE ONLY PROPER & CORRECT WAY TO MAKE & SERVE TEA

*A bit of Almanac advice from the turn of the century.*

1. Use a china or pottery pot, never a metal one.
2. Draw the water from the cold-water tap and bring it to a boil.
3. Pour the boiling water into the pot until it is nearly filled and allow it to stand until the pot is hot.
4. Throw away this water and put dry tea in the pot — a rounded teaspoon of loose tea for each cup.
5. Pour vigorously boiling water on the leaves, allow the tea to stand for about a minute, and then stir well.
6. Let the tea stand four to five minutes, then pour.
7. Tea should always be poured by a woman — and by the same woman until the party is over.
8. When it is time for a second or even a third cup of tea, always ask for "some tea." Never ask for "more tea."

## Tips on the Gentle Art of Listening

**Basic posture.** Place your left elbow on the table and rest your cheek in the palm of your left hand. Not only does this convey the impression of listening intently, but it allows easy use of one fingertip to prop up a heavy eyelid while drawing the lower lid down with another finger. Further, the position of the palm is appropriate for stifling an oncoming yawn.

**If a yawn cannot be suppressed.** Either upset a drink or drop a lighted cigarette behind the sofa. While on your hands and knees during the ensuing excitement, you can safely dispense with the yawn. If your timing is precise, it may be possible to continue creeping on all fours out of the room.

**Listening to a funny story.** Remember that it is important to laugh at the right place, particularly if the narrator is your employer. Sometimes you may be so eager to impress your boss that you jump the gun and burst into guffaws at the first pause in the narrative. A hasty effort to disguise your laugh as a hacking cough is hardly convincing, and the unfortunate bobble makes you so tense that the next time the boss stops for a breath, you go into even louder gales of laughter. In this situation, you will rarely be able to muster up anything better than a watery smile when the punch line actually arrives — joined, perhaps, by some lame remark such as, "I certainly have got to remember that one."

*Courtesy of Garnette Wassen.*

*Actress Marlene Dietrich demonstrates the good listener's basic posture.*

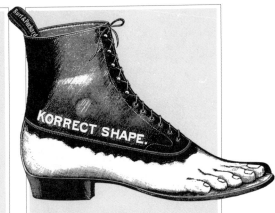

## Fixing Shoes That Pinch

THE LATE AUTHOR Roald Dahl once penned a letter to the venerable *Times* of London that the newspaper printed in full. Dahl wrote that he had recently purchased a pair of gym shoes and found that they pinched his toes. He said that fortunately he remembered his school physics course, which taught that "10 volumes of water at zero degrees centigrade expand to 11 volumes at freezing point. So I pushed a plastic bag deep into each shoe and filled it with water. I placed the shoes in the deep freezer compartment of the refrigerator and closed the door. The next morning the water inside the shoes had frozen solid and expanded in all directions by 10 percent." The shoes fit perfectly.

*Reprinted in* The Old Farmer's Almanac *courtesy of the* Boston Globe.

*Why is this woman smiling? Well, it's possible she just discovered another use for vinegar.*

# When in Doubt, Use Vinegar

*Whether it's cleaning, polishing, unclogging, deodorizing, or, well, you name it . . .* By Earl W. Proulx

**Bathtub film.** Wipe the tub with white vinegar and then baking soda. Rinse with water.

**Drip coffee makers.** To clean, fill the reservoir with white vinegar and run the coffee maker through a brewing cycle.

**Faucets.** Remove calcium deposits by soaking toilet tissue in white vinegar and placing it around the stains. Leave tissue in place for an hour or two.

**Garbage disposal.** If the rubber shield smells after much use, remove it and soak it in a pan of white vinegar.

**Oven.** Dampen a cleaning rag with vinegar and water and wipe out the interior. This will prevent grease build-up.

**Steam iron.** To clean, fill the tank with white vinegar and let it sit overnight, then rinse it out thoroughly with warm water. (Be sure to keep the cord dry.)

**Toilet bowl.** Clean and deodorize by pouring undiluted white vinegar into it. Let the vinegar stand for five minutes, then flush. Spray stubborn stains with vinegar, then scrub vigorously.

**No-wax vinyl flooring.** To clean and shine, wash with a mixture of ½ cup white vinegar and ½ gallon warm water.

**Painted and varnished surfaces.** Combine 1 cup ammonia, ½ cup white vinegar, ¼ cup baking soda, and 1 gallon warm water. Wash the surface with this mixture. No rinsing or drying is required, and the mixture will not dull the finish.

**Wood paneling.** To clean, mix ⅛ cup olive oil with ¼ cup white vinegar and 1 quart warm water. Dampen a soft cloth with this mixture and wipe the paneling; then wipe dry with a soft cloth.

**Aluminum pans.** Remove dark stains by boiling water containing 1 tablespoon white vinegar for each quart of water in the pans.

**Aluminum screens.** For corrosion, apply white vinegar, let it stand a few minutes, then scrub it off.

**Clogged drains.** Pour ½ cup baking soda down the drain, then ½ cup vinegar. Close the drain and let the mixture work for a while. Then open the drain and flush with hot water for three to four minutes.

**Greasy residue.** Filmy dirt and grease on top of the stove and refrigerator come clean with white vinegar.

**Salt and water stains.** White vinegar takes these stains off leather boots and shoes. Wipe over the stained area only, then polish.

**Baby clothes and diapers.** Add 1 cup vinegar to each wash load during the rinse cycle. Vinegar naturally breaks down uric acid and soapy residue, leaving clothes soft and fresh.

**Hair care.** After washing your hair, rinse it well with 1 cup water containing 1 tablespoon white vinegar. This removes soapy film.

**Relief from itching.** White vinegar is a time-honored remedy for wasp stings, bruises, sunburn, and hives. It relieves the itching of mosquito and other insect bites. Apply full-strength unless the area is raw.

**Smoke odors on clothes.** Fill the bathtub with hot water and add 1 cup white vinegar. Hang clothes above the steaming water. ✦

*The author wishes to thank the Vinegar Institute for its help.*

> One's dress should be a little inferior to one's condition.
>
> *1801*

# CHAPTER FIFTEEN

## *Did You Ever* WONDER . . .

> *Pretty! in amber to observe the forms*
> *Of hairs, or straws, or dirt, or grubs, or worms!*
> *The things, we know, are neither rich nor rare,*
> *But wonder how the devil they got there.*
> — Alexander Pope

SOMETIMES IT SEEMS THE MORE WE LEARN, THE MORE WE'RE inclined to wonder. Each nugget of truth that explains away a mystery is like a tiny window into the next level of an even larger mystery. But for two hundred years, the Almanac has never been shy about explaining things to its readers — things both useful and useless — that the editors of the Almanac feel they really ought to know. ✦

*Contemplating life's mysteries on a bluff overlooking New Haven, Connecticut, circa 1890.*

# Why Is the Midwest Square?

*Don't anyone take offense. Being square with the world means being solid, reliable, and having things pretty well squared away. But if you have to blame someone, blame Thomas Hutchins, this country's first geographer.* BY GENE LOGSDON

EVEN THOUGH OUR house is a conventional, solid brick structure that any bank would be glad to make a loan on, it makes my fellow Midwesterners nervous. It doesn't set "square with the world." Not to set square with the world is an affront to the senses in the Corn Belt, a callow lack of social grace, indicating probable tendencies toward secular humanism and other terminal diseases. People who do not build houses facing exactly east and west or north and south can hardly be trusted to be fair and square in their dealings. Worse than that, they might allow pictures on the wall to hang lopsided. Had the Leaning Tower of Pisa been built in northern Ohio, it would long ago have been razed to preserve the rectilinear sanity of our society.

At a party in our house, the conversation will soon drift from matters of national concern to important news such as who broke the window in the old Mifflin schoolhouse or the new paint job on Uncle Al's barn. Since such points of interest would be almost visible out our windows in daylight, the person talking will invariably nod or point in the direction of the subject under discussion — a habit of country folk who always know exactly where they stand in relation to everyone and everything in the area. Once a direction is so indicated, however, the conversation veers off into an argument:

"You talking about Al's barn?"

"That's what I said, ain't it?"

"Well, you're pointing more toward Carl's. Al's is a tad more easterly."

"You're both wrong. The way you're pointing, there's nothing but cornstalks all the way to Harpster."

"Well, now, just where do you think east is? This house doesn't set straight, you know." (Frowns all around.)

"Oh, that's right. It's the corners that point the directions."

"Not quite." (I am talking now, trying to, ha ha, set matters straight.) "The corners actually point a bit off the direction, too." No one seems to think that's as funny as I do.

Soon people are up, pacing nervously, peering out into the dark, trying to fix their location from the mercury vapor pole lights on the horizon. The house has turned into a spacecraft, yawing off into the universe with-

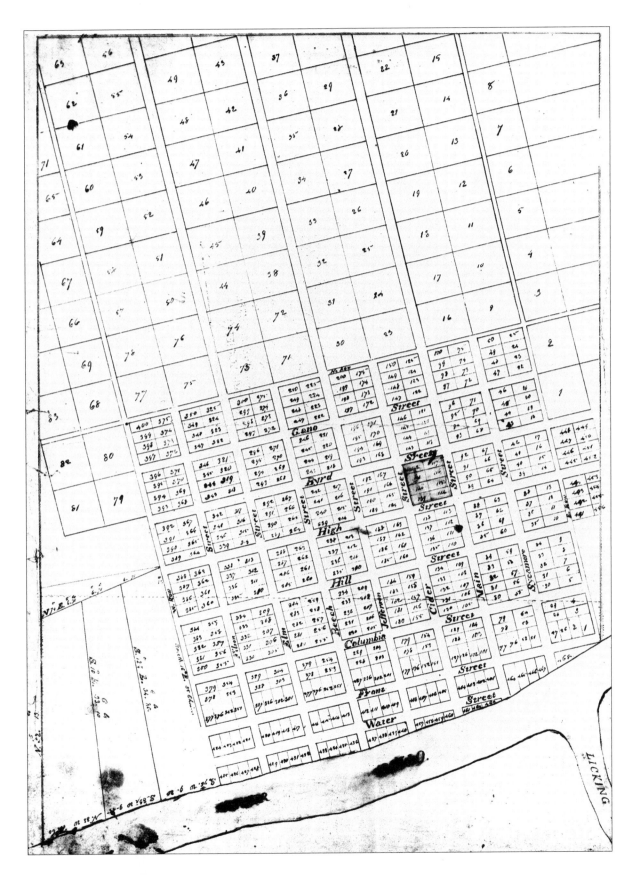

out a compass or gyroscope. The walls do not indicate "up north" or "down south." If Uncle Al's barn is not where it's supposed to be, what can you believe these days? They straighten lopsided pictures on my walls. They find excuses to go home early.

I live in the country of Squaredom, which begins here in north central Ohio and runs west at least to the Great Plains. This is the land of the square deal. Plaid shirts are always in style; paisley never. The new passive solar houses do not catch on here, not just because the sun rarely shines from November to April, but because the shapes of these structures are rhombic and trapezoidal rather than rectilinear. You can't depend on them — not solid, reliable, square. The world is divided into the competent, who have "everything squared away," and all those other idiots "running in circles."

Credit (or blame, depending on one's view) for the squaring of the Midwest is often given to Thomas Hutchins, the first geographer of the United States. Due partially to his influence, Congress, in 1785, two years before the Northwest Ordinance opened the Midwest to settlement, passed a law that stipulated the new lands would be surveyed in a grid pattern of six-mile squares, each square (or township) to be further subdivided into 36 one-mile squares (sections) of 640 acres each.

Surveying the first tract for the Ohio Company of Massachusetts, Hutchins stuck his Jacob's staff into the north bank of the Ohio, square on the Pennsylvania border, and ran a line due west forty-two miles to mark off the first seven ranges of townships from the Pennsylvania border. Thus began the pattern of land surveying that was to be used throughout the rest of the country except in West Virginia, Tennessee, Kentucky, Maine, Vermont, and Texas (and, of course, the thirteen original states, which were mostly already surveyed). By the time surveying had been completed in the Delaware Tract, wherein sits my catawampus house with its lopsided pictures, the six-mile square township of thirty-six sections, the sixteenth often reserved for a school, had become a permanent feature.

Henry Howe, the historian, called the system "one of the great American inventions." Whether that is true or not, it did provide a way to locate precisely any piece of land within a

*A 1909 survey team near Minnesota's Mud Lake prepares to "square off" Chippewa lands into 640-acre sections.*

tract to be surveyed. Thus Rufus Putnam and Manasseh Cutler, leaders of the Ohio Company and the real brains behind Hutchins's surveying, could sit comfortably in Mr. Brackett's Tavern, or more often in Cromwell's Head Tavern in Boston, and speak with great geographical lucidity about their land. If Hutchins said that the northwest quarter of section 12 in township 3, range 6 (counting ranges over from the Pennsylvania line and townships from Hutchins's first baseline survey) was a good place for a city someday and best not to sell it off too quick, everybody knew exactly whereof he spoke.

Unfortunately, playing checkers on a map does not tell one much about the real country involved, and only later would the Ohio Company realize that it had bought the poorest, most ragged up-and-down land in the state. Many had argued, to no avail, that "the squares would cut indiscriminately across streams, valleys, and ridges in undesirable and awkward ways." No matter. If your square straddled a hogback and your neighbor's covered all the good bottomland below, tough. If your square missed a good supply of water by twenty feet, leaving you forever at the mercy of your neighbor, that was kismet. If section 16 was an undrainable swamp, well, let the schools worry about that later.

Actually, the surveyors are not to blame for the squaring of the Midwest. It was the road builders who really did it. A survey line is only a mark on a map, not visible on the land like a river or three oak trees growing from one root. In hill country, delineations of property fence or roadway by necessity follow the lines of least resistance, with the result being more paisley than plaid, no matter what the survey system. But when the checkerboard squares reached flat northwestern Ohio and on into the flatter land of Indiana and Illinois, it became possible to mark them physically on the land. The roads were built on the section lines, and every section line had to have a road — all the way to Dubuque.

But why not? If the towns were all squares surrounded by streets, why not the country? Cleveland, Zanesville, and other towns, even before they were platted, were set aside as one-mile squares. Platting started with a public square, then little squares or blocks pushed out in all directions until they ran blindly into a river or lake, where they appeared to be sloughed off by the water and the remnants floated away.

*The divisions of Oregon's Hood River valley orchards, as viewed from eight thousand feet in 1928, clearly followed the unbending rules of the early geographers.*

WORLDWIDE REGULATIONS regarding heroic horse and rider statues are as follows:

- Horse standing on all four legs with rider mounted means the rider is a national hero.
- Horse with three legs on the ground and rider mounted means the rider died as a result of his wounds in battle.
- Horse with two legs on the ground and rider mounted means the rider died during the battle.
- In all the above positions, rider standing beside horse means the horse died also.

*Courtesy of Janet Cosgrove.*

*A rider who, according to the above rules, died in battle.*

City squares transferred to the country on a larger scale produce quintessential boredom for the traveler, but at least it is impossible to get lost. If you head west from my place on a township road and stick to it, you will still be heading west long past Indiana. If you count the perpendicular roads you pass, you know how many miles you have gone. Count the seconds between roads, and you know how fast you are going. You can do it from a 747, and I have. If the road you are on does end, as at a river, for example, you just make a right-angle turn and go until you find another east-west road that does cross the river. There are no surprises unless you fall asleep, an ever-present danger.

Unfortunately, you can't lay down a straight line on a curved surface for very far unless you dig a terrifically deep ditch. You can't apply a square piece of paper to an orange of equal plane surface, or, vice versa, you can't accurately transfer a globe to a flat surface. Furthermore, a magnetic compass will not keep to a consistently straight line over a great distance. It will vary in different areas and at different times. For both these reasons, Squaredom is not nearly as accurate as the square mind would like it to be. Very few 640-acre sections of land actually contain 640 acres. They contain a few more or sometimes a few less. These extra acres, from trying to make a square board fit a curved surface, may be added on to all the quarters of a section, or they may, as in Illinois, all be thrown into the northwest quarter, so that at least three-fourths of the land possesses pure and undefiled rectitude.

There is another kind of inaccuracy inherent in forcing imperfect earth into perfect geometric squares that gladdens the hearts of paisley-loving hill folk. Deeply undulating terrain contains considerably more surface area than flat terrain of the same survey dimensions. If a giant hand could press down a hill farm flat, it would stick out considerably more beyond its boundaries than a flatter farm would. Surprisingly, natives of Squaredom will resent this fact almost militantly, insisting only that "as far as records go, this difference is simply not considered." It is annoying to the Squaredom mind to realize that there are unnumbered acres out there, unbought and untaxed. What a lovely thought, though, for those of us whose dead furrows are always crooked, our mowed corners obtuse, our pictures lopsided, and our houses not square with the world. ✦

# How to Hypnotize a Lobster

### By Senator Edmund S. Muskie

**B**ACK WHEN I WAS campaigning for governor of Maine, I would occasionally be called upon to demonstrate a technique taught to me by a fisherman from Owls Head, Maine: I would hypnotize a lobster.

It's a simple procedure but be forewarned: there are a few things you must memorize before you mesmerize.

**1. Choosing a lobster.** I never met a lobster I didn't like. A couple of prerequisites are a firm grip and good eye contact. To add to the drama of the demonstration, make sure your lobster is vigorous —quite vigorous (see number 2).

**2. Getting to know your lobster.** Grasp him in your left hand, making sure you place your fingers just on the carapace (where the body and tail meet). Now see if your hand-held *Homarus americanus* is a flapper — you know, if the tail flaps quite a bit. If it does, you've got a good one. Presumably you're trying this in front of a crowd, so wait until everyone is duly impressed before you move on to number 3.

**3. Putting your lobster in a trance.** Now, when I was a senator, I listened to occasional speeches here and there that I thought were enough to put any self-respecting lobster to sleep. But here is an easier way. Holding the lobster in your left hand, start stroking (with your right) the lobster's tail in a downward motion, curling it as you go. Do this until the lobster is inert.

**4. Making your lobster do something lobsters normally wouldn't do.** Moving carefully, you may now stand your lobster on his head, using the claws for support. In other words, make a tripod. He'll stand like that until you wake him up.

**5. Waking up your lobster.** Grasp the lobster by the carapace and shake him. To arouse a particularly stubborn lobster, shake him and whisper, "Drawn butter, drawn butter."

# How Were States, Towns & Places Named?

*The state of Washington was about to be named Columbia when one legislator pointed out that the new state would always be confused with the District of Columbia. So they changed it to Washington.*

MORE THAN TWO hundred years ago, in March 1784, Thomas Jefferson proposed a number of names for new states to be formed out of the vast territory west of the Appalachian Mountains. Had his suggestions been followed, today's roll call of the states might include Chersonesus, Polypotamia, Assenisipia, and Pelisipia.

Instead the English custom of naming places according to local traditions held sway. That is why Indian names, though often misspelled and misinterpreted, dominate the more than two million place names recorded by the U.S. Geological Survey's Board of Geographic Names.

For example, Wisconsin comes from Quisconsing, which was how the French explorers Marquette and Joliet spelled the Indian word Mesconsing. But a careless French mapmaker in 1715 spelled it Ouariconsint, which some geographers think may have led to the naming of Oregon.

The American Revolution caused more than a few towns and places to be renamed and supplied many new heroes to memorialize. The greatest of them, of course, was George Washington, who still holds the record for the most place names in this or any other country — 1 state; 33 counties; 121 cities, towns, and villages; 257 townships; 10 lakes; 8 streams; 7 mountains; and thousands of streets and other manmade features. Strangely, the state of Washington was not named until 1853, although both Mississippi in 1817 and Minnesota in 1847 were almost named for him.

*Father Jacques Marquette and Louis Joliet, a trader, explore the Mississippi River in the mid-1600s. In 1817 the state of Mississippi was almost named Washington.*

When Washington finally entered the roll call of the states, it was an eleventh-hour substitution. The settlers in that state had asked Congress to accept the name Columbia, after Christopher Columbus and the great river that runs through the Northwest. Oddly enough, Congress decided on Washington instead — responding to one legislator's claim that otherwise the new state would be endlessly confused with the District of Columbia!

Such confused thinking also attended the christening of other western states. Residents of the Pike's Peak region petitioned Congress in 1861 to name their new state Idaho. Congress instead named it Colorado, on the ground that it was the source of the great Colorado River, which it was not (to rectify this, the state of Colorado later renamed the Grand River, a tributary of the Colorado that does rise in that state, the Colorado River). This act annoyed representatives of the Territory of Arizona (through which the Colorado does flow), who wished to name their state after the river.

Supporters of the name Idaho, which was thought to be an Indian word meaning Gem of the Mountains (it was not), got a second chance in 1863 when another territory was named. This time Idaho got the better of Montana (Latin for "mountainous"), which had to wait until the next year, when it was hung on the eastern section of the Idaho territory (which is mostly flat plains). The neighboring territory of Wyoming, which includes two formidable mountain ranges, was named for a valley in Pennsylvania; the term comes from an Eastern Indian name meaning "large plains." The tradition of geographical error continued with the name of sun-parched Nevada, which means "snowed upon."

By 1890 the frontier had officially been declared closed. There were no unnamed states or territories, and the federal government decided it was time to establish an official arbiter of place names. The Board of Geographic Names was founded to straighten out disputes over names and to approve new names where necessary. The board still exists, deliberating over more than one hundred proposed name changes or new names every month. It continues to generate controversy, such as when it changed the name of Cape Canaveral (which dates back to Ponce de León and is thus one of the oldest names in America) to Cape Kennedy in 1963 (Canaveral was restored in 1973).

If such controversies seem like making a mountain out of a molehill, rest assured there is a precedent for that. Acceding to the request of a West Virginia town's residents, the board not long ago changed the town's name from Mole Hill to Mountain. ✦

*Explorer Juan Ponce de León, who discovered Florida in 1513, named it for the Spanish* Pascua Florida, *or Feast of the Flowers.*

*The tradition of geographical error continued with the name of sun-parched Nevada, which means "snowed upon."*

# Is Your Eagle Dexter or Sinister?

*If you have a decorative eagle, should his head face sinister (to his left) or dexter (to his right) — which means to your right or left, respectively, as you face the bird? Is right wrong or right?*

## By Mrs. Mark Kunkel

THE BICENTENNIAL hoopla and its attendant gimmickry did quite a job of reviving interest in national symbols. I have seen the American bald eagle stamped, printed, appliquéd, painted, and carved on everything from coffee mugs to T-shirts, all of which brought to mind the extensive research I did on our national symbol some years ago.

It began because I wanted a carved wooden eagle to place between our McDonald and Kunkel coats of arms. We bought one in the city, but when I unwrapped it, something about it irritated me. It just didn't look right — but what was wrong with it? When I went to my faithful Merriam-Webster and turned to the colored plates of official seals, flags, arms, and so on, I was convinced that the reason I could not accept the plaque we had bought was that the eagle's head was turned sinister (to his left).

I found the eagle's head turned dexter (to his right) on our great seal, the president's seal and flag, the insignias of all the branches of the armed services, the West Point insignia, the one-dollar greenback, the silver dollar, the silver quarter, the U.S. Army and Navy distinguished service medals, and the U.S. Distinguished Service Cross.

My husband returned the plaque that night, went to another store, and brought home a carved fruitwood eagle, head right, made by Soroco of Syracuse, New York. I wrote to Soroco to see if the company could document what I felt to be fact. They very kindly referred my letter to their designer, who replied promptly, "We turn the head of the eagle to the right (his) except in two instances — in death and 'In Memoriam.'"

About the same time, I saw a picture in *American Legion Magazine* of the plaque hung in Paris in 1919 commemorating the organization of the first American Legion post. The plaque had our eagle across the top of it, wings spread from side to side and head turned to his left. I accepted this as one of Soroco's two exceptions — "In Memoriam." I wrote then to the magazine's art director, Mr. Marshall, and he answered me by saying, "On the Presidential Seal the eagle turns his head to his right (your left) during peace time because he is holding the palm branch (the symbol of peace) in his right talon. During war time his head turns to his left (your right) because he is holding the arrows (of war) in his left talon."

Mr. Marshall further suggested that I write to General Donald Bennett, former superintendent of West Point Military Academy. I did and soon received a reply.

The general had referred my letter to Philip M. Cavanaugh, museum technician, who was thoroughly interested and wrote at great length: "The rules of heraldry specify that charges (symbols) must always be depicted as facing or moving dexter (to their right) and never sinister (to their left). For this reason, the helmet charge on the Coat of Arms of the United States Military Academy was changed in 1923 from sinister to dexter. Unfortunately, the regulating text of the Great Seal of the United States does not specify that the eagle is to face dexter (to his right); however, there are only three renderings (official) of the Great Seal of the United States (1782, 1841, and 1902), all of which depict the eagle facing dexter (to his right). It would appear that when the regulations concerning the arms were written it was understood that, according to the rules of heraldry, the eagle could only face dexter, and it was not necessary to specify this in the regulations. An eagle device which is used for ornamentation need not necessarily conform exactly to the rules of heraldry."

But I still hadn't documented my findings, so I then wrote to the General Services Administration, National Archives. This time I was told that on October 25, 1945, President Harry S Truman had issued an executive order depicting the great seal and the presidential flag. I wrote to Mr. Cavanaugh at West Point and gave him the information. Mr. Cavanaugh was most grateful to know that the order had been executed, and Mr. Marshall, the art director of *American Legion Magazine*, said that he was thoroughly convinced that the Paris plaque was in error due to the lack of knowledge of heraldic rules on the part of the designers.

As long as I live, I shall see beautiful reproductions of eagles with heads sinister (to their left, my right), but as far as I am concerned, I shall abide by the rules. ✦

# How Long Should Life Be?

*Looking at life and death through the patient eyes of evolution,
we see them as the head and tail of a single coin . . .*

### By Guy Murchie

A
S WE GET ALONG IN years, increasingly the thought arises: when will
all this end? Or, if we have a choice, how long should life be?
Clearly it is not a simple philosophical question, and it is not one
that may ever be satisfyingly answered in this mortal phase of existence. It
raises such basic issues as the meaning and purpose of life, upon which there
is far from general agreement and which the ancients traditionally entrusted
to the gods.

To the extent that "how long" is a probe into time, an understanding
of time is vital to any judgment of the length or limit of a life. Einstein's
theory of relativity says in effect that neither space nor time is fundamental but more truly only an illusion of finitude. Space, therefore, may be viewed
as the relation of things to other things and time as the relation of things to
themselves. The latter concept, of course, involves identity, as the relation

between you as a child and you as a grown-up, bringing all these periods together in the self that merges your life into a continuum. That is what may be reasonably considered a human lifetime on earth.

People have dreamed of vastly elongating life since time immemorial, as is revealed in the beliefs of the Taoists of ancient China, *Tir na nog* of the ancient Celts, the Hindu Pool of Youth, and the Hebrew River of Immortality. Meanwhile, with the progressive accumulation of knowledge and the acceleration of scientific discoveries, the length of an average human life has tripled since the time of Christ and doubled in this century. Besides, the miracle of genetic engineering is fast moving from fiction to fact, and the scarcely imaginable transplantation of brains has moved into the realm of research with primitive animals. (This, inevitably, brings up the troublesome question of consciousness. For if consciousness actually depends on the brain as is widely assumed, then transplanting a brain into another body is the same thing as transplanting a body onto another brain, and who would be you after such an operation? Or who would you be? And might not your brain actually survive and persist through a long succession of bodies of which you could theoretically be conscious for millenniums?)

*Convicted in about 399 B.C. of "impiety," corruption of the young, and neglect of the gods, Socrates preferred death to exile; following the custom in Athens for men so condemned, he "drank the hemlock." Socrates maintained that most humans miss true happiness during their lives on earth because, in spite of a universal wish for it, they do not know what it is.*

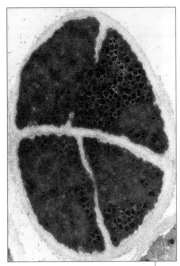

*Microscopic organisms like these may have been the earliest forms of life on earth. Instead of dying when they reached maturity, they merely divided and kept on dividing while each portion was rejuvenated.*

*Slime mold . . . feeds most of the time in the form of millions of independent cells that can be considered immortal.*

Few of us seem aware of it, but immortality is already present among us on earth. I am thinking of the soil amoeba *Dictyostelium discordeum,* known collectively as the slime mold that lives in rotting wood and dead leaves, feeding most of the time in the form of millions of separate, independent, invisible cells that can be considered immortal because they don't have to die. Occasionally, when it has had enough of its bacterial food, this nebulous population swarms and solidifies into a dense, coordinated, visible, mortal mass that oozes about as a small garden slug before suddenly sprouting into a thin-stemmed flower full of spores. In this stage, it spews out clouds of fertile powder that drift on the wind to land and start new colonies for miles around. Then the stem shifts into reverse and thickens again, pulling the flower back down into the shape of a slug, whence it disintegrates once more into its constituent amoebas in order to feed. It flips regularly from mortality to immortality, from visibility to invisibility, and, one might almost say, from finitude to infinitude as it alternately propagates and feeds.

Now let us expand our perspective outward into the full sweep of evolution, from where it is obvious that death is far from inevitable, for the kind of death we humans have to deal with (a disintegration of cells) did not even appear in evolution until the latter days of multicelled organisms. The creatures of early evolution — amoebas, bacteria, viruses — were all microscopic. And instead of dying when they reached maturity, they merely divided and kept on dividing while each portion was rejuvenated, leaving no corpse. So true death evolved only in the more advanced colonial and macroscopic stages of life, when cells started organizing themselves into complex organisms such as sponges, jellyfish, and worms and learned to diverge into sexes. At the same time, mind you, they kept on evolving, as often as not in unsuitable ways that could not be sustained. In other words, they needed death to eliminate deformed individuals and misfits and to steer evolution most of the time into more efficient directions. By this means death evolved, and over hundreds of millions of years it became solidly established because, from an evolutionary standpoint, it had survival value. Complex creatures such as our own primate ancestors urgently needed it — and ultimately they could not get along without it. In that sense, death has long been an indispensable part of life.

Looking at life and death through the patient eyes of evolution, we see them as the head and tail of a single coin, something like the traditional yin-yang polarity of ancient China or the crest and trough of an ocean wave that might be considered the symbolic wave of total being. If we accept such life-death polarity, longevity is diminished in its appeal, and the relatively subtle goal of life's quality may even overshadow the more obvious goal of its quantity. These interrelationships are both natural and reasonable. After all, if one is surely going to die (still our normal expectation), does it much matter when? Whatever the answer, if you feel confident that you will likely be happier in your soul during your future years on earth than you have been in past years, then it makes sense to live as long as you can. But if your ailments, frustrations, and spiritual failures are increasingly weighing you down, wouldn't it almost surely be a blessing if your life ended soon?

Arranging the time of your death, if it should come to that, may not be easy, especially if you are not distressed enough to commit suicide. But you probably do have some choices of action that could alter your expectancy. You might change jobs or even lifestyles. You could decide to buckle up or forget your seat belt, to avoid or accept risks, to cultivate new friends, to treat or ignore your ailments, to live cautiously or dangerously. You might even take to pondering the spiritual maturity of Socrates, who preferred death to exile.

If you are capable of broadening your perspective enough to contemplate life not as a mere individual but from the viewpoint of all humankind, then many things might come into your ken. Population control, for example, could become a serious consideration, along with resolving the related world pollution problem that's beginning to be known as the three Bs (for babies, bombs, and blight).

The main thing to realize is that the fate of our world is largely up to us humans. We are at the cutting edge of evolution in this present unique period, when our planet is germinating; when the speed of travel and communication has exploded; when earth at last has completed the exploration and mapping of itself, opened the atom, cracked the genetic code, leapt into space, and is now moving with some pain and uncertainty toward global freedom and oneness.

Is it not worth living a little longer if you can actually participate in this worldwide movement and help it fulfill its spiritual purpose? If you can say yes and really let yourself get absorbed in the universal cause, you will progressively forget yourself and think of all humankind, of all life and more. And you may even burst outside your finite aura of space and time so that it will no longer matter when you die or how long you live. In deepest truth, you will then just exist — for all anyone knows, forever. ✦

*A Buddha appears to contemplate the mysteries of eternity. Disciples of Buddhism aim at complete purity of thought and life, believing that if they achieve that state, they will be freed from the necessity of rebirth and be ready for Nirvana.*

# Which Really Came First — the Chicken or the Egg?

*Finally, after all these years, we have the answer.*
*Well, unless you want to be pedantic . . .*

## BY GUY MURCHIE

CHICKEN OR EGG? WHICH ONE STARTED IT ALL?

First let me say that although the chicken, like all other living creatures, is mysterious enough, the egg is even more so. For an egg not only contains the equivalent of a clock, a compass, nest-building instructions, menus, sheet music, and sometimes a map of the stars, but it also can talk and hold a conversation, and it is immortal.

Would a talking egg surprise you? Consider the fact that most eggs, particularly birds' eggs, are laid one at a time, and a clutch of them may appear during a span of a week or more. Yet it is vital that they hatch within a few hours of each other so the last baby bird to emerge will not be trampled to death by its much older and bigger brothers and sisters. For this reason the eggs of many different ages somehow coordinate their hatching, which is done by direct communication — egg to egg and often egg to mother and mother to egg. For a day or two before the egg hatches, some air accumulates in it, and in this air the developing chick starts to utter peeping sounds and eventually to peck against the shell. Since eggs in a nest generally touch each other, the sounds in them are easily transmitted from one to another as a sort of telegraphic code.

The immortality of an egg derives from the abstract nature of its genes, for these can produce a bird that, even if kept indoors and prevented from seeing or hearing any other bird, can nevertheless sing the songs of its species and navigate by stars it never knew existed. Furthermore, the egg does not have to die, for it normally grows into an adult bird, specifically a bird that in turn may lay eggs that prolong life indefinitely — showing that, from the egg's viewpoint, a chicken is primarily a lonely egg's way of getting another egg.

This line of thinking leads us to our long-awaited answer to the ancient dilemma of "Which came first, the chicken or the egg?" The egg wins hands down — literally by half a billion years! It is well known to evolutionists that eggs are more than ten times older than chickens because eggs antedate chickens by well over 400 million years. In fact, fish have been laying eggs almost since Cambrian times 500 million years ago. Then came the first bugs, followed by amphibians and reptiles, all of which lay eggs, as well as many birds older than the relatively recent barnyard fowl that evolved into what's known as the order of Galliformes a mere 40 million years ago.

Of course, some pedants argue that the egg in the original question has to be a chicken egg, not just any old egg. But I'd say that if you want to be pedantic, as well as logical, you really should define your terms — in which case you can create any outcome you choose (or no outcome) depending on your definitions. Should you, for example, insist on a chicken egg and define it as "an egg capable of hatching a chicken," the egg still wins. But if you define a chicken egg as "an egg laid by a chicken," the chicken beats the egg because the first chicken could not have hatched from a chicken egg, since there were no

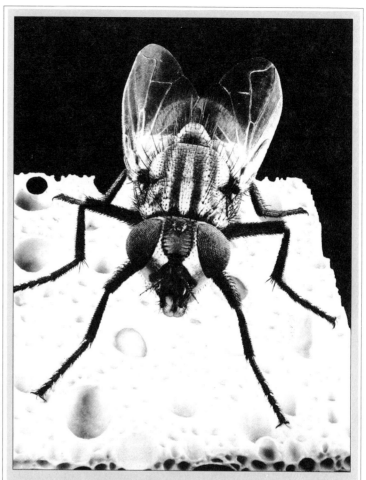

### How Many Children Can a Mother Housefly Have in Six Months?

UNDER IDEAL conditions, authorities say, 336 trillion houseflies could develop from a single pair in one April-to-September season — just nine generations — if they all survived.

*Courtesy of Herb Sanford.*

previous chickens around to have laid it. If, however, your definition requires that all chickens be hatched from chicken eggs, which in turn can only have been laid by chickens, then the sequence of egg-chicken-egg-chicken-egg must go back endlessly into history without any beginning — something no evolutionist would accept, nor any reasonable mortal living in a finite world! ✦

## Is It Remotely Possible for a Rich Man Ever to Get into Heaven?

"It is easier for a camel to go through the eye of a needle, than for a rich man to enter into the kingdom of God" (Matt. 19:24).

This passage from the New Testament has perplexed many people, who have taken it literally. These days the metaphor is a bold one, but the sense in which it was understood by those who heard it originally was quite different from a literal interpretation today. In Oriental cities, there are in the large gates small, very low openings called, metaphorically, "needles' eyes." These entrances are too narrow for a laden camel to pass through in the ordinary manner. When a camel has to pass through one of these entrances, it kneels down, its load is removed, and it shuffles through on its knees. "Yesterday," wrote one Lady Duff-Gordon from Cairo, "I saw a camel go through the eye of a needle — that is, the low-arched door of an enclosure. He must kneel and bow his head to creep through; and thus the rich man must humble himself."

*Courtesy of Dorothy C. Quinan.*

# Text Credits

GRATEFUL ACKNOWLEDGMENT IS made to the following for permission to reprint previously published material.

*Marcia Barnard Chandler:* "Why My Great-Uncle Gave Up the Ministry" by Marcia Barnard Chandler from the 1984 edition of *The Old Farmer's Almanac.* Reprinted by permission of the author.

*Fred E. Crockett:* "How the Doughnut Was Invented — for Sure" by Fred E. Crockett from the 1981 edition of *The Old Farmer's Almanac.* Reprinted by permission of the author.

*The Estate of Warren Evans c/o Florence Evans:* "The Ol' Goosebone Method" by Warren Evans from the 1980 edition of *The Old Farmer's Almanac.* Reprinted by permission of Florence Evans.

*Rick Horowitz:* "Friday the 13th: The Luckiest or Unluckiest Day of All," originally published as "Have a Happy Friday the 13th," by Rick Horowitz from the 1985 edition of *The Old Farmer's Almanac.* Reprinted by permission of the author.

*Bernard Lamere:* "The First Case of Artificial Insemination by a Bullet" by Bernard Lamere from the 1981 edition of *The Old Farmer's Almanac.* Reprinted by permission of the author.

*Ralph W. Leavitt:* "Expert Advice on Catching, Keeping, Measuring & Cooking Your Favorite Fish" by Ralph W. Leavitt from the 1975 edition of *The Old Farmer's Almanac.* Reprinted by permission of the author.

*T. R. LeMaire:* "The Greatest Single Prediction of All Time," originally published as "The Incredible Saxby-Allison Hurricane Forecast," by T. R. LeMaire from the 1975 edition of *The Old Farmer's Almanac.* Reprinted by permission of the author.

*Gene Logsdon:* "Why Is the Midwest Square?" originally published as "Why the Midwest Is Square" by Gene Logsdon from the 1987 edition of *The Old Farmer's Almanac.* Reprinted by permission of the author.

*Guy Murchie:* "Which Really Came First — the Chicken or the Egg?" from the 1979 edition of *The Old Farmer's Almanac* and "How Long Should Life Be?" from the 1989 edition of *The Old Farmer's Almanac.* Reprinted by permission of the author.

*Edmund S. Muskie:* "How to Hypnotize a Lobster, " originally published as "The Only Foolproof Way to Hypnotize a Lobster," by Edmund S. Muskie from the 1989 edition of *The Old Farmer's Almanac.* Reprinted by permission of the author.

*Gordon Peery:* "The Seeds Your Grandfather Used to Grow" by Gordon Peery from the 1987 edition of *The Old Farmer's Almanac.* Reprinted by permission of the author.

*Robert W. Pelton:* "The Girl Who Struck Out Babe Ruth" by Robert W. Pelton from the 1982 edition of *The Old Farmer's Almanac.* Reprinted by permission of the author.

# Picture Credits

*Chapter One.* Pages 3, 4: Yankee Archives. Page 5: The American Antiquarian Society. Pages 6, 7, 8: Yankee Archives. Page 9: John Huehnergarth. Pages 10, 11, 12, 13: Yankee Archives. Page 14: Culver Pictures. Pages 15, 16: John Huehnergarth. Pages 17 (both), 18 (both), 19: Yankee Archives. Page 21: The American Antiquarian Society.

*Chapter Two.* Pages 22–23: Yankee Archives, courtesy Harry Packard. Page 24: *Prometheus,* by Rockwell Kent, from *Rockwellkentiana,* Harcourt, Brace and Co., New York

1933. Page 25 (both): Yankee Archives. Page 26: John Huehnergarth. Page 27 (left): © 1962 Estate of Norman Rockwell, reprinted courtesy The Norman Rockwell Family Trust. Page 27 (right): Yankee Archives. Page 28: Culver Pictures. Page 29: John Huehnergarth. Page 30: Culver Pictures. Page 31: Yankee Archives. Page 32: courtesy Allyn Chase. Page 33: John Huehnergarth. Pages 34, 35, 36: Culver Pictures. Page 37: John Huehnergarth.

*Chapter Three.* Pages 38–39: Yankee Archives. Pages 40–41: AP/Wide World Photos. Page 42: John Huehnergarth. Page 43: Yankee Archives. Page 44: The National Archives. Page 45: Yankee Archives. Page 46: John Huehnergarth. Page 47: courtesy The Norton Company, Worcester, Massachusetts, photograph by N.C. Flink. Page 49: AP/Wide World Photos. Page 50: Yankee Archives. Page 51: AP/Wide World Photos. Page 52: John Huehnergarth. Page 53: Yankee Archives, gift of Walt Kelly, © 1968. Page 54: John Huehnergarth. Pages 55, 56: Yankee Archives.

*Chapter Four.* Page 59: AP/Wide World Photos. Pages 60, 61, 62, 63: Yankee Archives. Pages 64-65 (top): The New Haven Colony Historical Society. Page 65 (bottom): AP/Wide World Photos. Pages 66, 67: courtesy The Jericho, Vermont, Historical Society. Page 69: Yankee Archives. Page 70: Culver Pictures.

*Chapter Five.* Pages 72–73: The New Haven Colony Historical Society. Pages 74, 75, 76, 77, 78: Culver Pictures. Page 79: Yankee Archives. Pages 80, 81: Culver Pictures. Page 83: Yankee Archives. Page 84: The National Archives. Page 85: The New Haven Colony Historical Society. Page 86 (top): Yankee Archives. Page 86 (bottom):

H. Armstrong Roberts. Page 87: The Emmons/Stanley Collection, courtesy Marius B. Péladeau and Samuel Pennington.

*Chapter Six.* Pages 88–89: courtesy Universal Studios via Movie Stills Archives. Pages 90, 91, 92, 93 (both), 94: Yankee Archives. Page 95 (top): *The Seven Ages of Man: Youth*, by Rockwell Kent, from *Rockwellkentiana*, Harcourt, Brace and Co., New York, 1933. Page 95 (bottom): Culver Pictures.

*Chapter Seven.* Pages 96–97: The New Haven Colony Historical Society. Page 99: Culver Pictures. Pages 100, 102, 103: Yankee Archives. Pages 104–05: The State Historical Society of Wisconsin. Page 107: Dover Publications. Pages 109, 110: Culver Pictures. Page 111: Dr. C. Keith Wilbur, from *Revolutionary Medicine*, the Globe Pequot Press. Page 113: Yankee Archives. Page 114: Culver Pictures. Page 115: Yankee Archives. Page 116: Culver Pictures. Page 117: Yankee Archives. Page 118: Dover Publications. Page 119: Culver Pictures.

*Chapter Eight.* Pages 120–21: The New Haven Colony Historical Society. Page 123: from The Sherman Collection, courtesy The National Park Service, Ellis Island Immigration Museum. Page 124: Yankee Archives. Page 125: Dover Publications. Page 126: courtesy Mrs. Nina Donatello. Page 127 (top): Yankee Archives. Page 127 (bottom): Craig MacCormack. Page 128: H. Armstrong Roberts. Page 131: Norman Rockwell for Maxwell House, courtesy of General Foods Corp. and The Norman Rockwell

Family Trust. Page 132: Craig MacCormack. Page 133 (both): Culver Pictures. Pages 134–35: The American Antiquarian Society. Pages 136 (both), 137, 139: Yankee Archives.

*Chapter Nine.* Pages 140–41: from The Sherman Collection, courtesy The National Park Service, Ellis Island Immigration Museum. Pages 142, 143: Culver Pictures. Pages 144, 145, 146: Yankee Archives. Page 147: courtesy The Library of Congress. Pages 148, 149, 150, 151: Culver Pictures. Page 153: Yankee Archives. Pages 154, 155: Culver Pictures.

*Chapter Ten.* Pages 156–57: H. Armstrong Roberts. Page 158: Culver Pictures. Page 159: The New Haven Colony Historical Society. Pages 160–61: Don Bousquet. Page 162: Culver Pictures. Page 163: Yankee Archives. Page 164: Alan Ferguson. Page 165 (both): Culver Pictures. Page 166 (top): courtesy the Bridgeport Public Library. Page 166 (bottom left): Yankee Archives. Page 166 (bottom right): courtesy Jim Kageleiry.

*Chapter Eleven.* Pages 168–69: AP/Wide World Photos. Pages 170, 171: Culver Pictures. Page 172: Carl Kirkpatrick. Page 173: Yankee Archives. Pages 174, 175, 176, 177: Culver Pictures. Page 178 (top): Yankee Archives. Page 178 (bottom): Culver Pictures. Page 179: courtesy The Library of Congress.

*Chapter Twelve.* Pages 180–81: The New Haven Colony Historical Society. Page 182: Culver Pictures. Pages 183, 184: Yankee Archives. Page 185: AP/Wide World Photos. Pages 186, 187: Bruce Hammond. Pages 188 (all), 189, 190: Culver

Pictures. Page 191: Bruce Hammond. Page 192: Yankee Archives. Pages 193, 194: Bruce Hammond.

*Chapter Thirteen.* Pages 196–97: The New Haven Colony Historical Society. Page 199: Culver Pictures. Page 201: The State Historical Society of Wisconsin. Page 202: Grant Wood lithograph, courtesy the Cedar Rapids Museum of Art, gift of Mr. Peter O. Stamats and Mr. Larry K. Zirbel. Page 204: Dover Publications. Page 205: Yankee Archives. Page 206: Bob Johnson. Page 207: courtesy the Collection of E. Morgan Williams. Pages 209, 211: Yankee Archives.

*Chapter Fourteen.* Pages 212–13: Culver Pictures. Pages 214, 216: Yankee Archives. Page 218: courtesy the Collection of E. Morgan Williams. Pages 220, 221 (bottom): Culver Pictures. Page 221 (top): Dover Publications. Page 222: Culver Pictures.

*Chapter Fifteen.* Pages 225–26: The New Haven Colony Historical Society. Page 227: The Cincinnati Historical Society. Pages 228, 229, 230: Culver Pictures. Page 231: Pamela Carroll. Pages 232, 233: Culver Pictures. Page 235: AP/Wide World Photos. Pages 236–37: Culver Pictures. Page 238: AP/Wide World Photos. Pages 239, 240: Dover Publications. Pages 241, 242: Culver Pictures.

*Note:* Diligence was exercised in locating owners of all images used. If an image was uncredited or mistakenly credited, please contact the publisher and effort will be made to include credit in future printings.